American Furniture

AMERICAN FURNITURE 2019

Edited by Luke Beckerdite

Published by the CHIPSTONE FOUNDATION

Milwaukee

Distributed by Oxbow Books

Cover   Charles Willson Peale, *Colonel George Washington*, Virginia, 1772. Oil on canvas. 50" x 40". (Courtesy, Washington-Custis-Lee Collection, Washington and Lee University, Lexington, Virginia.)

Design and production   Wynne Patterson, VT
Copyediting   Richard Lindemann, ME
Typesetting   Jo Ann Langone, NH and Wynne Patterson

Published by the Chipstone Foundation
Distributed by Oxbow Books
oxbowbooks.com

© 2019 by the Chipstone Foundation
All rights reserved
Printed in Czech Republic   5 4 3 2 1
ISSN 1069–4188
ISBN 978–0–9863857–6–6

Contents

Editorial Statement

American Furniture is an interdisciplinary journal dedicated to advancing knowledge of furniture made or used in the Americas from the seventeenth century to the present. Authors are encouraged to submit articles on any aspect of furniture history, essays on conservation and historic technology, reproductions or transcripts of documents, annotated photographs of new furniture discoveries, and book and exhibition reviews. References for compiling an annual bibliography also are welcome.

Manuscripts must be double-spaced, illustrated with black-and-white prints, transparencies, or high resolution digital images, and prepared in accordance with the Chipstone style guide. The Foundation will offer significant honoraria for manuscripts accepted for publication and reimburse authors for all photography approved in writing by the editor.

Luke Beckerdite

American Furniture

Adam T. Erby

"Mostly new, and very elegant": The Several Lives of George William and Sally Fairfaxes' London-Made Furniture

▼ ON A WARM SUMMER DAY in 1763, a London-made carriage pulled by four of the finest horses in the Virginia Colony rounded the carriage circle of a large brick mansion. The enslaved postilion dressed in the red-and-white livery of the Washington family eased the horses to a stop just in front of a massive paneled door. George and Martha Washington, the passengers, knew this mansion, called Belvoir, quite well, as it was the home of their closest friends and nearest neighbors, George William and Sally Fairfax. The Washingtons had not seen their friends in three years because the couple had been on an extended trip to England. The Fairfaxes' butler greeted the Washingtons and showed them into the dining room, but as the couple passed through the house they noticed major changes. The Fairfaxes had emptied Belvoir, one of the grander dwellings on the Potomac, of its furniture, stripped much of its architectural detail, and made the house ready for a full redecorating campaign. Sixty massive wooden crates, stenciled with the cypher "GWFx" for George William Fairfax, were piled high in the first-floor rooms. The crates contained furniture, upholstered goods, looking glasses, wallpaper, mantels, and papier-mâché ceiling ornament sufficient to furnish the entire house.

These are mere imaginings of the way in which the Washingtons first encountered the Fairfaxes' purchases. Unfortunately, George Washington's diary for that summer is lost but, given the two couples' close friendship and proximity of their respective homes, it is entirely plausible that the Washingtons called on the Fairfaxes soon after their homecoming. On that first visit, the Washingtons were likely astounded at what they saw. Although George and Martha were accustomed to receiving shipments of furniture from their London factors—a set of chairs or a few tables in one shipment or the other—they had never seen anything on this scale. The Fairfaxes had commissioned the entire contents of their house from a London upholsterer, the interior designer of the day, and had them shipped 3,000 miles across the Atlantic Ocean. The Fairfaxes no doubt intended that these imported furnishings would confirm their status as taste-makers at the apex of Virginia society. To date there is no other known instance of an American colonist furnishing an entire house from an English upholsterer. While the Washingtons did not record their impressions of the Belvoir renovation, they signaled their approval in a different manner. Just over a decade later, when the Fairfaxes moved permanently to England at the outbreak of the American Revolution, the Washingtons either purchased or were given nearly a third of the London-made furniture from Belvoir, and they continued to use much of it for the rest of their lives.

In September 2013 George William Fairfax's account book surfaced at auction, and the Mount Vernon Ladies' Association purchased it. The document lists all the purchases the Fairfaxes made in London between 1760 and 1772, offering remarkable insight into the material lives of one of the wealthier families in colonial America. Belvoir burned in 1783, leaving behind only a foundation and archaeological remains. Although scholars have long acknowledged Belvoir as the most architecturally significant and influential

Figure 1   William Fairfax and George William Fairfax Account Book, 1742, 1748, 1760–1772. Account book B kept by George William Fairfax "Containing Tradesmen Shop Notes & c from the Year 1760 to the Year [1772]." (Courtesy, Mount Vernon Ladies' Association; photo, Gavin Ashworth.)

Figure 2   Invoice for furniture and upholstered goods purchased by George William Fairfax from the London firm William Gomm and Son and Company on March 31, 1763, on pp. 1–2 in George William Fairfax's account book. (Courtesy, Mount Vernon Ladies' Association; photo, Gavin Ashworth.) The goods are listed with their prices on the right and the numbers of their shipping crates on the left.

eighteenth-century house in Fairfax County, Virginia, its loss, the absence of images, and a dearth of documentary references have prevented a full understanding of the property. The emergence of the Fairfax account book and its subsequent examination in conjunction with the archaeological record have revealed incredible detail about the rooms at Belvoir and the manner in which the Fairfaxes furnished them. The first four pages of the volume are the most significant to understanding the house: they feature an invoice for furniture and upholstered goods purchased from the London firm of William Gomm and Son and Company for use at Belvoir (figs. 1–3).

Figure 3 Invoice for furniture and upholstered goods purchased by George William Fairfax from William Gomm and Son and Company on March 31, 1763, on pp. 3–4 in George William Fairfax's account book. (Courtesy, Mount Vernon Ladies' Association; photo, Gavin Ashworth.)

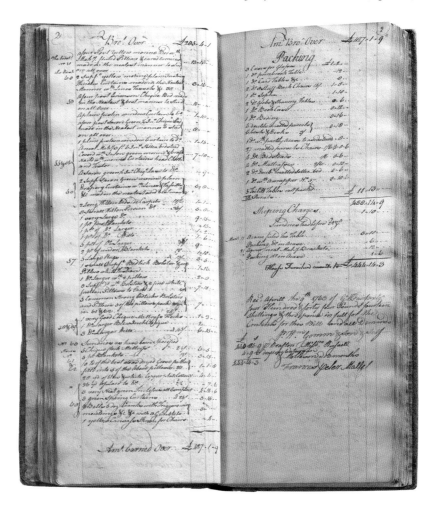

Read in conjunction with the archaeological remains of the house, a 1773 inventory held by the Virginia Historical Society, and a few surviving furnishings, the account book allows modern scholars to reconstruct much of Belvoir's appearance. By positioning George William and Sally Fairfax's material choices within the context of their biographies, their social aspirations, and their family dynamic, a new image emerges of a couple utilizing material goods to establish and confirm their position in society.[1]

This article traces the story of the Fairfax furnishings and the critical role they played in the lives of George William and Sally Fairfax, and later, the lives of George and Martha Washington. The central narrative is George

William's declining relationship with his cousin, Thomas, Lord Fairfax, and his continuing attempts to regain Thomas's favor. Lord Fairfax owned the largest land grant in Virginia, known as the Northern Neck Proprietary, and his patronage through position and inheritance was critical to George William's success in life. At a critical juncture in the narrative, George William becomes heir apparent to his cousin's title—a title with no fortune—and the couple decides to use the furnishings of their Virginia home to assert their status as English aristocrats in the British colonies. They construct two exceptional rooms, a dressing room and a bedchamber, for Lord Fairfax's use, in an effort to bring them back into his good graces. In so doing, the couple fails to see that the aristocratic behaviors embodied in the furnishings of these two rooms are no longer suited to the rapidly changing perspectives of Virginia colonists as the Revolutionary War approaches. Defeated and outmoded, the couple moves permanently to England in 1773, and their furniture takes on new life.

The furniture is sold at auction, presenting an excellent opportunity for local planters to acquire fashionable British goods at a time when trade is cut off to the mother country. George and Martha Washington utilize this opportunity as they expand Mount Vernon to update two of the more public rooms in the house, their dining room and front parlor. For the Washingtons, the furniture represents an opportunity to furnish their rooms with goods that have been tried and approved by one of the grandest families in the colony. Now, the rediscovery of the Fairfax account book and a reexamination of the corresponding documentary record allow scholars to trace those furnishings through time and space and to examine their every detail at a granular level in a manner previously not seen in American houses. By melding furniture, style, and personal biography into a single narrative, the Fairfax furnishings offer a lens into the lives of two of the most important families in Virginia and how they used furniture to define themselves and their standing in society.[2]

Fairfax Proprietary

George William Fairfax's father, Colonel William Fairfax, moved to Virginia in 1734 to act as land agent for his cousin Thomas, 6th Lord Fairfax of Cameron, the single largest landowner in colonial Virginia. Lord Fairfax owned the Northern Neck Proprietary, which consisted of all of the land between the Potomac and Rappahannock Rivers from their emergence in Chesapeake Bay to their headwaters. Thomas, 6th Lord Fairfax managed the land through a series of proprietary land agents resident in the colony (fig. 4). Lord Fairfax might have left his Virginia lands to the management of others had it not been for a series of three unfortunate circumstances. First, his father, Thomas, 5th Lord Fairfax, had squandered much of the Fairfax estate in England, leaving little money and diminished lands to meet the baron's many financial obligations and forcing the young squire to be frugal at an early age. Second, Lord Fairfax learned that his land agent, Robert "King" Carter of Corotoman, had unduly enriched himself by issuing hundreds of thousands of acres of proprietary land to himself,

Figure 4   Chimney back, Marlboro Furnace, Frederick County, Virginia, ca. 1770. Cast iron. 34½" x 31". (Courtesy, United States Army Engineer Museum, Fort Belvoir, Virginia; photo, Robert Hinds.) Thomas, 6th Lord Fairfax commissioned a set of chimney backs, represented by this example, for his home at Greenway Court in Clarke County, Virginia. The arms are those of Fairfax, featuring a lion rampant, impaling Culpeper, featuring a bend or diagonal stripe. The Culpeper arms are those of Lord Fairfax's mother, Catherine, Lady Culpeper, the heir to the Northern Neck Proprietary.

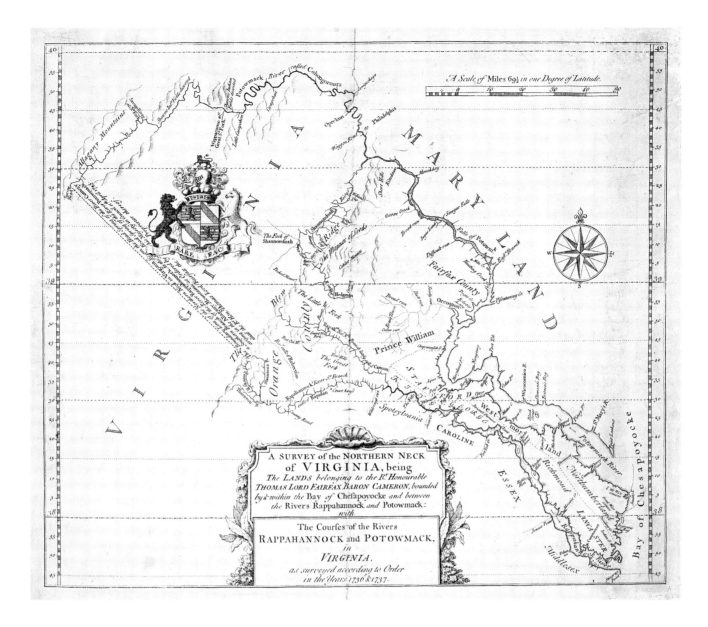

Figure 5 John Warner, *A Survey of the Northern Neck of Virginia, being the lands belonging to the R.t. Honourable Thomas Lord Fairfax Baron Cameron, bounded by & within the BAY of Chesapoyocke and between the Rivers Rappahannock and Potowmack, in Virginia* (London, 1745). 12" x 14". Engraving on paper. (Courtesy, Colonial Williamsburg Foundation.) According to the terms of the Northern Neck grant, Lord Fairfax owned all of the land between the Rappahannock and Potomac Rivers, a claim disputed by Virginia's colonial government. Fairfax requested that the Privy Council resolve the dispute, and the two sides employed surveyors to determine the bounds in 1736 and 1737. The Privy Council ruled in Lord Fairfax's favor in 1745, leaving him with more than five million acres of land.

his children, and his grandchildren, making him the wealthiest man in Virginia. Third, the exact boundaries of the proprietary were not firmly established, and the Virginia Colony began questioning the boundaries after Robert "King" Carter's death in 1732. The Potomac and Rappahannock Rivers had numerous tributaries, and determining exactly which ones constituted the "headwaters" would make a crucial difference in the total acreage owned by the baron (fig. 5).[3]

Lord Fairfax required an administrator to help consolidate power and make the proprietary profitable, and he hired his first cousin and childhood friend, Colonel William Fairfax, to leave his post in Massachusetts and come to take control of Lord Fairfax's Virginia lands. Colonel William Fairfax had all of the necessary skills. At an early age, William had embarked on a career in the colonies and held a series of lucrative public offices. He began as collector of customs for Barbados before becoming the chief justice and later governor of the Bahamas. He then moved to the Massachusetts Bay

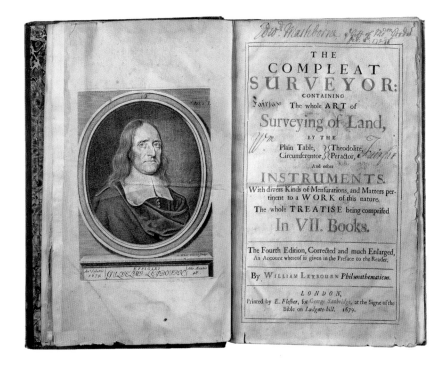

Colony where he served as collector of customs for Salem and Marblehead. In these positions, he proved himself an able bookkeeper capable of tracking customs revenue for the Crown. He also had learned the art of surveying while young, a skill that would prove vital in Virginia, where he oversaw the establishment of the proprietary's boundaries and approved the many surveys that accompanied individual land patents (fig. 6). In 1734 William Fairfax moved his young family to Virginia in order to take stock of Lord Fairfax's land holdings and prepare for the 1735 Lord's arrival in the colony. He immediately assumed the post of collector of customs for the South Potomac. William was later elected to the House of Burgesses and eventually appointed president of the Governor's Council. In each of these Virginia offices, he served as an advocate for the interests of the proprietary.[4]

After thoroughly exploring the lands in his charge, Col. Fairfax began amassing property at the heart of the bustling proprietary in 1736. On the Potomac River in Prince William County, he planned to build a large house to establish permanently his family and to serve as the proprietary land office. Located on the edge of the Tidewater region, Prince William County opened for settlement in 1722, attracting colonists from the lower Chesapeake desperate for fertile tobacco-growing land. Within a decade of the colonel's initial purchases, Prince William County's population had grown so large that the legislature resolved to divide it into several counties. The area north of the Occuquan River, which included the colonel's land, became the County of Fairfax. In 1748 the inhabitants of Fairfax County petitioned the House of Burgesses to establish a town and port at the head of navigable waters on the Potomac. They named the town Alexandria and hoped it would serve as an entrepôt for trade with the Ohio Territory.[5]

Belvoir

Sometime between 1736 and 1741 William Fairfax built the first prodigy house in the region, naming it Belvoir after a family holding in Yorkshire. For him, the house and surrounding grounds were more than an aspirational statement; they confirmed his status as a member of the trans-Atlantic British elite. The fourth son of a baron's second son had built his reputation, and a large income, as a colonial administrator, and he was prepared to set down roots and permanently establish his family in Virginia. Colonel Fairfax intended to impress when he built a grand two-story Georgian double-pile house that likely had five bays. Constructed of brick with a molded water table and a footprint of 56' x 37', the house immediately signified its role as both the dynastic seat of the Fairfax family and the administrative center of the Fairfax proprietary. In size and degree of finish, it compared favorably with many of the larger brick dwellings of the lower Tidewater region (namely, Sabine Hall, 1738; Shirley, 1738; and Cleve, 1746). The first floor of Belvoir contained "four convenient Rooms" on either side of "a large passage," which most likely stretched through the house and included a large central staircase (fig. 7). During Col. Fairfax's ownership, the four rooms on the first floor likely included a large dining room, a smaller parlor, a bedchamber, and a study or office. The second floor had "five Rooms," almost certainly all bedchambers and storage, and a stair passage.[6]

Figure 7 Conjectural first-floor plan of Belvoir, ca. 1740–1763, reflecting changes made by George William and Sally Fairfax in 1763.

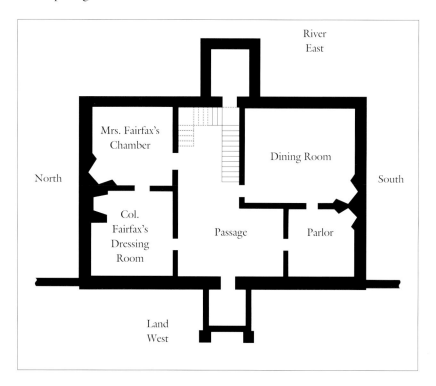

The grounds surrounding the house were among the more highly cultivated in the colony. The mansion house occupied a dramatic bluff at the crest of a ridge overlooking the Potomac River. On the land side, there was a large carriage circle flanked by two outbuildings, likely the proprietary

Figure 8 Anne Byrd Carter, attributed to William Dering, probably Charles City County, Virginia, 1742–1746. Oil on canvas. 50½" x 40". (Courtesy, Colonial Williamsburg Foundation.) The garden setting, likely at Westover in Charles City County, Virginia, closely resembles that found archaeologically at Belvoir.

land office and kitchen. Curved brick walls connected the two buildings to the main block of the house and to the brick walled court or garden on the river side. The archaeological remains of the riverside court likely closely resembled the one depicted in William Dering's 1742–1746 portrait of Anne Byrd Carter (Mrs. Charles Carter) (fig. 8). In that picture, Carter stands before a court of carefully manicured grass surrounded by a brick wall with wooden palings. In the distance, a small brick garden house frames the view. To maintain symmetry, there was likely a matching building on the other side, as there was at Belvoir. A curved brick wall extends between the two buildings and there was almost certainly a gate at the center, as at Belvoir. At Belvoir, the curved wall sat at the edge of the bluff overlooking the river, accentuating the view from the house (fig. 9).[7]

Colonel William Fairfax's Family
Although Lord Fairfax had no wife or children, Col. Fairfax did. By the time the latter moved to Belvoir, he had six children by two marriages. By his first wife, Bahamian Sarah Walker, Fairfax had four children: George William, Thomas, Anne, and Sarah. Sarah, his wife, died in childbirth in

Figure 9 R. E. Collins, conjectural view of Belvoir and gardens, 1940–1950. (Courtesy, Library of Congress.) While fanciful, this drawing illustrates the major features of Belvoir as found archaeologically. The garden had a central pathway, but the remaining divisions are conjectural.

1731, and William quickly married Deborah Clarke of Salem, Massachusetts, by whom he had three children: Bryan, William Henry, and Hannah. The two daughters from the first marriage wed prominent citizens of Fairfax County. Anne married Lawrence Washington of Mount Vernon, the elder half-brother of George Washington, and Sarah married British merchant John Carlyle of Alexandria. The two surviving sons, George William and Bryan, married two sisters, Sarah (Sally) and Elizabeth Cary, daughters of Colonel Wilson Cary of Ceelys, one of the wealthier men in Virginia and a member of the Governor's Council.[8]

Lord Fairfax took an early interest in the colonel's eldest son and heir, George William Fairfax, and sent him to England at age eleven to be educated at his expense. Once George William's schooling was complete, Lord Fairfax appointed him deputy land agent and brought him back to Virginia, setting him up to assume his father's role and eventually to take over management of the proprietary. In 1746 George William accompanied his father and representatives of both Lord Fairfax and the colony to run the boundary line of the proprietary. Two years later, during the rush to issue land grants after the boundary's finalization, William Fairfax sent George William and sixteen-year-old George Washington to survey a number of plots of land across the Blue Ridge Mountains. While this trip whetted George Washington's appetite for the American frontier, it seems to have had the opposite effect on George William. That same year, he married Sally (Sarah) Cary and settled into the domestic life of a Tidewater gentleman at his father's home on the banks of the Potomac River. George William's preference for the genteel Chesapeake lifestyle was at odds with the needs of the proprietary and Lord Fairfax, who required a land agent close by to the major land grants.[9]

Although George William Fairfax was not as much of a frontiersman as his father, he was far from idle. At Belvoir, he managed a 2,000-acre tobacco plantation, a commercial fishery, and stone quarries, all worked by enslaved laborers. At his "Shenandoah" property in Frederick County, he built an iron foundry while also speculating in western lands as a member of the Ohio Company. He continued to serve the political interests of the proprietary through his election to the House of Burgesses as a representative for Frederick County, where he also served as justice of the peace and a colonel of the county militia during the French and Indian War. He eventually became a member of the Governor's Council in 1768, a position that allowed him to advocate for the interests of the proprietary.[10]

In 1745 the Privy Council finalized the boundaries of the Northern Neck Proprietary as surveyed, allowing Lord Fairfax to open the western lands to settlement. Lord Fairfax recognized the economic necessity of moving closer to his new land grants. In 1749 the baron erected a small log cabin on a plot of land he called Greenway Court near the fledgling town of Winchester (fig. 10). Winchester occupied a strategic location on the Great Wagon Road, the thoroughfare taken by large numbers of German and

Figure 10 Greenway Court, Clarke County (formerly part of Frederick County), Virginia, illustrated in Henry Howe, *Historical Collections of Virginia* (Charleston, S.C.: S. C. Babcock and Co., 1845), p. 235. (Courtesy, Mount Vernon Ladies' Association.) Lord Fairfax lived at Greenway Court with his nephew Thomas Bryan Martin. The roof collapsed in 1834, and the house was torn down.

Greenway Court, the seat of Lord Fairfax.

Scotch-Irish immigrants eager to settle the fertile farmland beyond the Blue Ridge Mountains. George William chose to remain at Belvoir rather than follow Lord Fairfax, an act that created a rift between the two men from which they never recovered. As long as Col. Fairfax lived, however, the proprietary land office remained at Belvoir and the agent's title in George William's hands. In the meantime, Lord Fairfax sought someone to help manage the burgeoning western business at Greenway Court, and he brought his nephew Thomas Bryan Martin from England in 1751 to live with him and train in the business. George William viewed Martin's presence as a threat to his position as land agent, and the two men quickly developed a hostile relationship.[11]

In 1747 George William became heir presumptive to his cousin's title, elevating his status in English society. In the British peerage, most titles descend in the direct male line. If the current holder fails to produce a male heir, the title passes to the closest male relative of the peer in a direct male line from the original holder. Although Thomas, 6th Lord Fairfax was a confirmed bachelor, his brother, Robert (later 7th Lord Fairfax) had produced a male heir, presumably securing the Fairfax title in the Culpeper line. After the child's death in 1747, Robert sought a second wife and married Dorothy Best on July 15, 1749. Her death the next year and Robert's subsequent failure to remarry left George William all but certain that he would inherit the title, albeit one with no fortune. The Fairfax lands in Yorkshire were no more, and Lady Fairfax's five-sixth share in the proprietary would pass to the nearest Culpeper relations. George William could only hope that he would be left the one-sixth share that Lord Fairfax inherited in his own right as a means of maintaining a lifestyle appropriate to the title.[12]

On September 3, 1757, Colonel William Fairfax died after leading the proprietary through the transition from an ill-defined land grant producing little income to a fully surveyed grant of more than five million acres with rapidly expanding settlement and increased revenue. His loss left a hole in the lives of both the proprietor and the Fairfax family and further complicated the ties between Lord Fairfax and George William. George William inherited all of his father's land at Belvoir, all of his household goods, and three slaves. Almost immediately after his father's death, George William boarded a ship bound for England to appeal to the Board of Trade for his father's former post as collector of customs for the South Potomac, a position worth between £500 and £600 annually.[13]

George William Fairfax returned to Virginia in 1758, having secured his position as collector of customs for the South Potomac. Not long after, he received word from Yorkshire that his uncle Henry Fairfax of Towlston Grange, his father's eldest brother and heir to the family fortune, had died, leaving him a sizable Yorkshire estate as next in line. The Reverend Thomas Moseley, caretaker of the property, was almost jubilant when he wrote to George William with news of Henry's death. He noted that George William needed "to bring no more money into England than what is necessary to defray yr voyage here" and hinted that his uncle's affairs turned out to be "greatly beyond [his] expectation." Moseley refused to "properly condole with [George William] for his Departure," suggesting that Henry Fairfax's "life was of no service to his relations" and that Henry "was daily surrounded with a set of low, mean men." Less than two years after his previous visit to England, George William and Sally prepared to embark for the mother country yet again "to put a stop to the foreclosing of the Mortgage on the Redness Estate," one of his grandmother's mortgaged estates. He wrote hastily to Lord Fairfax on May 1, 1760, requesting another leave of absence, this time for between twelve and eighteen months. Yet again, the proprietary would be left without a land agent. After missing Lord Fairfax in Williamsburg in the summer of 1760, George William wrote again, but this time he noted that Lord Fairfax could send written consent for his absence to his agent in London. Lord Fairfax never replied to either letter, and George William and Sally sailed for London. By the time the couple embarked, George William complained to Lord Fairfax that the income at the Belvoir land office had slowed so much that he could barely pay for a clerk and stationery.[14]

Purchasing in London

With inheritances from his father and uncle and revenue from both his new post and his fees as land agent, George William could sustain a substantial lifestyle—but not quite the one he believed was most suited to his position as heir presumptive to his cousin's barony. George William had an encumbered financial position, and he wrote to Lord Fairfax complaining that should he survive Lord Fairfax and his brother "the great Estates formerly annexed to the Titles have long since changed their Channel." He worried that it would be his lot "to drag Titles which I can by no means Support the dignity of." Rather than live within their means, George William and Sally chose to improve their material surroundings to accord with their new social station in a manner appropriate to the dignity of the title. As material culture scholars have shown, men and women with small mercantile and landed estates attempted to confirm their social standing by building houses and purchasing furnishings appropriate to their station rather than presuming to ape the upper echelons of aristocracy. By residing in the proper classical home and furnishing it with the correct goods, the Fairfaxes participated in a universal British language of polite sociability. They hoped that Lord Fairfax would leave them the one-sixth share of the proprietary that he controlled in his own right to support the title.[15]

The Fairfaxes remained in York with family and attempted to resolve complex inheritance issues for the next two and one half years. Although the couple likely always intended to return to Virginia in the spring of 1763, they hastened their preparations when they learned that on February 10, 1763, the British had signed the Treaty of Paris, officially ending the French and Indian War. With the Atlantic Ocean once again open to uninhibited trade and French vessels no longer threatening their British rivals, the couple quickly realized that "ships would sail as they could get ready" rather than wait for escort by vessels from the British Navy. Concerned that they would not be able to purchase all of the goods they needed before the vessel on which they intended to travel departed, George William and Sally boarded their horse-drawn chaise on February 15 and began the four-day overland journey to London.[16]

Two days after arriving in London, George William and Sally visited the warerooms of William Gomm and Son and Company. Their London agent, Samuel Athawes, or one of their relatives might have recommended the firm to the couple. London upholsterers by then had evolved as a trade beyond the traditional role of fitting up "Beds, Window-Curtains, and Hangings" and covering "Chairs that have stuffed Bottoms" to become con-

noisseurs "in every Article that belongs to a House" (fig. 11). Upholsterers either employed or marshaled a diverse range of tradesmen, including chair makers, cabinetmakers, glass grinders, carvers, finish specialists, woolen drapers, paper stainers, and metal smiths. In 1763 London cabinetmakers and upholsterers were at the height of their trade. The year before, Thomas Chippendale issued the third edition of *The Gentleman and Cabinet-Maker's Director*, a publication that a decade before had established cabinetmakers and upholsters as taste-makers in their own right. Over the next ten days, George William and Sally worked with the Gomm firm and other suppliers to outfit completely their Virginia home.[17]

While upholsterers with aristocratic connections, such as Chippendale or Vile and Cobb, occupied warerooms in the fashionable shopping district behind St. Paul's Cathedral, second-tier firms, including Gomm and Son, often set up shop on the outskirts of the city, where land was cheaper and space more plentiful. In 1736 William Gomm moved into Newcastle House, former home to the Dukes of Newcastle, in Clerkenwell Close on the northern edge of the city and set up shop as a cabinetmaker (fig. 12). Clerkenwell Close had once been an aristocratic enclave, but during the late seventeenth and early eighteenth centuries it transitioned into a working-class neigh-

Figure 12   Newcastle House, Clerkenwell Close, London, illustrated in William J. Pinks, *The History of Clerkenwell*, edited by Edward J. Wood (London: J. T. Pickburn, 1865), p. 97. (Courtesy, British Library.)

Figure 13   J. Sanders, Gomm and Company warerooms, Old St. James's Church, Clerkenwell Close, London, 1786. (Courtesy, Society of Antiquaries.) Gomm and Company built its warerooms with continuous north-facing windows atop the south cloister of Old St. James's Church. The "Gothick" arcade incorporates trefoils to harmonize with the style of the cloister. The firm sold furniture with gothic arches similar to those seen on the ground floor of their warerooms.

borhood occupied by tradesmen. The outdated aristocratic house offered a home for William Gomm, and the firm used Newcastle House as the address for its "cabinet wareroom." Nearby, on the remains of the medieval cloister of St. Mary's nunnery, William and Richard Gomm built "the most compleat & extensive Suit of Ware-rooms in London," a two-story wooden building with continuous north-facing windows (figs. 13–14). Their work-rooms occupied additions built above the old Nuns' Hall (fig. 15). The Gomms spent more than £5,000 improving their properties in the close, and while there is little information regarding the number of tradesmen they employed, the sheer scale of the firm's property suggests that their output was massive.[18]

Typically, the upholsterer visited the home of a client to take measurements and make preliminary sketches before presenting his ideas to the

Figure 14   J. Sanders, Old St. James's Church, remains of the south cloister, Clerkenwell Close, London, 1786. (Courtesy, Society of Antiquaries.) Gomm and Company added the "Gothick" screen at the end of the arcade.

Figure 15   Gomm and Company workrooms, Nuns' Hall, Clerkenwell Close, London, illustrated in James Charles Crowle's edition of Thomas Pennant, *Some Account of London* (London: Robert Faulder, 1793). (Courtesy, British Museum.) Gomm and Company built its work rooms atop the medieval remains of Nuns' Hall.

client. Consumers who had fewer resources or lived in distant locales could reduce costs by taking the measurements themselves and hiring local craftsmen for installation. This approach entailed additional risk: if the goods arrived and they did not fit, the burden was on the client rather than the upholsterer. When the Fairfaxes visited Gomm and Son, the couple must have brought a floor plan with detailed measurements of Belvoir's rooms to facilitate the purchase of window curtains, carpets, and furniture in the proper sizes. With that degree of information, the Gomms could design and furnish virtually every aspect of an interior. Evidence suggests that the firm did precisely that for each room at Belvoir.[19]

Figure 16 William Gomm, *The Side of a Drawing Room*, London, 1761. Ink and watercolor on paper. 7¾" x 15 ¾". (Courtesy, Winterthur Library, Joseph Downs Collection of Manuscripts and Printed Ephemera.) Gomm's depictions of four elevations of a room were probably for a potential client. The drawings demonstrate his knowledge of the latest design books, his ability to create new elements, and his capacity to furnish a room tastefully in its entirety.

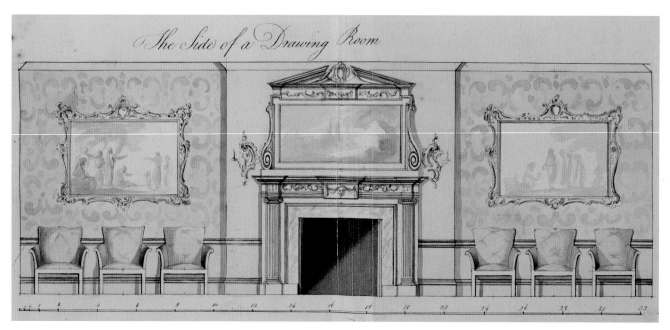

Figure 17 William Gomm, *The Side of a Drawing Room*, London, 1761. Ink and watercolor on paper. 8¼" x 16". (Courtesy, Winterthur Library, Joseph Downs Collection of Manuscripts and Printed Ephemera.)

Figure 18 William Gomm, *The Entrance of a Drawing Room*, London, 1761. Ink and watercolor on paper. 7" x 10½". (Courtesy, Winterthur Library, Joseph Downs Collection of Manuscripts and Printed Ephemera.)

Figure 19 William Gomm, *The Upper End of a Drawing Room*, London, 1761. Ink and watercolor on paper. 7¼" x 11¼". (Courtesy, Winterthur Library, Joseph Downs Collection of Manuscripts and Printed Ephemera.) English designers often created a focal wall in a room utilizing a sofa, candle branches, and looking glasses or pictures.

The ability to furnish a room en suite was a defining attribute of the eighteenth-century upholsterer. Four sketches executed by William Gomm (likely the younger) in 1761 illustrate the type of work his family firm offered its clients (figs. 16–19). The furnishings and decorations depicted in the sketches are probably more elaborate than those provided for Belvoir, but they show how upholsterers like the Gomms achieved harmony and resonance: there are ten matching chairs, a sofa, and window curtains with identical red fabric; a pair of pier tables with pagodas echoing those on the mirrors above; a "modern" or rococo looking glass with ornament similar to that on the large paintings and the window cornices; and a red damask (either wallpaper or fabric) covering the walls that pulls the entire composition together. In the colonies, achieving this level of coordination was difficult, even in the cities, where inhabitants were forced to rely upon goods—particularly textiles and wallpapers—imported from abroad.[20]

Figure 20 William Gomm, *A Cloath's Press*, London, July 18, 1761. Ink and watercolor on paper. 8¾" x 8¼". (Courtesy, Winterthur Library, Joseph Downs Collection of Manuscripts and Printed Ephemera.) The primary output of the Gomm firm was likely neat and plain pieces like this clothes press.

On February 24 George William Fairfax, almost certainly accompanied by Sally, returned to Gomm's warerooms "to choose Furniture &c in order to have an Estimate." The process of selecting furnishings for an entire house must have taken all day, and the couple did not return to their lodgings until dinner. While the Gomm firm could have produced almost anything in the rococo taste for the Fairfaxes, the couple's time constraints, the prevailing aesthetic of their social stratum, and budget seem to have pushed them towards stock items. Eighteenth-century British cabinetmakers and upholsterers kept well-made but conservatively designed items on hand to supply the middle-class market and to furnish lesser rooms of the aristocracy. Such stock-in-trade tended to be "neat," or "elegant, but without dignity," and "plain," or "void of ornament, simple." The vast majority of the furniture enumerated in the Fairfax estimate appears to have been in this "neat and plain" style (figs. 20–21). The distinguishing features of this type of furniture were high quality primary woods and hardware, and proportions, shapes, and moldings based on the classical orders.[21]

Figure 21 William Gomm, *A Desk & Bookcase*, London, August 15, 1761. Ink and watercolor on paper. 10¾" x 9¾". (Courtesy, Winterthur Library, Joseph Downs Collection of Manuscripts and Printed Ephemera.)

Like so many of their contemporaries, the Fairfaxes went to London to familiarize themselves with the latest tastes, but they were willing to buy their furnishings elsewhere if they could find similar items for less money. British consumers often found these cheaper prices in smaller cities, where cabinetmakers and upholsterers could operate with less overhead and less competition. The Fairfaxes, who were based in Yorkshire, considered acquiring some of their furnishings in York. George William's "List of Household & Kitchen Goods to be Purchased" has headings designated "London Price" and "York Price." The former records the prices received from Gomm and Son, but the latter is not filled out. Apparently, comparison shopping required more time and effort than the Fairfaxes could afford before returning to Virginia.[22]

While Gomm and Son could provide many of the necessary furnishings in-house, they did not stock wallpaper, papier-mâché ornament, or architectural woodwork. For wallpaper and papier-mâché ornament, the firm worked with Robert Stark, a paper stainer with a wareroom at Ludgate

Hill, a fashionable shopping district near St. Paul's Cathedral (fig. 22). Stark described himself as a "paper hanging maker" who sold "all Sorts of Paper Hangings for Rooms." His inventory probably included papers

Figure 22 Thomas Sherborn, trade card for Robert Stark, London, ca. 1765. (Courtesy, British Museum.)

Figure 23 Papier-mâché ceiling in the first-floor, southeast parlor of Philipse Manor, Yonkers, New York, ca. 1750. (Courtesy, Philipse Manor Hall State Historic Site, administered by the New York State Office of Parks, Recreation and Historic Preservation; photo, Steven Spandle.)

made both in his shop and from other English and French establishments, as well as expensive "India," or Chinese, papers. Stark also advertised papers "to [match] Damasks & Linens" and "a great Variety of papier mache . . . Ornaments modern and antique" (fig. 23). The Fairfaxes purchased enough wallpaper and border to outfit six rooms, papier-mâché ornament for the ceilings of two of the more formal spaces, and a variety of "branches," girandoles, and brackets. For architectural woodwork, they turned to London carver Thomas Speer, although it is not certain that he was part of the Gomm network. Speer sold the couple "3 New Viend [veined] Marble Pieces" with varying amounts of ornament to fit inside three carved "[wood] Mantils wth. frees & Cornice" for three of the finer rooms in Belvoir. The mantels and friezes probably resembled the one drawn by Gomm in his plan of the mantel wall of a room.[23]

Returning to Belvoir

When the Fairfaxes set sail with their furnishings in the spring of 1763, trouble was brewing back in Virginia. Lord Fairfax had cut off communication with George William and moved permanently to the western frontier, depriving the latter of his job as land agent. In 1761 Lord Fairfax had a new land office constructed at Greenway Court, and he named Thomas Bryan

Figure 24 Greenway Court Land Office, Clarke County, Virginia. (Courtesy, Dennis Pogue.)

Martin as land agent (fig. 24). There the two men lived in danger as the French and Indian War played out around them, and many of their neighbors fended off attacks from Native Americans. George William had urged Lord Fairfax to move to Belvoir for several years, and he was stunned by these developments. For the remainder of his life, he failed to see that his failure to move to the backcountry with his cousin to act as land agent was the main cause of the two men's strained relations, and he believed that Martin had turned the proprietor against him.[24]

Through their purchases and the manner in which they furnished Belvoir, George William and Sally signaled their intention to live according to their station in society, but in doing so, their choices became an implicit criticism of the current Lord Fairfax's lifestyle. Robert Fairfax of Leeds Castle, Lord Fairfax's brother, visited Virginia and recorded his concern about how Lord Fairfax lived, and those thoughts almost certainly mirrored George William's. Robert wrote that at Greenway Court the "House, Furniture, and Manner of Living is past all conception." He claimed that there was "not a gentleman within sixty miles," and that they were "surrounded by nothing but Buckskins, people that first settled here to kill deer for the sake of their skins, the most strange brutish people you ever saw." The nearest town, Winchester, was full of "Dutch & Germans," who were mostly "dissenters of different denominations," while the "Established Church," the true mark of British civilization, had only "one parson" to service five chapels in a county "a hundred miles long & forty broad." Consequently, each chapel met "once in five weeks," and "if the day proves Hot or Rainy, no parson." These observations on life in the backcountry stood in stark contrast to the increasing gentility of Fairfax County.[25]

As the Fairfaxes' enslaved workers unpacked the crates filled with furniture, textiles, wallpaper, architectural woodwork, and silver, Greenway Court could not have felt farther away. By 1763 Fairfax County was firmly established as home to the planter elite and was no longer the frontier that Colonel William Fairfax first encountered. The river towns of Alexandria, Colchester, and Dumfries offered taverns for entertainment and small shops stocked with necessary goods, while wealthy tobacco planters began to build large, highly refined houses around the county. House owners and guests looked to these houses and their furnishings as markers of social standing. These neighboring houses, such as George Mason's Gunston Hall (1752), John Carlyle's Alexandria house (1751), and George Washington's Mount Vernon (expanded 1757–1759), formed the foundations of polite society. They were more than people's homes; they were centers of hospitality where elite Virginians entertained their social equals through traditional rituals such as dinners, the taking of tea, and elaborate parties. Prior to leaving Britain, George William wrote home and ordered all of his father's household furnishings sold to make way for the London goods he planned to buy. With the new goods they brought with them, the Fairfaxes sought to assert their standing at the height of colonial society and to draw Lord Fairfax back to live at Belvoir through a pair of rooms created for his own use: the Blue "Dressing Room" and the "Chintz Chamber."[26]

Layout of Belvoir

While the furnishings for the rooms were exceptional for colonial Virginia, the floor plan and types of spaces at Belvoir were nearly all typical of those found in other homes of the Virginia gentry. The disposition of the rooms can be reconstructed using four specific pieces of evidence: a 1774 rental advertisement in the *Virginia Gazette*; archaeology; George William Fairfax's 1773 inventory of the house; and Robert Stark's 1763 wallpaper invoice. The advertisement describes the typical arrangement of rooms in a double-pile Virginia house, wherein the "lower Floor" consisted of "four convenient Rooms and a large Passage." In large gentry houses, the second floor almost always had a floor plan similar to that of the first. At Belvoir, the floor plan is also reflected in the division of rooms found archaeologically in the cellar, which is often seen in brick dwellings (fig. 25). There are four rooms of uneven size, two on either side of a large passage. The question then remains, which room was which? While George William Fairfax did not mention the floors in his inventory of the house, he appears to have listed them in the order one encountered them in the house. The first four rooms—the dining room, the parlor, "Col. Fairfax's D[ressin]g Room," and "Mrs. Fairfax's Chamber"—are listed before the remaining bedchambers and "The Dressing Chamber (see appendix)." Given typical Virginia practice, the first four rooms were almost certainly on the first floor (see fig. 7).[27]

The dimensions of the largest room, on the east, or river, front correspond with the measurements for a papier-mâché ceiling, purchased from Robert Stark along with "fine varnished Green" wallpaper for the space. Based on George William's inventory, which lists twelve chairs, two card

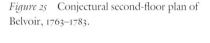

Figure 25 Conjectural second-floor plan of Belvoir, 1763–1783.

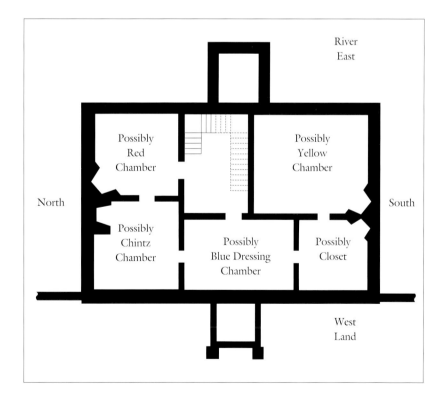

tables, and a sideboard table, this room—most likely the dining room—was the most heavily furnished space in Belvoir. The room also had three sets of window curtains, more than any other space on the first floor. The curtains were made of red moreen, the same fabric used to cover the chairs. Red and green were often used together during the period, making the moreen a logical choice to complement the green wallpaper provided by Stark. As in other Virginia dwellings, including Carlyle House, which Colonel William Fairfax's son-in-law built on nearly the same floor plan as Belvoir, there was probably a division between public and private spaces delineated by the central passage. This suggests that Col. Fairfax's Dressing Room and Mrs. Fairfax's Chamber occupied the two rooms on the other (north) side of the central passage. The remaining space, probably the parlor, was on the south side of the house. Parlors diminished in importance in Virginia interiors as dining rooms took precedence. The parlor at Belvoir had only eight chairs, a spider-leg table, a dining table, and a few smaller items.[28]

On the second floor, the disposition of the five rooms—blue "Dressing Room," "Red Chamber," "Chintz Chamber," "Yellow Chamber," and an unknown space likely used as a lumber room—is more difficult to discern. According to George William's inventory, the blue Dressing Room had three sets of window curtains and more furniture than any other space on the second floor. That number of windows and furnishings suggest that the blue dressing room either occupied room at the head of the stairs or the space above the dining room. The room likely functioned in tandem with an adjoining bedchamber, which was almost certainly the best bedchamber in the house, the "Chintz Chamber." As decorative arts scholar John Cornforth has noted, these "best rooms" were places for entertaining or conducting business with the most important guests. This pair of spaces likely functioned as the domestic equivalent of "state rooms." At the Governor's Palace in Williamsburg, Lord Botetourt used two rooms on the second floor for a similar purpose. The room at the head of the stairs on the second floor served as his dressing room, while his bedchamber directly adjoined the space. The Governor's Palace is the only other known instance of the use of such elaborate rooms in Virginia, a testament to the ostentation of these spaces at Belvoir. If the blue Dressing Chamber at Belvoir occupied the room at the head of the stairs and the "Chintz Chamber" occupied the large room beside it, perhaps the two remaining bedchambers, the "Red Chamber" and the "Yellow Chamber" occupied the two rooms on the east side of the house. The remaining room likely served as either a closet or a lumber room.[29]

Principal Entertaining Spaces

As with most Virginia great houses of the mid-eighteenth century, the principal entertaining spaces at Belvoir were the central passage, dining room, and parlor on the first floor. These spaces functioned in tandem and were almost always the most ornate rooms in the house. The central passage served as a room for social filtering and as one of the more important living spaces in the house. At Belvoir, the butler, who was likely one of the

Fairfaxes' enslaved people, opened the door for visitors and made the critical judgment of where to take them. For elite guests, the butler most often conducted them directly to the parlor, while those of lower rank remained in the passage where they would wait for the owner or another member of his family. The central passage also functioned as an informal living space because of the cross-breeze produced by opening the front and back doors. In such spaces, Virginia planters and their families often dressed more informally to take full advantage of the cooler air.[30]

At Belvoir, the passage was particularly spacious. There the Fairfaxes chose to imitate the stuccowork and stone entryways of grand English halls and entryways by installing "8 Pieces of Painted Stucco" wallpaper edged with "8 doz. borders." As decorative arts scholar Margaret Pritchard sug-

Figure 26   An Interior with Members of a Family, attributed to Strickland Lowry, Ireland, ca. 1770s. Oil on canvas. 25" x 30" (Courtesy, National Gallery of Ireland.) The architectural wallpaper printed *en grisaille* is one of a number of patterns that could have been called "Painted Stucco." The "Square Top Chairs" are likely similar to those in the central passage and Mrs. Fairfax's chamber at Belvoir.

Figure 27   Chairs in perspective illustrated on pl. 9 in Thomas Chippendale, *The Gentleman and Cabinet-Maker's Director* (London, 1754). (Courtesy, Winterthur Library, Printed Book and Periodical Collection.)

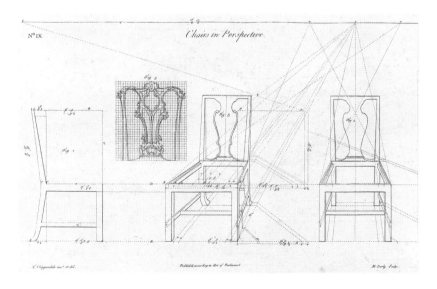

Figure 28 Wallpaper fragment recovered at Captain Lord Mansion, Kennebunkport, Maine, 1790–1810. Paint and polish or varnish on paper. (Courtesy, Historic New England.)

gests, "stucco papers" were likely printed architectural patterns painted *en grisaille* (fig. 26). Passages were often furnished with sets of chairs. The "14 Mahy. Marlborough Square Top Chairs [with] pin [cushion] seats" that Gomm and Son sold to the Fairfaxes for the room likely resembled the simple, square topped chairs illustrated in perspective in Thomas Chippendale's *Gentleman and Cabinet-Maker's Director* (fig. 27). Chairs of that basic design were popular in Virginia and Maryland and are represented by both locally made and imported seating. While the mahogany used for the Fairfaxes' chairs conveyed elite status, the simple design of that seating alluded to the more casual nature of the passage. "Figured Showhair," or horsehair, covered the slip seats, providing a resilient and easy-to-clean surface for chairs in constant use. While there were probably other objects in the space, such as old dining tables and possibly prints, the central passage or "The Passage below Stairs" is one of only three spaces whose furnishings are not listed in George William's inventory (the others are a small room on the second floor and "The Lobby," likely the second-floor stair hall).[31]

The dining room and parlor were the most formal spaces on the first floor, and entry required that a guest first pass through the central passage. By mid-century, dining rooms and parlors were often roughly equivalent in size and importance, representing the male and female spheres, respectively, but at Belvoir the dining room (20' 3" x 16' 5") was almost double the size of the parlor and was far more elaborate. For George William Fairfax, the dining room was the physical manifestation of his hospitality. There he presided over the table at dinner—the central social event of the day—and displayed the abundance of his estate through the many dishes of meat and vegetables arrayed on the table. He also exhibited his wealth through the many specialized accoutrements associated with meals: sets of spoons emblazoned with his crest, sets of English and Chinese ceramics, and sets of glassware for drinking. The room was one of the more architecturally elaborate in the house, with an entire ceiling covered in papier-mâché ornament; a chimneypiece likely consisting of a marble mantle with an ornamental frieze (a tablet flanked by appliques and trusses) surmounted by a carved wooden overmantle (an architrave with appliques or trusses and pediment with tablet, frieze, and central ornaments); "fine varnished Green" wallpaper; and upholstery and curtains in rich "Crimson morine" (fig. 28).[32]

The furniture in the room demonstrates that the space served multiple purposes. In the inventory, George William lists chairs, a sideboard, and a pair of card tables, indicating the room's use for dining and entertaining—but there were no dining tables. The dining tables were likely kept in the passage when not in use and only brought in for meals in accordance with established English fashion. The twelve mahogany chairs were the most expensive examples with wooden backs in the house. The set was upholstered over-the-rail with brass nails and had loose covers made from "Rich Crimson Chiq." The fixed and loose covers were made of wool and linen respectively which, fabrics that were durable, easy to clean, and were frequently used for dining chairs. The dining room also had the most expensive looking glass in the house, a "Large Sconce Glass the frame carvd &

Gilt in Burnished Gold," and a mahogany sideboard table "with fretwork upon the Edge of the Top, Astragal Mound[ing]s & Brackets." The dining tables were likely standard English models with turned legs and pad feet or straight legs, but following British precedent. When not used for dining, the room served as a place for other forms of entertainment. When George William left for England in 1773, the dining room at Belvoir contained a pair of "Mahy. 3ft. [wide] Square Card Tables lind wth Green Cloth." The tables were fairly simple, but they had "Astragal mouldings & open brack-

Figure 29 Johan Zoffany, *Sir Lawrence Dundas with His Grandson*, England, 1769–1770. Oil on canvas. 40" x 50" (Courtesy, Zetland Collection.) The carpet depicted by Zoffany would have been called a "Wilton Persian carpet" in the eighteenth century. Carpets of that type were based on Middle Eastern designs.

ets" that may have matched those on the sideboard table. Complementing all of these furnishings was a large and costly "Wilton Persian Carpet," a British copy of a Middle Eastern design (fig. 29).[33]

The parlor offered a less formal setting and was furnished more simply. During the middle of the eighteenth century, dining rooms and parlors

Figure 30 Spider-leg table, England, 1750–1770. Mahogany with mahogany and unidentified conifer. H. 27½", W. 28", D. 26⅞". (Courtesy, Mount Vernon Ladies' Association; photo, Gavin Ashworth.)

Figure 31 View showing the spider-leg table illustrated in fig. 30 with swing legs retracted and leaves down. (Photo, Gavin Ashworth.)

were often interchangeable spaces. The Fairfaxes, who kept a dining table in the parlor, probably ate there frequently. That room was also furnished with a "Strong fine Mahy. Spider Leg Table" on which Sally almost certainly served tea, which was the sole purview of the lady of the house (figs. 30–31).

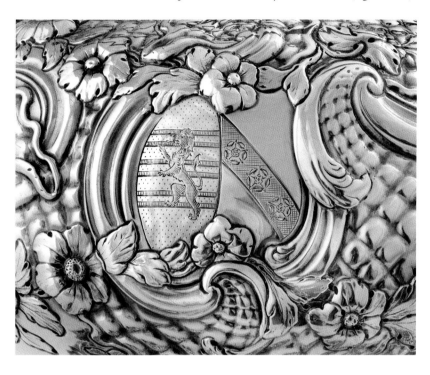

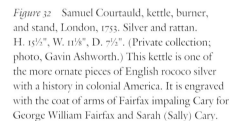

Figure 32   Samuel Courtauld, kettle, burner, and stand, London, 1753. Silver and rattan. H. 15½", W. 11⅛", D. 7½". (Private collection; photo, Gavin Ashworth.) This kettle is one of the more ornate pieces of English rococo silver with a history in colonial America. It is engraved with the coat of arms of Fairfax impaling Cary for George William Fairfax and Sarah (Sally) Cary.

Figure 33   Detail of the coat of arms on the kettle, burner, and stand illustrated in fig. 32. (Photo, Gavin Ashworth.)

The set of six chairs in that space was made of mahogany and "Covered over the rail wth. figured Horse hair & Brass naild." Their individual value was less than that of the dining chairs listed in George William's inventory. The most expensive seating in the parlor was the pair of "Mahy. Hollow Suff Back & Seat arm Chairs Coverd wth figured hair." Likely resembling French elbow chairs, those objects were likely intended to differentiate the owners from their guests. The parlor does not appear to have had wallpaper, although it was furnished with a pair of curtains in Saxon green moreen with line and tassel to pull up in drapery. A silver hot water kettle, urn, and stand survives with the arms of Fairfax-impaling-Cary, which the couple likely used in this space (figs. 32–33). It is one of the more ornate extant examples of English rococo silver with a history in colonial America, a testament to the Faifaxes' lavish lifestyle at Belvoir.[34]

Family Spaces

The private spaces, "Mrs. Fairfax's Chamber" and "Col. Fairfax's D[resin]g Room," functioned in tandem and were the nexus of family life. In eighteenth-century Virginia, the bedchamber occupied by the owners was often located on the first floor and served as the domain of the lady of the house. From this room, she had a prime vantage point to the dining room, the kitchen, and domestic outbuildings, enabling her to manage the household affairs within her purview. Often these rooms had closets to store

Figure 34 William Gomm and Company, chest-on-chest, London, 1763. Mahogany with oak and an unidentified conifer. H. 72½", W. 46¼", D. 26" (Courtesy, Tudor Place Historic House and Garden; photo, Gavin Ashworth.)

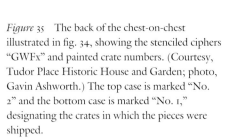

Figure 35 The back of the chest-on-chest illustrated in fig. 34, showing the stenciled ciphers "GWFx" and painted crate numbers. (Courtesy, Tudor Place Historic House and Garden; photo, Gavin Ashworth.) The top case is marked "No. 2" and the bottom case is marked "No. 1," designating the crates in which the pieces were shipped.

linens, spices, and other valuable commodities, and the lady kept the key. The paucity of case furniture listed in George William's inventory suggests that Belvoir had closets, although Mrs. Fairfax's Chamber did contain a "Mahy. 3 ft. 9 in. Double Chest of Drawers with Square Ends." That object, which is one of the few Fairfax pieces known, was probably for storage of Sally's clothing and some of the household linens. Made of mahogany in the "neat and plain" taste, the chest's high quality locks would have kept expensive textiles secure. The chest has George William's cipher "GEFx" and the shipping crate numbers painted on the back, markings which correspond with notes in the Fairfax account book (figs. 34–37).[35]

As in most eighteenth-century bedchambers, the bed with its expensive textiles was the most valuable object in the room. Mrs. Fairfax's chamber housed the least expensive bed in the house: the "four post" bed with curtains made from "Saxon Green ½ In[c]h Chique [sic]" from Gomm and Son. The bedstead was probably made from an inexpensive conifer, and its hangings were most likely linen, one of the less expensive fibers available,

Figure 36 Detail of the back of the of chest-on-chest illustrated in fig. 34 showing the stenciled cipher "GWFx" and painted crate number "No. 2." (Courtesy, Tudor Place Historic House and Garden; photo, Gavin Ashworth.)

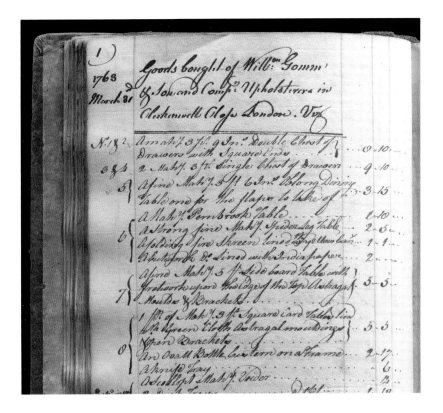

Figure 37 William Fairfax and George William Fairfax Account Book, 1742, 1748, 1760–1772. (Courtesy, Mount Vernon Ladies' Association; photo, Gavin Ashworth.) The account entry is for the double chest of drawers illustrated in figs. 34–36 along with crate numbers listed on the left.

with little to no trim aside from a stitched edge. "Saxon green" was a newly fashionable emerald color made by boiling a textile dyed Saxon blue in fustic. A set of four "Mahy. Square Top Chairs" similar to those in the central passage accompanied the bed, making the room suitable for entertaining close friends and family. The seats of the chairs were covered in canvas and were among the less expensive seating listed in George William's inventory. "Cases," or slipcovers, made of the same Saxon green linen check as the bed hangings and a single festooned window curtain furnished by Gomm and Son made the bedroom ensemble appear en suite. The dressing table listed in the 1773 inventory does not correspond to any object on the Gomm invoice, but it was one of the more expensive objects in Belvoir.[36]

Col. Fairfax's Dressing Room served as a study and his center of operations in the house. In the period, Virginia men occasionally had dedicated studies, but most often they simply used a desk set up in the dining room. At Belvoir, George William elevated the standing of his study by calling it his dressing room. It was a place for conducting business, entertaining guests, storing his clothing, and dressing, which he likely accomplished with the assistance of an enslaved valet. Belvoir had a separate office for the proprietary outside the house. George William's study was more lavishly furnished than Mrs. Fairfax's chamber, containing the most expensive piece of case

Figure 38 William Gomm and Company, shaving desk, London, 1763. Mahogany with oak and an unidentified conifer. H. 33¼", W. 15½", D. 15½" (closed). (Courtesy, Mount Vernon Ladies' Association; photo, Gavin Ashworth.)

Figure 39 Open view of the shaving desk illustrated in fig. 38. (Courtesy, Mount Vernon Ladies' Association; photo, Gavin Ashworth.) The lid and shelf are restored.

Figure 40 Open and expanded view of the shaving desk illustrated in fig. 38. (Courtesy, Mount Vernon Ladies' Association; photo, Gavin Ashworth.) The outer frame is original, with mortices indicating the positions of the mirror and the central brace.

furniture in the house: a "Mahy 3 ft. 6 Inh. [wide] Desk" surmounted by a "Bookcase wth. pidement head," "Gilt Ornaments" on the frieze, and doors "wired wth. Green Silk behind." That object was where George William housed his personal correspondence and business accounts. His study also contained "A Mahy. Shaveing Table & Glass" (figs. 38–40), a set of

Figure 41 Settee bedstead, England, 1760–1780. Mahogany with beech; leather, wool, linen, brass, iron. H. 49½", W. 40⅞", D. 28¼" (closed). (Courtesy, Sotheby's.)

Figure 42 Open view of the settee bedstead illustrated in fig. 41. (Courtesy, Sotheby's.) The curtains slide on an iron compass rod that is bent into a square, obviating the need for three separate curtains and keeping more heat inside. This feature occurs frequently on beds where the compass rod extends around the outside of the footposts and beneath the cornice.

four mahogany chairs, and a mahogany "Settea bedstead," which was a standard settee that opened up to form a bed large enough for one person (figs. 41–42). The bed was probably intended for George William's use when his wife was ill, but it could also have been used to create an extra bedchamber when there was a surplus of visitors. The chairs were slightly more elaborate than those in Mrs. Fairfax's chamber, indicating the space's more public nature. The Gomms covered their pincushion, or slip, seats and the settee bed with "Green morine," a worsted wool cloth often with a waved or stamped finish. The fabric was more expensive than linen. The entire suite of seating furniture also received loose covers of Saxon green check to protect the morine from light and dirt.[37]

Upstairs Bedchambers

In keeping with English custom, guests at Belvoir were assigned bedchambers based on their social station; the more important the visitor, the more elaborate the room. The differences among the bedchambers were often subtle, but they would have been readily apparent to the Fairfaxes' guests, who would have recognized variations in the furniture, upholstery, bed hangings, and window treatments. At Belvoir, the best bedroom was the "Chintz Chamber," distinguished by having curtains and bed hangings made from one of the more valuable textiles in the house. The textiles most likely to have been described as "chintz" were a multi-colored, printed and hand-painted Indian cotton, an English derivative, or an English or European printed copper plate design. The same material was used to make slipcovers for the four backstools in that bedchamber, which are valued higher than any of the bedchamber side chairs in George William's inventory. Second in the hierarchy of sleeping rooms was the "Yellow Chamber," which had window curtains, bed hangings, and slip covers for four mahogany side chairs made of "yellow morine." That textile was less expensive than printed chintz but costlier than linen check. The bed was made of mahogany, with "fluted Pillars" and a "carvd cornice." Although it is possible that all of the posts were fluted, those at the head of the bed were most likely plain. A pair of Wilton bedside carpets and a "Wilton Persian Carpet," enhanced the comfort of the space, but only the chintz and yellow bedchambers had carpeting. The "Red Chamber" held the third rank, with simple bed hangings of red check. The bedstead was likely made of an inexpensive wood and had no cornice, while the mahogany chairs were worth one shilling more per chair than those in Mrs. Fairfax's chamber. Like those chairs, the Gomms covered the mahogany chairs in canvas and provided them with slipcovers in the same material used on the bed.[38]

Ceremonial Spaces

The blue "Dressing Chamber" and "Chintz Chamber" in Belvoir were anomalies in eighteenth-century Virginia houses. The pair of spaces functioned as state rooms, or "best rooms," reserved for the use of the Fairfaxes' most important visitors. At Belvoir, George William and Sally Fairfax almost certainly intended these rooms as accommodations for Lord

Fairfax, and they hoped that their creation would entice him to move permanently to Belvoir. In England, gentlemen of rank often created such spaces for themselves, along with a more elaborate room or suite of rooms to accommodate royalty or visitors whose social status exceeded that of the estate's owner. In the most elevated settings, state rooms often consisted of an enfilade of spaces approaching the bedchamber of the king or the aristocrat. In this arrangement, the two most important spaces were the bedchamber and the dressing room. In the morning, the room's resident would rise in the bedchamber, where his valets dressed him in the company of his highest ranking guests. He then proceeded to the dressing chamber to hold a levee, a formal ceremony in which his valets applied the final touches to his outfit and wig while he sat at a dressing table. During the levee, the gentleman conducted the business of the day. According to Isaac Ware, the "dressing-room in the house of a person of fashion" was essential "for its natural use in being the place for dressing, but [also] for the several persons who are seen there." Mornings were often reserved "for dispatching business." Because men of rank were "not supposed to wait" for those of lower station, the latter were given "orders to come about a certain hour" and admitted while the former were dressing.[39]

Although Ware spoke to an audience of wealthy men and women beyond the aristocracy, such spaces are only known to have been used by aristocrats in colonial Virginia. George William attempted to transplant the trappings of the English landed elite to the colonies, where there was little appetite for such elevated spaces. The Belvoir suite is only the second recorded example of such an elaborate dressing room/chamber combination; the other belonged to Lord Botetourt, the royal governor of Virginia. The presence of such a space at Belvoir is a testament to the important position George William believed Lord Fairfax occupied in Virginia, and Ware's description must have encapsulated the former's vision of the way a man of Lord Fairfax's stature should conduct business in the colonies. As such, the arrangement and furnishings of the "Dressing Chamber" and "Chintz Chamber" rooms can be interpreted as "state rooms" and as a criticism of Lord Fairfax's casual lifestyle on the Virginia frontier. There can be little doubt that George William also intended to use these rooms when he acceded to his cousin's title at Lord Fairfax's death. As a man forced to live a frugal existence at an early age, Lord Fairfax seems to have chafed at the ostentation of these spaces, further dividing the two men.

The elaborate nature of the furniture and the color of the textiles and wallpaper made the dressing chamber visually striking. The room contained "8 Mahy. Marlboroug Stuff back Chairs" (backstools) and a "Large Sofa," one of the earliest documented in the Tidewater region. Backstools and sofas were among the more expensive seating purchased by colonists, and their use was typically reserved for the finest rooms. Examples from only three sets with Virginia histories are known. One set belonged to Robert Beverly of Blandfield in Essex County, one to William Byrd III of Westover in Charles City County, and one to the colonial government. Backstools introduced a level of comfort previously unseen in colonial Virginia, where chairs with wooden backs were the norm and easy chairs were expensive anomalies. Settees and sofas were even scarcer. A settee that descended in the Page family of Rosewell in Essex County survives, but no extant sofa with a colonial Virginia history is known. While couches with one arm and an open back were common, it remains unclear why sofas do not appear in Virginia inventories until the 1790s. The form was popular in the mid-Atlantic and northern colonies, as both imported and locally made examples attest. Perhaps, the reluctance to adopt such forms relates to the new, more relaxed style of seating that sofas introduced. As John Singleton Copley's portrait of an unknown lady demonstrates, sofas allowed sitters to relax and sink into the upholstery and strike a less formal, and even scandalous, pose than previous furniture forms allowed (fig. 43). Commentators and satirists in England and France remarked on the dangers posed by the new form, whose comfort might encourage one to spend the day relaxing in its cushions rather than applying oneself to productive pursuits. Regardless of the reason for their typical absence, the presence of this sofa further highlighted the aristocratic nature of the space. Among the other lavish furnishings were

Figure 43 John Singleton Copley, *Portrait of a Lady,* probably Boston, Massachusetts, 1771. Oil on canvas. 50" x 40". (Courtesy, Los Angeles County Museum of Art.)

an "India Skreen," a "Compass Japannd Dressing Glass," a "Large Ovall Glass" with a mahogany frame "painted lead white," a large looking glass, and a pair of "Girandoles" with "single branches." The looking glass may have been flanked by the girandoles and hung over the sofa, an arrangement common during the period (fig. 19). Underfoot, the Fairfaxes placed the largest carpet, which was likely a Wilton, given its high value.[40]

Textiles accounted for much of the expense of backstools and sofas. An ordinary side chair might require a little more than half a yard of fabric to cover a slip seat, while a backstool required approximately two yards of show fabric for the front and another yard of the same fabric or a less expensive textile for the back. Sofas required even larger amounts. The labor involved in upholstering backstools and sofas also contributed to their cost. Both forms required a base layer of webbing before the application of multiple layers of grass and horsehair, which were stitched between linen or coarser buckram. The craftsman who upholstered the Fairfaxes' backstools described those objects as "Mahy. Marlboroug Stuff back chairs stuffd in the best French manner." The "French manner" referred to the square, or boxed, shape of the seat and back. "Round Stuffed" chairs, like those provided for the Chintz Chamber, were less labor-intensive. The blue Dressing Room chairs were "cush[ion]ed," a term suggesting higher padding, and "Borderd & wilted," meaning that the seat sides were covered with a fabric panel different from that on the top and finished with a narrow welt at the seams. The upholsterer ornamented the show cloth with "2 Rows [of] No. 3" polished brass nails. The sofa was made "to match" and included "2 bolsters." Because no separate mattress or cushions are mentioned, the piece likely had a seat built up with horsehair like that on the chairs and had an overstuffed back. Sixty-seven yards of "Superf[in]e. Saxon Blew Mixd Damask" were used to upholster this seating and fabricate the three window curtains, which were trimmed with "the best silk Cover'd Lace" (tape) and fringe and fitted with "6 Silk & worsted Tassells" and cords so they could be drawn up in drapery. The chairs and sofa also received loose covers of "Superf[in]e Saxon Blew In[ch]. Chiq.," likely made of linen.[41]

The Fairfaxes used a striking color combinations in the blue Dressing Room. The Saxon blue damask of the furniture and curtains was meant to coordinate with plain blue verditer wallpaper of nearly the same color. Upholsterers could only achieve such exact color combinations when wallpaper manufacturers matched the hue of the textile, a feat only accomplished in the greater metropolitan areas. This particular color combination was extremely popular when the Fairfaxes were furnishing Belvoir. Johann Zoffany's *Sir Lawrence Dundas and His Grandson* (fig. 29), painted just a few years after the Fairfaxes returned from London to Virginia, depicts an interior with both decorative treatments. The curtains are woven in a damask pattern, while the wallpaper approximates the same color but has no pattern. Developed by a German scientist in 1743, Saxon blue was one of the first semi-synthetic dyes produced in Europe. Consisting of indigo dissolved in oil of vitriol (sulfuric acid), that dye produced a vivid turquoise blue. At Belvoir, the Gomm firm heightened the effect by using Saxon blue

on all of the furniture, rather than just the curtains as seen in Zoffany's painting. The blues in the dressing room would have stood out against the architectural components, which were probably painted a "stone" or cream color, and the "72 yds White [paper] mashe border" that created a fillet edging the wallpaper (fig. 44). The white border would also have picked up on the "painted lead white" detailing of the large oval looking glass.[42]

The Chintz Chamber was no less elaborate than its mate, the Dressing Chamber. The Gomm and Son upholsterer used "81 yds. of fine Chintz"

cotton to make the bed curtains, slipcovers, and window curtains. Robert Stark provided "6 pcs Chintz [wallpaper] to pattern," indicating that he made the wallpaper to match the chintz fabric. While this practice was common in elite English homes, no other instance has been documented in colonial America. The bed in the "Chintz Chamber" had "Mahy. fluted Pillows" (pillars or foot posts) and a tester frame fitted with a compass rod, an ingenuous fitting that allowed the curtains to travel freely around three sides of the bed; individual rods only allowed the curtains to travel their

Figure 46 Reproduction bed in the chintz chamber in Mount Vernon, Mount Vernon, Virginia. (Courtesy, Mount Vernon Ladies' Association; photo, Matthew Briney.) This bed is a conjectural reproduction of the chintz bed with drapery curtains George Washington purchased from Philadelphia upholsterer John Ross in 1773. The drapery curtains are tacked to the cornice and raised and lowered with line secured to brass rings on a pulley system installed in the cornice. This type of bed was the most expensive and complicated in the period.

length. The curtains on the chintz-draped bed were lined with white cotton chintz for extra warmth, and the bed included sixteen yards of buckram to stiffen a valance. All of the curtains were edged with "the best mixd worsted lace" and made to draw up in drapery (figs. 45–46). The chairs in the room were round stuffed backstools with loose covers made of the same chintz, rather than a less expensive fabric as was typically the case. Other furnishings included a single chest of drawers, a basin stand, a compass-shaped table, and bedside Wilton carpets.[43]

George William and Sally lived at Belvoir in splendor for the next decade, but George William's relationship with Lord Fairfax failed to improve. Meanwhile, the chancery case involving Henry Fairfax's estate dragged on, and George William was unable to collect his inheritance. By January 1773 the Fairfaxes began making plans to move to England, though they were not certain how long they would stay. The couple also had health problems, and they believed they could receive better care from English doctors. In early July, George William and Sally left Belvoir to visit her family at Ceelys in Elizabeth City County, Virginia, before boarding an England-bound ship in Norfolk in August.[44]

In a January 10, 1774, letter to George Washington, George William wrote that he and Sally would remain in England for the foreseeable future and not return to Belvoir. Although Washington may have predicted that outcome, seeing it in writing from his friend must have been difficult. Washington later wrote that he had spent "the happiest moments" of his life at Belvoir. In the Fairfaxes' absence, he acted as their power of attorney. George William requested that Washington and his farm manager, Francis Willis, rent Belvoir to a tenant and sell the furniture in the mansion. The Belvoir furnishings represented a substantial investment, and George William wanted to ensure that he could recoup as much as possible. Fairfax gave Washington specific instructions for the sale; the former wanted items sold for the Virginia currency equivalent of what he had paid for the pieces in pounds sterling, which was approximately twenty-three percent less. He also

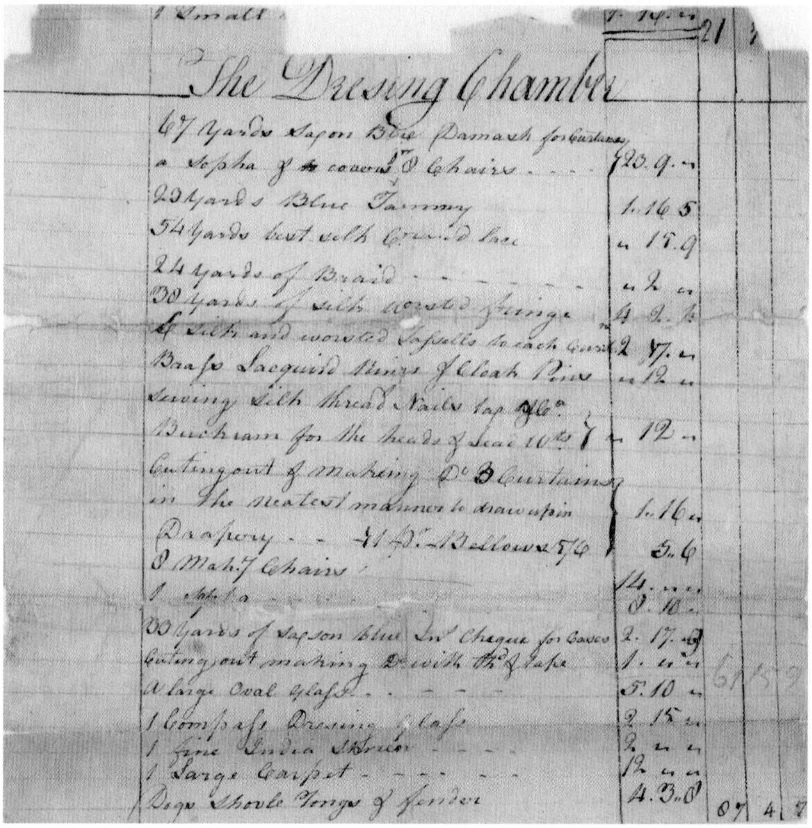

Figure 47 "The Dressing Chamber" from George William Fairfax's inventory of Belvoir, 1773. (Courtesy, Virginia Museum of History and Culture.)

requested that the furniture in the dining room and dressing chamber not be split up if possible, as the furnishings were more valuable as a group.[45]

Before departing, George William had prepared carefully for an eventual auction by leaving three detailed documents with Francis Willis. These included "Shop Notes" recording his 1763 London purchases; a detailed room-by-room inventory of the furnishings (fig. 47); and "a written direction for the Sale," which was probably a draft for newspaper advertisements. The inventory allowed Washington and Willis to see the value of each object at a glance. George William must have walked from room to room to jot notes on the furnishings of each. He then would have matched the items in each space with those in the shop notes and listed them in an inventory with an abbreviated description taken directly from the document and its corresponding price.[46]

Auction

With Fairfax's information in hand, Washington and Willis placed an advertisement, which was printed on June 2, 1774, in Mrs. Rind's *Virginia Gazette*:

> To be SOLD *at* Belvoir, *the Seat of the Honourable* George William Fairfax, Esq: in Fairfax *County, on* Monday *the 15th of* August *next (pursuant to his Direction)* ALL *his* HOUSEHOLD *and* KITCHEN FURNITURE *of* every Kind, consisting of Beds and their Furniture, Tables, Chairs, and every other necessary Article, mostly new, and very elegant. — Ready Money will be expected from every Purchaser under 5 £. and twelve Months Credit allowed those who exceed that Sum, upon their giving Bond and approved Security, to carry Interest from the Date, if the Money is not paid within forty Days after it becomes due.

The "mostly new, and very elegant" furniture was actually more than a decade old. While this may seem like false advertising, the furniture would have been considered reasonably new because the textiles were kept under slipcovers and the bedding was stored when not in use. Additionally, the neoclassical taste was barely beginning to arrive in Virginia, and the relatively conservative styles of the previous decade had not changed substantially.[47]

The first auction was well attended and included some of the more prominent members of the local community: George Washington, John Carlyle, George Mason, Doctor James Craik, and John Parke Custis. The most sought-after items were bedding, carpets, metal kitchen utensils, and fire equipment—the types of objects colonial Virginians would have typically bought as imports retailed locally or through agents abroad (fig. 48). Only three purchasers spent more than ten pounds, with George Washington leading at £169.12.6. At the conclusion of the auction, only one of the three most expensive suites of furnishings, the dining room, had sold. The minimum amount required to purchase the remaining two—the blue dressing chamber and the chintz chamber—was higher, which probably accounted for their failure to sell. Washington and Willis conducted a second sale on December 5, 1774, where they sold mostly livestock and agricultural equipment along with a few pieces of furniture. Again, the furnishings of the chintz chamber and blue dressing room did not sell.[48]

Figure 48 John Watts, pewter hot water plates, London, ca. 1765. Pewter. H. 9⁷/₁₆", W.11³/₁₆", D. 1⁷/₈". (Courtesy, Mount Vernon Ladies' Association; photo, Gavin Ashworth.) These may be three of the "10 Pewter Water plates" Washington purchased at the Belvoir auction along with other kitchen items.

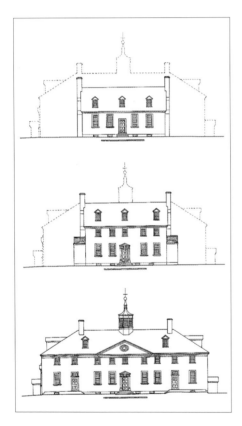

Figure 49 Mount Vernon, Mount Vernon, Virginia, 1734–1787. (Courtesy, Mount Vernon Ladies' Association.) George Washington expanded Mount Vernon, the house his father built in 1734, twice. He first added a second story and a garret between 1757 and 1759. Then, in 1774 George began building two wings, a project he completed in 1787. (Courtesy, Mount Vernon Ladies' Association.)

Fairfax Furnishings at Mount Vernon

The Fairfax auction came at a particularly opportune moment for George and Martha Washington. In 1773 the couple finalized their plans for major additions to Mount Vernon (fig. 49). They intended to extend the main house by adding two wings, one on the south to accommodate a first-floor study for George, a new bedchamber for the couple on the second, and a servant's hall in the basement; and one on the north, which would feature a two-story dining room for showcasing the family's hospitality and largesse. George and Martha may also have contemplated upgrading the small dining room, but those changes would not occur until 1775. This expansion was made possible by an inheritance of £8,000 received after the death of Martha's daughter Martha "Patsy" Parke Custis in 1773. With those funds, George settled his accounts with Robert Cary and Company in London and began purchasing window glass, plank flooring, and other goods for these additions (figs. 50–51).[49]

By the time the first Fairfax sale occurred on August 15, 1774, construction of Mount Vernon's south wing was well underway, but the American political climate was rapidly deteriorating and the couple could not import goods from England as they had done in the past. The previous December, patriots dumped tea into Boston Harbor to protest England's tax policy and the Crown closed the port, crippling Massachusetts's economy. That spring George Washington attended a session of the Virginia House of Burgesses and voted to support a day of fasting in solidarity with Massachusetts colonists, which resulted in the royal governor dissolving the assembly. In such uncertain times, the Fairfax auction offered the Washingtons exactly what they needed: access to expensive, well made, and fashionable London-made goods at a lesser cost and without the entanglements of importation.[50]

At this critical juncture, the Washingtons chose to upgrade the two finest rooms in their house, the dining room and front parlor, with the most expensive suites of furnishings from Belvoir, the dining room and blue dressing

Figure 50 Charles Willson Peale, *Colonel George Washington*, Virginia , 1772. Oil on canvas. 50" x 40". (Courtesy, Washington-Custis-Lee Collection, Washington and Lee University, Lexington, Virginia.)

Figure 51 Charles Willson Peale, *Martha Washington*, Virginia, 1772; refashioned ca. 1790. Watercolor on ivory, gold, copper alloy, glass. 2⅜" x 1¹³/₁₆". (Courtesy, Mount Vernon Ladies' Association; photo, Gavin Ashworth.)

chamber, which they acquired through purchase and gift. They also obtained furnishings from George William's dressing room for George's new study at Mount Vernon along with a few individual objects. Although the Washingtons could have bought new furnishings when they traveled to Philadelphia in 1774, the objects from Belvoir were familiar to them and were appropriate to their status. Additionally, the Fairfaxes' furniture had been well received by the couples' social peers, giving the Washingtons confidence to use the objects they acquired from Belvoir in their own home. Throughout their marriage, George and Martha appeared to be most comfortable adopting the latest fashions after seeing them in the homes of their friends. They followed the same approach during George's presidency when he and Martha acquired furnishings owned by the French minister to the United States, a story chronicled in this volume by Amy Hudson Henderson.[51]

From Dining Room to Dining Room

The availability of the Fairfax furnishings offered the Washingtons an opportunity to upgrade their existing (small) dining room. While there is no documentary evidence that George and Martha planned to alter that space prior to the Fairfax sale, the dining room, as executed, has several features noted in written descriptions of Belvoir's: a richly carved chimneypiece, ornamental ceiling, and "green varnished" walls (fig. 52). It was likely inspired by it. Work began sometime in 1775, when George gave his farm manager Lund Washington explicit instructions for the execution of the space. Rather than use imported English woodwork, as the Fairfaxes had, Washington commissioned carver William Bernard Sears, who had previously worked

Figure 52 "Small Dining Room" at Mount Vernon, Mount Vernon, Virginia. (Courtesy, Mount Vernon Ladies' Association; photo, Walter Smalling.)

for architect William Buckland, to carve the lower half of a chimneypiece taken directly from plate L in Abraham Swan's *The British Architect* (1745) (fig. 53). Sears executed his work in black walnut, a wood rarely used for architectural carving, even though the chimneypiece was to be painted. An anonymous immigrant stucco worker indentured to Washington and Fielding Lewis was responsible for the upper section of the chimneypiece as well as the ceiling ornaments. Sears appears to have either carved some of the patterns for the stucco worker or recut some of his ornaments to make the upper and lower sections of the chimneypiece

Figure 53   William Bernard Sears and anonymous "stucco man," chimneypiece in the "Small Dining Room," Mount Vernon, 1774. (Courtesy, Mount Vernon Ladies' Association; photo, Gavin Ashworth.)

harmonious. The ceiling ornaments created an effect even richer than those rendered in papier-mâché at Belvoir. Plasterwork was more expensive than papier-mâché because the medium required more labor, and it allowed for crisper detail and higher relief. The endeavor was made more expensive by the cost of the indenture and the craftsman's expenses. Sears painted the walls and mantel in the dining room a cream or stone color in 1775, but shortly thereafter Washington had the color changed to verdigris green. With its varnished surface, the green paint would have closely resembled the green varnished wallpaper of Belvoir's dining room.[52]

The Washingtons appear to have moved almost all of the objects in Belvoir's dining room into the small dining room at Mount Vernon. Although they declined to purchase the Fairfaxes' dining tables because they owned

Figure 54 Sideboard table, England, 1740–1757. Black walnut; marble. H. 29⅞", W. 28¼" D. 25⅞". (Courtesy Mount Vernon Ladies' Association; photo, Gavin Ashworth.) The knee blocks are missing.

Figure 55 Sideboard table, Pembroke table, and punch bowl illustrated in Benson J. Lossing, *Mount Vernon and Its Associations: Historical, Biographical, and Pictorial* (New York: W. A. Townsend and Company, 1859), p. 317. The author illustrated the Fairfax sideboard when it was at Arlington House, but his depictions are only partially accurate. Gomm and Company's invoice notes that the sideboard table they provided had no inlay.

SIDEBOARD, TEA-TABLE, AND PUNCH-BOWL.

Figure 56 Reconstruction (1952) of the bottle cistern William Gomm and Company furnished for George William and Sally Fairfax in 1763. Mahogany; lead, brass. H. 18⅜" x W. 23" D. 21¼". (Courtesy, Mount Vernon Ladies' Association; photo, Gavin Ashworth.) The brass bands, the lion mask handles, and the staves to which the handles are attached are the only surviving components of the "Ovall Bottle Cistern on a Frame" George Washington purchased from George William Fairfax.

a pair that George had purchased as a bachelor in 1757, Fairfax furnishings displaced many other objects previously in use in the Washingtons' dining room. The set of twelve chairs with crimson moreen upholstery and red check slipcovers from Belvoir took the place of an earlier set of English chairs, and the Fairfaxes' sideboard table replaced an earlier example with cabriole legs and turned pad feet (figs. 54–55). The fenestration in the dining room and conventional usage suggest that the Washingtons probably hung the carved and gilded sconce glass from Belvoir between two windows, which would have been a prominent location. Some of the items they purchased would have required alteration; the curtains were probably cut down to fit Mount Vernon's smaller windows. Other Belvoir objects used in the Washingtons' dining room included a knife tray, dish trays, a mahogany voider, a mahogany sweetmeat basket, and an oval mahogany cistern (fig. 56).[53]

From Col. Fairfax's Dressing Room to George Washington's Study
Before the 1774 addition to Mount Vernon, George Washington may have corresponded and managed his affairs using a desk in the dining room. That changed when he purchased the contents of George William Fairfax's dressing room and moved them into his new study in the south wing (fig. 57). Following British practice, he used that space to dress and to transact business. George Washington Parke Custis noted that his step-grandfather

Figure 57 George Washington's study, Mount Vernon, Mount Vernon, Virginia. (Courtesy, Mount Vernon Ladies' Association; photo, Robert Lautman.) George Washington added the built-in bookcase in 1786.

came to the study "two hours before day, in winter, and at daybreak in summer." There "a single servant prepared his clothes" and the general "shaved and dressed himself." The contents of Washington's study probably included the four mahogany chairs, settee bedstead, and shaving table brought from George William's dressing room at Belvoir. In his inventory, George William instructs that his desk "be sent to Col. Washn.," but there is no indication that the latter received it. By the time Washington died, he had updated his study's furnishings several times, relegating the furniture from Belvoir to other rooms in Mount Vernon.[54]

Other Purchases

At the Fairfax sale, the Washingtons purchased a variety of objects for use in their bedchambers, including the mahogany chest-on-chest from Sally's bed chamber, "1 wash stand & bottle & ca," and "1 Mahogany Close Stool." George also referred to the purchase of the "Mahogy. Spider made tea table" that formerly sat in the first-floor parlor in Belvoir. Like many of the participants in the Fairfax sale, the Washingtons also acquired goods of the type typically purchased as imports locally or through agents abroad: carpets, "1 bed, a pr blankets & ca," (mattresses and blanket for a bed), fireplace equipment, and metal kitchenware.[55]

From the Blue Dressing Room to the Front Parlor

In a March 2, 1775, letter to George Washington, George William Fairfax instructed his friend regarding the disposition of the final objects that remained unsold:

> As to the Furniture Remaing I can only repeat, that unless we can get near the Value of that in the Chinch [sic] Room, I should like to have it sent Over if Possible, meaning only the Curtains, Counterpains, and Covers of the Chairs, and that entire in the Blue or Dressing Room, I must beg your acceptance of, and the sooner its taken away the better.

George William's gift of the contents of the blue dressing room almost certainly arose from his affection for the Washingtons. The furnishings consisted of the eight backstools, sofa, and three sets of curtains covered with Saxon blue damask. Lund Washington probably oversaw shipment of the furnishings of the "Chintz Room" back to England. On August 14, 1775, the Fairfaxes' London agent, Samuel Athawes, reported that he had sent the curtains to his "upholsterers to be cleand & repaird" before having them delivered to George William at his residence in Yorkshire.[56]

In June 1786 George William Fairfax wrote George Washington to ask what had happened to the "blue damask Furniture out of Belvoir House." The latter responded:

> For the furniture of your blue room—which had been removed to this place . . . during my absence—for which I intend to allow whatever you might think it was worth (as we were under the necessity, it seems, of using it)—and of which you have been pleased to request my acceptance, my grateful acknowledgments of thanks are due—but as it was under full expectation of paying for it I am very willing, & ready to pay for it accordingly.

Washington acknowledged that he had simply moved the furniture to Mount Vernon after the sale. His phrasing implies that Martha decided to keep the furniture rather than him.[57]

The Washingtons had no need for the aristocratic trappings of a dressing room, but their parlor furniture was old and well used by the end of the Revolutionary War. The couple used the aristocratic furnishings of the dressing chamber to update their front parlor. In doing so, they transformed what had been a typical Virginia parlor with wooden splat chairs that could have been used for a variety of functions, including dining, into a distinguished space that could only have been used for elite entertaining. While they brought the furniture to Mount Vernon before the war, they

Figure 58 Front parlor, Mount Vernon, Mount Vernon, Virginia. (Courtesy, Mount Vernon Ladies' Association; photo, Gavin Ashworth.) The front parlor sofa, chairs, and window curtains are recreated utilizing the documentary evidence provided by the Fairfax account book and comparison with surviving period pieces with similar features.

were only able to integrate it into the space at its conclusion. At that time, they decided to redecorate their front parlor with the furnishings from the blue bedchamber and replace the old paint scheme—cream on the panels with window and door surrounds, and the mantel picked out in Spanish brown—with an overall cream, which was more in keeping with the Saxon blue upholstery fabrics on the furniture from Belvoir (figs. 58–60). Concurrent with this refurnishing and the completion of the "New Room," or large dining room, the function of the front parlor changed. Rather than

Figure 59 Front parlor, Mount Vernon, Mount Vernon, Virginia. (Courtesy, Mount Vernon Ladies' Association; photo, Gavin Ashworth.) Guests arrived through the central passage visible in the distance.

Figure 60 Front parlor, Mount Vernon, Mount Vernon, Virginia. (Courtesy, Mount Vernon Ladies' Association; photo, Gavin Ashworth.) The front parlor became the formal entry to the two-story New Room visible through the doorway.

Figure 61   New Room, Mount Vernon, Mount
Vernon, Virginia. (Courtesy, Mount Vernon
Ladies' Association; photo, Gavin Ashworth.)

serving as a space for multiple functions, the front parlor became the nexus
of a suite of rooms leading to the new addition (fig. 61). To further update
and elevate the status of the parlor, George commissioned John Rawlins,
the Baltimore stuccoman who was then adding the plasterwork to the New
Room, to install a ceiling featuring a neoclassical medallion with husks,
swags, and drapes (fig. 62).[58]

The Washingtons used the Fairfax furniture for the rest of their lives; it
was a poignant reminder for them of the happy times they had spent at Belvoir. During the Revolutionary War, Belvoir burned to the ground. Shortly
after George returned from the conflict, he rode to the site to inspect the
damage. On February 27, 1785, he wrote George William that "the dwelling
house & the two brick buildings in front, underwent the ravages of the fire;
the walls of which are very much injured" and "I believe [they] are now
scarcely worth repairing." Washington consoled his friend adding that the
"happiest moments of [his] life had been spent there" and that when "he
could not trace a room in the house" he "was obliged to fly from them; &
came home with painful sensations." Washington implored the Fairfaxes
to move back to Virginia, but he and Martha never saw their friends again.
George William remained sickly and lived in diminished circumstances in

Bath for the remainder of his life. He died in 1787, six years before he would have inherited the title from his cousin, Robert, 7th Lord Fairfax. George William lived long enough to learn that he and his branch would not inherit the one-sixth interest in the proprietary from the 6th Lord Fairfax, and he was crushed when his uncle's chancery cause did not conclude in his favor. Sally maintained a lively correspondence with the Washingtons for the rest of their lives and died in 1811 at the age of eighty-one.[59]

The Fairfax furniture had a long and tangled journey from the warerooms of William Gomm and Son to George and Martha Washington and the homes of their peers. While little of the Fairfax furniture survives today, its corresponding documentary evidence provides insights into two of the more influential families in colonial Virginia. The men and women who

Figure 62 Richard Tharpe for John Rawlins, front parlor ceiling, Mount Vernon, Mount Vernon, Virginia, 1787. (Courtesy, Mount Vernon Ladies' Association; photo, Gavin Ashworth.) George Washington updated the ceiling with neoclassical ornament to unite the space visually with the New Room.

owned those furnishings imbued them with new meaning to make a statement about themselves and their rank in society. For George William and Sally Fairfax, their furnishings were also central to their plans to secure the friendship and affection of Lord Fairfax and to prepare Belvoir to take on a new role as the home of a future member of the peerage. Although the couple's plans failed, their furnishings took on new use and meaning after being dispersed at auction. For George and Martha Washington, the objects they purchased and received as gifts allowed them to update old and new rooms in Mount Vernon and were constant reminders of their life-long friendship with the Fairfaxes.

ACKNOWLEDGMENTS   For assistance with this article, the author would like to thank Douglas Bradburn, Lydia Brandt, Matthew Briney, Nancy Britton, Molly Kerr, The Honorable Hugh Fairfax, Leroy Graves, Amy Hudson Henderson, Amanda Isaac, Elizabeth Jamieson, Natalie Larson, Luke Peroraro, Dennis Pogue, Thomas Reinhart, Susan Schoelwer, Jeanne Solensky, Michelle Lee Silverman, Steven Spandle, Kate Smith, Samantha Snyder, Mary Thompson, Annabel Westman, Esther White, Lucy Wood

1. Work on Belvoir was underway by July 1763, when George Washington informed George William Fairfax that he had no lath available to send. Washington also indicated that his enslaved servant, Smart, would bring buckets and other supplies but that the staples and hasps for Belvoir's locks, which were being made by another slave named Peter, were not ready for delivery (George Washington to George William Fairfax, July 20, 1763, transcribed in *The Papers of George Washington, Digital Edition*, edited by Theodore J. Crackel et al. [Charlottesville: University of Virginia Press, 2007–] [hereafter PGW Digital]). William Fairfax and George William Fairfax Account Book, 1742, 1748, 1760–1772, bound MSS, Fred W. Smith National Library for the Study of George Washington (hereafter Washington Library), Mount Vernon, Va., p. 6. Thomas Tileston Waterman, one of Virginia's early architectural historians, commented on the importance of Belvoir in his *The Mansions of Virginia: 1706–1776* (New York: Bonanza Books, 1945), pp. 330–34. The date Belvoir burned and the cause of the fire are not certain.

2. For more on Virginia great houses and status, see Dell Upton, "White and Black Landscapes in Eighteenth-Century Virginia," *Places* 2, no. 2 (1984): 59–72; Rhys Isaac, *The Transformation of Virginia, 1740–1790* (Chapel Hill: University of North Carolina Press for the Institute of Early American History and Culture, 1982); Dell Upton, *Holy Things and Profane: Anglican Parish Churches in Colonial Virginia* (New Haven and London: Yale University Press, 1986); and *The Chesapeake House: Architectural Investigation by Colonial Williamsburg*, edited by Cary Carson and Carl R. Lounsbury (Chapel Hill: University of North Carolina Press in association with the Colonial Williamsburg Foundation, 2013).

3. In 1649 at the height of the English Civil War, Charles II granted the land to seven loyalist lords proprietors including members of the influential Culpeper family. Recognizing the value of the land, Lord Fairfax's grandfather, Thomas, 2nd Baron Culpeper of Thoresway, one-time governor of Virginia, consolidated five of the six shares in his own name, and upon his death bequeathed them to his only daughter, Catherine, Lady Fairfax. William Fairfax to Brian Fairfax, July 20, 1734, MSS 30306, British Library (hereafter BL). The best accounts of the origins of the Fairfax proprietary are "The Northern Neck Proprietary to 1745," in Douglas Southall Freeman, *George Washington: A Biography*, 7 vols. (New York: Charles Scribner's Sons: 1948–1957), 1: 447–512; and Warren R. Hofstra, *The Planting of New Virginia: Settlement and Landscape in the Shenandoah Valley* (Baltimore: Johns Hopkins University Press, 2004), pp. 143–79.The most complete biography of Thomas, Lord Fairfax is Stuart E. Brown, *Virginia Baron: The Story of Thomas 6th Lord Fairfax* (Berryville, Va.: Chesapeake Book Company, 1965). Robert "King" Carter's death is recorded in the *Gentleman's Magazine, or, Monthly Intelligencer* 2, no. 23 (November 1732): 1082. The obituary lists his death on August 4 and records that "he was president of the Council, and left among his Children above 300,000 Acres of Land, about 1000 Negroes, and 10,0000 l." The largest share of the proprietary was entailed to descendants of Sir Thomas Culpeper, while Catherine Culpeper Fairfax inherited the other one-sixth in her own right. Thomas, 6th Lord Fairfax inherited this share from his mother, and he was free to dispose of it as he pleased. For a full history of the Fairfax title, see Hugh Fairfax, *Fairfax of Virginia: The Forgotten Story of America's Only Peerage, 1690–1960* (London: Published privately by the Fairfax Family, 2017).

4. Bruce A. Ragsdale, "William Fairfax (1691–1757)," *Dictionary of Virginia Biography*, Library of Virginia (1998–), published 2016, http://www.lva.virginia.gov/public/dvb/bio.asp?b=Fairfax_William, accessed February 26, 2019. The Mount Vernon Ladies' Association owns Colonel William Fairfax's personal copy of William Leybourn, *The Compleat Surveyor* (London, 1679). He inscribed his edition and later lent it to George Washington, who learned surveying using that book.

5. For dates of land purchases, see Brown, *Virginia Baron,* p. 101. Fairfax Harrison, *Landmarks of Old Prince William: A Study of Origins in Northern Virginia* (Berryville, Va.: Chesapeake Book Company, 1964), pp. 311–26, 405–9.

6. William Fairfax first wrote that he was "of Truro" Parish in November 1741 (Brown, *Virginia Baron*, p. 101). The Belvoir house site has been excavated four times. The first dig, chronicled in Colonel Edward H. Schulz, *Belvoir on the Potomac: Fort Humphreys, Virginia* (Fort Humphreys, Va., 1933), established the footprint of the house, the layout of the garden walls, and the positions of the two flanking outbuildings. The second dig, chronicled in George C. Shott, *U.S. Army Engineer Museum Archaeological Investigations of Belvoir Site* (Fort Belvoir, Va.: Department of the Army, U.S. Army Engineer Center and Fort Belvoir, 1973), uncovered the house and a number of dependencies as well as garden walls and brick drains. Shott uncovered a number of significant ceramic assemblages. The third dig began in 1990 when the Directorate of Engineering and Housing at Fort Belvoir contracted Mid-Atlantic Archaeological Research Associates, Inc., to search for the location of two garden sites near the mansion. Archaeologists found evidence of a kitchen garden to the east of the kitchen. For more on their work, see "Phase II Archaeological Investigations at the Belvoir Ruins and Garden Sites Fort Belvoir, Fairfax County, Virginia" (report prepared for Department of the Army, Fort Belvoir, Directorate of Engineering and Housing, Mid-Atlantic Archaeological Research Associates, Inc., 1992). James River Archaeology conducted the final dig in 1994 to explore the formal gardens, several outbuildings, and to locate the carriage turn-around. They identified ornamental structures in the formal garden and a number of intact archeological features and foundations. For more on their work, see "Final Report on Archaeological Investigations at U. S. Army Garrison Fort Belvoir, Site 44FX4, Belvoir Manor, Fort Belvoir, Virginia" (report prepared for CDM Federal Programs Corporation, James River Institute for Archaeology, Inc., June 28, 1994). Although the military and professional architects have dug the site on multiple occasions, it remains largely intact and ripe for further study. The layout of Belvoir is given in rental advertisements in the Purdie and Dixon and Rind publications of the *Virginia Gazette*, both on June 2, 1774 and the *Maryland Gazette*, December 15, 1774: "The Mansion House is of Brick, two Stories high, with four convenient Rooms and a large Passage on the lower Floor, five Rooms and a Passage on the second, and a Servants Hall and Cellars below, convenient Offices, Stables, and Coach House adjoining, as also a large and well-furnished Garden, stored with a great Variety of valuable Fruits, in good order." For more on the role of small classical houses in confirming status, see Stephen Hague, *The Gentleman's House in the British Atlantic World, 1680–1780* (Hampshire, Eng.: Palgrave MacMillan, 2015), pp. 57–63.

7. The most salient description of the mansion and gardens is in Waterman, *The Mansions of Virginia*, pp. 330–34.

8. Ragsdale, "William Fairfax (1691–1757)." Colonel William Fairfax's son-in-law John Carlyle completed his own home in Alexandria, Virginia, in 1753 with a floor plan heavily influenced by Belvoir. The house measures 52' 3" x 34' 10", just slightly smaller than Belvoir's outer dimensions of 56' 8½" x 36' 9". As at Belvoir, the largest room on the first floor was probably the dining room, which was adjacent to a much smaller parlor, an unusual arrangement in Virginia houses. For more information on Carlyle House, see Robert H. Garber, "The John Carlyle House, Alexandria, Virginia" (restoration report for the Northern Virginia Regional Park Authority, Fauber Garbee, Inc., Architects, July 1980); and Robert A. Leath and Betty C. Leviner, "A Proposal for Revisions to the John Carlyle House Historic Furnishings Plan" (report for the Northern Virginia Regional Park Authority, May 11, 2005).

9. In 1745 the Privy Council defined the headwaters of the Shenandoah and Rapidan Rivers as the origins of the Potomac and Rappahannock Rivers, respectively, concluding years of debate over the size of the grant. Soon after, Lord Fairfax opened the western reaches of the proprietary to settlement. For more on George William Fairfax's education, see William Fairfax to Bryan Fairfax, July 19, 1735, BL. For more on Washington and Fairfax surveying for the proprietary, see *The Diaries of George Washington*, edited by Donald Jackson and Dorothy Twohig, 6 vols. (Charlottesville: University of Virginia Press, 1976–1978), 1: 1–23.

10. For a concise biography of George William Fairfax, see Mary V. Thompson, "George William Fairfax (1724–1787)," *Dictionary of Virginia Biography*, Library of Virginia (1998-), http://www.lva.virginia.gov/public/dvb/bio.asp?b=Fairfax_George_William, accessed February 27, 2019.

11. For more on settling the Shenandoah Valley, see Hofstra, *The Planting of New Virginia*, pp. 94–142. Brown, *Virginia Baron*, pp. 119–22. For more on Greenway Court, see Henry Howe, *Historical Collections of Virginia* (Charleston, S.C.: William R. Babcock, 1852), pp. 233–237; and Stephen Lissandrello, *National Register of Historic Places Nomination: Greenway Court, White Post, Virginia* (Washington, D.C., March 15, 1975).

12. Brown, *Virginia Baron*, pp. 97, 118.

13. Will of William Fairfax, Fairfax County Will Book B, 171–74, Historic Records Center,

Fairfax, Va. For more on George William Fairfax's plan to seek that post, see draft of George William Fairfax to Mr. Pullyn, December 6, 1757, reel 585, Fairfax of Cameron Manuscripts (hereafter FCM), Virginia Colonial Records Project.

14. George William Fairfax wrote in December 1757 that he planned to return to Virginia when the British fleet sailed the next spring. George William Fairfax to Mr. Pullyn, draft, December 6, 1757, FCM. George William Fairfax's family questioned his racial background during his lifetime. Sally Fairfax addressed these rumors in a letter to her nephew. She wrote that Henry Fairfax, George William's uncle, "would have left it [his estate] to your uncle Wm. Henry Fairfax [younger brother of George William], from an impression that my husband's mother [Sarah Walker Fairfax] was a black woman, if my Fairfax had not come over to see his uncle and convinced him he was not a negroe's son." Quoted in Wilson Miles Cary, *Sally Cary: A Long Hidden Romance of Washington's Life* (New York: De Vinne Press, 1916), pp. 50–51. Fairfax's mother, the Bahamian Sara Walker, was the daughter of English Captain Thomas Walker and his wife Ann, whose ancestry is not known. For more, see Brown, *Virginia Baron*, pp. 59–60. Thomas Moseley to George William Fairfax, December 1, 1759, FCM. George William Fairfax requested leave in George William Fairfax to Thomas, Lord Fairfax, May 1, 1760, FCM; and George William Fairfax to Thomas, Lord Fairfax, undated draft, FCM. More than a year after arriving in England, George William Fairfax wrote a letter to Lord Fairfax from York on March 30, 1762, expressing frustration at not having heard from Lord Fairfax. "A Copy of a letter from G[eorge] F[airfa]x when in England to L[ord] F[airfa]x Dated from York March 30, 1762," undated, *Wykeham-Martin Family Papers, 1672–1810*, Kent Archives Office (hereafter KAO), Maidstone, Eng., microfilm. The couple left for England in August 1760 and returned to Virginia in the spring of 1763. George William Fairfax to Thomas, Lord Fairfax, draft, May 1, 1760, FCM.

15. For more on Americans identifying as Britons, see Margaret Pritchard and Virginia Sites, *William Byrd II and His Lost History: Engravings of the Americas* (Williamsburg, Va.: Colonial Williamsburg Foundation, 1993), pp. 19–48. For more on appropriate decorative choices based upon station in society and room in the house, see Amanda Vickery, "'Neat and Not Too Showey': Words and Wallpaper in Regency England," in *Gender, Taste, and Material Culture in Britain and North America, 1700–1830*, edited by John Styles and Amanda Vickery (New Haven: Published for Yale Center for British Art and Paul Mellon Centre for Studies in British Art by Yale University Press, 2006), pp. 201–224. For more on polite sociability, see Richard Bushman, *The Refinement of America: Persons, Houses, Cities* (New York: Vintage Books, 1993), pp. 61–91; and Amanda Vickery, *Behind Closed Doors: At Home in Georgian England* (New Haven and London: Yale University Press, 2009). For more on the British trans-Atlantic language of polite sociability, see Bernard L. Herman, *Town House: Architecture and Material Life in the Early American City, 1780–1830* (Chapel Hill: University of North Carolina Press, 2005); and Zara Anishanslin, *Portrait of a Woman in Silk: Hidden Histories of the British Atlantic World* (New Haven and London: Yale University Press, 2016). George William Fairfax wrote to Lord Fairfax while in England encouraging Lord Fairfax to move to Belvoir and complaining that he had not received a letter from him. He also complained that Thomas Bryan Martin had turned Lord Fairfax against him and bemoaned the fact that he would inherit a title with no estates to support it. "A Copy of a letter from G[eorge] F[airfa]x when in England to L[ord] F[airfa]x Dated from York March 30, 1762," KAO.

16. Draft of George William Fairfax to unnamed correspondent, February 26, 1763, FCM. George William chronicled his time in England in *The Daily Journal, or, The Gentleman's and Tradesman's Complete Annual Accompt-Book* (London, 1763) (hereafter GWFJ). Fairfax included a drawing of the Cary coat of arms in the opening pages of the book, likely for use when purchasing silver. Mary Cary Ambler, Fairfax's sister-in-law, kept a journal in the remaining pages of George William's. Mary Cary Ambler Journal, 1763–1770, Personal Papers, acc. 30647, Virginia Historical Society, Richmond, Va.

17. Robert Campbell, *The London Tradesman* (London: T. Gardner, 1747), p. 170. For more on the upholsterer's practice, see Christopher Gilbert, *The Life and Work of Thomas Chippendale* (London: Studio Vista, 1978), pp. 25–27.

18. Lindsay Boynton, "William and Richard Gomm," *Burlington Magazine* 122, no. 927 (June 1980): 395–402. Geoffrey Beard and Christopher Gilbert, *Dictionary of English Furniture Makers* (Leeds: W. S. Maney and Son Ltd., 1986), pp. 349–50. *Public Advertiser,* June 5, 1776, as cited in "Clerkenwell Close Area: Introduction; St Mary's Nunnery Site," in Survey of London: Volume 46, South and East Clerkenwell, edited by Philip Temple (London, 2008), pp. 28-39, *British History Online*, http://www.british-history.ac.uk/survey-london/vol46/pp28-39, accessed February 28, 2019.

19. Invoice from Robert Stark to George William Fairfax, 1763, Papers of the Fairfax Family, 1760–1799, MSS, Gunston Hall Library and Archives, Lorton, Va. William Fairfax and George William Fairfax Account Book, p. 6. George William Fairfax, Inventory of the Furniture of the Several Rooms at Belvoir, ca. 1773, MSS, Fairfax Family Papers, 1756–1787, Series MSS2F1619B (hereafter Fairfax Family Papers), Virginia Historical Society, Richmond, Va. The wallpaper invoice and account book entry for Thomas Speer both have letters beside groups of items that correspond with specific rooms, indicating the presence of a detailed floor plan. The colors of the wallpaper can be matched with the rooms listed in the inventory to determine the furnishings, wallpaper, and architectural details of specific rooms.

20. William Gomm, Sundry Drawings of Cabinet Ware & c., 1761, drawings, Collection 266, Joseph Downs Collection of Manuscripts and Printed Ephemera, Winterthur Library, Winterthur, Del. Although rooms with unified architectural details, finishes, and furnishings had long existed in England, they were more difficult to achieve in the colonies, where access to specialized labor and manufactured goods was more restricted. In Virginia, exceptions included Gunston Hall (1756–1761) and Mount Airy (1761–1771), where architect William Buckland designed furniture to complement his interior architectural details (Luke Beckerdite, "Architect-Designed Furniture in Eighteenth-Century Virginia: The Work of William Buckland and William Bernard Sears," in *American Furniture*, edited by Luke Beckerdite [Hanover, N.H.: University Press of New England for the Chipstone Foundation, 1994], pp. 29–48). For one of the more thoroughly documented efforts to create a unified decorative scheme, see Nicholas B. Wainwright, *Colonial Grandeur in Philadelphia: The House and Furniture of John Cadwallader* (Philadelphia: Historical Society of Pennsylvania, 1964).

21. GWFJ. Adam Bowett, *Early Georgian Furniture, 1715–1740* (Woodbridge, Suffolk, Eng.: Antiques Collectors' Club, 2009), p. 120. William Gomm, Sundry Drawings of Cabinet Ware & c., 1761, drawings, Collection 266, Winterthur Library.

22. Susan E. Stuart, *Gillows of Lancaster and London*, 2 vols. (Woodbridge, Suffolk, Eng.: Antique Collectors' Club, 2008), 1: 61. Samuel Johnson, *A Dictionary of the English Language*, 2 vols. (London: Printed by W. Strahan, 1755), 2: 1353, 1511. George William Fairfax, "List of Houshold & Kitchen Goods to be Purchased," FCM. Fairfax did not record the date he finalized his purchases.

23. Robert Stark trade card, Trade Cards 91.53, British Museum. *Public Advertiser*, March 9, 1784, as quoted in Phillippa Mapes, "The English Wallpaper Trade, 1750–1830" (Ph.D. dissertation, University of Leicester, U.K., 2016), p. 93. "Bought of Thomas Speer," William Fairfax and George William Fairfax Account Book, p. 5. Invoice from Robert Stark to George William Fairfax, 1763, Papers of the Fairfax Family, 1760–1799, MSS, Gunston Hall Library and Archives, Lorton, Va. Stark submitted a copy of the 1763 invoice on May 6, 1767, after failing to receive payment. The later invoice includes a note from Gomm suggesting that Fairfax may have mistakenly assumed "that it [his charge from 1763] was included in our bill." This account demonstrates the close relationship between Stark and Gomm.

24. Brown, *Virginia Baron*, pp. 135–154; George William Fairfax wrote Robert Fairfax after Lord Fairfax's death expressing his shock at not receiving Lord Fairfax's one-sixth share of the proprietary in his will. He wrote that Lord Fairfax visited Belvoir before George William moved to England and said he was sensible "of the great injustice that had been done to my branch of the Family by Alienating the Estates in Yorkshire that properly belonged to it, that He was sorry it was not in his power to Compensate us for those losses, but that he would certainly do every thing he could by leaving the sixth part of the Northern Neck, the Manner of Leeds, and the South Branch to go with the Title." George William Fairfax to Robert, Lord Fairfax, March 1783, KAO.

25. Robert Fairfax to unknown recipient, July 17–19, 1769, MSS Fairfax 35, Bodleian Library.

26. Draft of George William Fairfax to Thomas, 6th Lord Fairfax, June 2, 1761, FCM. George William learned from John Carlyle that a date and time had been set for the sale of his father's furniture. On May 1, 1762, George Washington acquired "a Tea Table and Appurt[enance]s" and "1 Tea Board" "from Belvoir" from Benjamin Grayson, a Colchester merchant, for £7.15 and £2.10, respectively. At the same time, Washington acquired "1 Sett Tea China" from Grayson for 64s. Washington credited these acquisitions against debts Grayson owed. What the "appurtenances" were is not apparent, but their presence seems to have added substantially to the cost of the table; they may have been additional tea china or equipment such as a hot water urn. George Washington Ledger Book A, 1750–1772, p. 129, The Papers of George Washington, Series 5: Financial Papers, Library of Congress, Washington, D.C.

27. All quotations in the section describing the contents of Belvoir are taken from Wil-

liam Fairfax and George William Fairfax Account Book, Washington Library. The contents of rooms are as described in George William Fairfax, Belvoir Inventory, Virginia Historical Society. For more on the disposition of rooms in Virginia houses, see Mark R. Wenger, "Town House & Country House: Eighteenth and Early Nineteenth Centuries," in *The Chesapeake House: Architectural Investigation by Colonial Williamsburg*, edited by Cary Carson and Carl Lounsbury (Chapel Hill: University of North Carolina Press for the Colonial Williamsburg Foundation, 2013), pp. 128–155.

28. For more on the disposition of rooms at Carlyle House, see Leath and Leviner, "A Proposal for Revisions to the John Carlyle House Historic Furnishings Plan."

29. At Mount Vernon, a small room that served as a lumber room and a bed chamber is carved off from the space of the second floor of the passage. John Cornforth provides a concise explanation of "state rooms" in his *Early Georgian Interiors* (New Haven and London: Yale University Press, 1995), pp. 13–19. He explains that "state rooms" or "best rooms" were often intended to honor special guests.

30. Mark R. Wenger, "The Central Passage in Virginia: Evolution of an Eighteenth-Century Living Space," *Perspectives in Vernacular Architecture* 2 (1986): 137–49.

31. Margaret Beck Pritchard, "Wallpaper," in *The Chesapeake House*, pp. 383–86. This study relies heavily on room usage as described in Elizabeth Donaghy Garrett, *At Home: The American Family, 1750–1870* (New York: Harry N. Abrams, Inc., 1990).

32. Only the blue dressing room and the chintz bedchamber had such elaborate chimneypieces. Mark R. Wenger, "The Dining Room in Early Virginia," *Perspectives in Vernacular Architecture* 3 (1989): 149–59. Mark R. Wenger, "Town House & Country House," p. 128.

33. The room also contained: "An Oval Bottle Cistern on a Frame;" "A Knife Tray;" "A Scallopt. Mahy. Voider;" "2 Dish Trays;" "1 Mahy cutrim [cut rim] Tea Tray;" and andirons, a shovel, tongs, and a fender. For more on gendered spaces, see Garrett, *At Home*, pp. 39–94.

34. Wenger, "Town House & Country House," p. 123. Wenger, "The Dining Room," pp. 149–59.

35. The most important study on room use in eighteenth-century Virginia is Susan Borchert et al., "Gunston Hall Room Use Study," Report Prepared for the Board of Regents of Gunston Hall Plantation, http://www.gunstonhall.org/mansion/room_use_study/methodology. html, accessed March 3, 2019. This section relies heavily upon the room use the authors discovered in their comprehensive examination of Virginia and Maryland probate inventories of the upper Tidewater from the second half of the eighteenth century.

36. Matthijs de Keijzer et al., "Indigo Carmine: Understanding a Problematic Blue Dye," *Studies in Conservation* 57, suppl. 1 (2012): S87–S95. The dressing table was valued at £10.

37. For more on the use of dining rooms for business and the creation of independent studies, see Susan Borchert et al., "Domestic Spaces," in "Gunston Hall Room Use Study." George William Fairfax to George Washington, January 10, 1759, PGW Digital. Nicholas A. Brawer, *British Campaign Furniture: Elegance under Canvas, 1740–1914* (New York: Harry N. Abrams, 2001), pp. 154–55. Florence M. Montgomery, *Textiles in America, 1650–1870* (New York: W. W. Norton and Company, 2007), p. 300. The settee bedstead was described as "A Neat Mahy. 3ft. 6in. [wide] Settea bedstead Cover'd wth. Saxon Green morine & Brass nail'd wth. morine Curatains, head Cloth and Tester." There were no curtains in the study. For a discussion of pincushion seats, see Lucy Wood, *The Upholstered Furniture in the Lady Lever Art Gallery*, 2 vols. (New Haven: Yale University Press for the National Museums Liverpool, 2009), 1: 12–13.

38. Scholars rarely discuss the ranked usage of bedchambers and the corresponding social implications, but it is apparent in the values of objects in period inventories. For more information on the English practice, see Cornforth, *Early Georgian Interiors*, pp. 91–92. When George Washington purchased a new bed in 1759, his London agent referred to copper plate textiles as "Chintz Blew plate Cotton furniture" (Invoice from Robert Cary and Company, August 6, 1759, PGW Digital). The difficulties of nomenclature are described in Linda Eaton, *Printed Textiles: British and American Cottons and Linens, 1700–1850* (New York: Monacelli Press, 2014), pp. 17–39.

39. By the middle of the eighteenth century, the concept of a suite of rooms leading to the bedchamber had been condensed to the dressing room and bedchamber. For more on the formal plan of rooms in English houses, see Mark Girouard, *Life in the English Country House* (New Haven: Yale University Press, 1978), pp. 126–35. Lord Botetourt, royal governor of Virginia, had the only other documented dressing chamber in Virginia (Graham Hood, *The Governor's Palace in Virginia: A Cultural Study* [Williamsburg, Va.: Colonial Williamsburg Foundation, 1991], pp. 98–117). Much of the analysis in this article is indebted to Hood's work. Isaac Ware, *A Complete Body of Architecture: Adorned with Plans and Elevations from Original Designs* (London: T. Osborne, 1756), p. 432.

40. Ronald Hurst and Jonathan Prown, *Southern Furniture 1680–1830: The Colonial Williamsburg Collection* (New York: Harry N. Abrams for the Colonial Williamsburg Foundation, 1997), pp. 79–80, 147. For more on the introduction of sofas to England, see Adam Bowett, *English Furniture 1660–1714: From Charles II to Queen Anne* (Woodbridge, Suffolk, Eng.: Antique Collectors' Club, 2002), pp. 251–253. For more on the widespread use of the sofa in eighteenth-century France, see Joan DeJean, *The Age of Comfort: When Paris Discovered Casual and the Modern Home Began* (New York: Bloomsbury USA, 2009), pp. 93–102.

41. For a concise description of backstools and square-edged upholstery, see Wood, *The Upholstered Furniture in the Lady Lever Art Gallery,* 1: 16–18. Other methods of achieving a much lower profile are described in Wallace Gusler, Leroy Graves, and Mark Anderson, "The Technique of 18th-Century Over-the-Rail Upholstery," in *Upholstery in America & Europe from the Seventeenth Century to World War I,* edited by Edward S. Cooke Jr. (New York: W. W. Norton, 1987), pp. 91–96; and Leroy Graves, *Early Seating Furniture: Reading the Evidence* (Williamsburg, Va.: Colonial Williamsburg Foundation, 2015), pp. 116–25.

42. Keijzer et al., "Indigo Carmine," ibid. These observations on Saxon blue rely on dye samples made by Kate Smith of Eaton Hill Weavers in Marshfield, Vermont. Smith used period dye recipes to recreate the color. Thomas Chippendale furnished Lady Winn of Nostell Priory "garter blue" upholstered furniture and bed and window hangings for her bedchamber. The term "garter blue" referred to the sashes worn by members of the Order of the Garter and was another designation for Saxon blue. Wainwright, *Colonial Grandeur in Philadelphia,* p. 41. Saxon blue dye was used for silk and wool but did not adhere properly to linen without modification of the recipe. The author thanks Kate Smith of Eaton Hill Weavers in Marshfield, Vermont, for information on the formulation and use of Saxon blue dye.

43. For more information on bed hangings, see Abbott Lowell Cummings, *Bed Hangings: A Treatise on Fabrics and Styles in the Curtaining of Beds, 1650–1850* (Boston: Society for the Preservation of New England Antiquities, 1994).

44. George William Fairfax to George Washington, August 3, 1778, and George William Fairfax to George Washington, August 5, 1773, PGW Digital. George William Fairfax to Samuel Athawes, September 5, 1773, FCM.

45. George William Fairfax to George Washington, January 10, 1774, and George William Fairfax to George Washington, August 5, 1773, PGW Digital. John J. McCusker, *Money and Exchange in Europe and America, 1600–1775* (Chapel Hill: University of North Carolina Press for the Institute of Early American History and Culture, 1978), p. 212. In 1774 £130.30 in Virginia currency was worth £100 sterling.

46. William Fairfax and George William Fairfax Account Book. George William Fairfax to George Washington, January 10, 1774, PGW Digital. George William Fairfax, Inventory of the Furniture of the Several Rooms at Belvoir, ca. 1773, Fairfax Family Papers.

47. *Virginia Gazette* (Purdie and Dixon), June 2, 1774; *Virginia Gazette* (Rind), June 2, 1774. The eighteenth-century understanding of how quickly a piece of furniture became outdated is quite different from our own. For instance, a 1764 inventory of Chatsworth described a Neo-Palladian cut-velvet bed after a 1749 design by John Vardy as "new" even though it was likely made nearly fifteen years before and its style was outmoded. For more on the "Vardy Bed," see Annabel Westman, "'Snug at the Hall': Beds and Canopies and the 6th Duke," in *Hardwick Hall: A Great Old Castle of Romance,* edited by David Adshead and David A. H. B. Taylor (New Haven and London: Yale University Press published for the Paul Mellon Centre for Studies in British Art and the National Trust, 2016), pp. 278–281. For a discussion of the introduction of neoclassicism to Virginia furniture, see Wallace B. Gusler, *Furniture of Williamsburg and Eastern Virginia, 1710–1790* (Richmond: Virginia Museum, 1979), pp. 7–10.

48. The auctioneers kept two accounts of the sale: an item-by-item listing that probably followed the order of the sale, and a list by purchaser. The accounts are "Sales of Furniture at Belvoir, August 15th, 1774," MSS, MS-5306, Washington Library; and "Accot. of Sales, August 15th, 1774 at Belvoir," Fairfax Family Papers, respectively. For the second auction, see "Account of Sales at Belvoir, Decem. 5th, 1774," Fairfax Family Papers.

49. Robert F. Dalzell and Lee Baldwin Dalzell, *George Washington's Mount Vernon: At Home in Revolutionary America* (New York: Oxford University Press, 1998), pp. 68–69; Messick, Cohen, Waite, "Mount Vernon Historic Structure Report," 3 vols. (report prepared for the Mount Vernon Ladies' Association, 1993), pp. 19–23.

50. Messick, Cohen, Waite, "Mount Vernon Historic Structure Report." For more on this time in George Washington's life, see Ron Chernow, *Washington: A Life* (New York: Penguin Press, 2010), pp. 165–193. George Washington took over the management of the estate of

Daniel Parke Custis when he married Custis's widow, Martha Dandridge Custis, on January 6, 1759. The Daniel Parke Custis estate included 17,880 acres of land, almost 300 enslaved people, thousands worth of personal property, and a large sterling reserve. Because Custis died without a will, his estate was divided according to law. Martha inherited one-third of Custis's personal property and lifetime rights to one-third of his land and enslaved workforce; their son John Parke "Jacky" Custis inherited one-third of his father's personal property and all of his land and enslaved people; and Martha Parke "Patsy" Custis inherited one-third of her father's personal property. Martha Parke Custis's inheritance was valued at £8,000 upon her death from an epileptic seizure in 1773.

51. On September 23, 1774, George Washington visited Philadelphia upholsterer John Ross and left him £15 cash "to buy furniture [textiles] with & to be accounted for." On September 30 he paid an additional £9 for "2 pcs. Callico Bed furniture," and on October 10 he paid the remainder of his bill for bed furniture from September 28, which totaled £29.17.6. September 23 and 30 and October 10, 1774, entries, Cash Memoranda, March–October 1774, 1749–1806, George Washington Collection, 1749–1806, Huntington Library, Art Collections, and Botanical Gardens, San Marino, Calif. George Washington accounted for the purchases in his ledger book as £55 for "Bed Furniture & Makg," and he paid for the "3 Bedsteads" separately at a cost of £12. George Washington Ledger Book B, 1772–1793, p. 121, Papers of George Washington. George Washington dined with Benjamin Chew on September 22, 1774, the day before he placed his order with John Ross. Chew had recently purchased beds and bed furniture from Ross, and Washington likely learned of the upholsterer through him. George Washington Diary Entry, September 22, 1774. The author thanks Amanda Isaac for these references. For more on the Chew purchases, see Nancy E. Richards, "The City Home of Benjamin Chew, Sr.; and His Family: A Case Study of the Textures of Life" (report created for Cliveden of the National Trust, Inc., 1996). George Washington wrote to Gouverneur Morris requesting a mirrored plateau for the presidential dining table, recalling similar examples he had seen in the homes of friends. He specifically requested that if his memory were "defective recur to what you have seen on Mr Robert Morris's table for my ideas generally," indicating that the source of his ideas was one of the more fashionable households in town. George Washington to Gouvernour Morris, October 13, 1789, PGW Digital.

52. For a complete description of William Bernard Sears's work in the Mount Vernon dining room, see Luke Beckerdite, "William Buckland and William Bernard Sears: The Designer and the Carver," *Journal of Early Southern Decorative Arts* 8, no. 2 (1982): 29–36. Susan Buck found verdigris green as the second generation of paint on the walls, the third generation on the mantel and overmantel, and the fourth generation on the mantel and overmantel. Susan Buck, "Small Dining Room Paint Analysis" (report prepared for P. Gardiner Hallock, Manager of Restoration, Mount Vernon Estate and Gardens by Historic Paint and Architectural Services, Newton Centre, Mass., July 15, 2000). George Washington noted the color of the dining room while in Philadelphia for the Constitutional Convention in September 1787. He said, "I am sorry to find that the Green paint which was got to give the dining room another Coat, should have turned out so bad; such impositions (besides the disappointment) are really shameful." George Washington to George Augustine Washington, September 2, 1787, PGW Digital. Susan Borchert et al., "Public Spaces," in "Gunston Hall Room Use Study." Referred to as "the Stoco Man," this craftsman is known only through his surviving work at Mount Vernon and Kenmore, the home of Washington's brother-in-law Colonel Fielding Lewis. George Washington to George Augustine Washington, September 2, 1787, and George Augustine Washington to George Washington, April 15–16, 1792, PGW Digital. Washington's nephew wrote of the problems with the verdigris oxidizing: "the chimney smokes in such a manner that it destroys the room." He understood that the room should be painted the same color "on acct of the furniture," an important admission that George Washington intended to maintain the same combination of furniture and paint decoration that the Fairfaxes had used in their dining room using the same furniture.

53. George Washington wrote to Richard Washington requesting "Two neat Mahagony Tables 4½ feet square when spread and to join occasionally" (Invoice to Richard Washington, April 15, 1757, PGW Digital). Joseph T. Shipley, *Dictionary of Early English* (New York: Philosophical Library, 1955), p. 712. Although the Washingtons also acquired the pair of card tables, they may have used them in the front parlor at Mount Vernon rather than in the dining room. George Washington purchased one card table at auction and the other from Colonel Henry Lee. The table from Belvoir was subsequently moved to Arlington House, where antiquarian Benson Lossing first saw it. George Washington did not purchase the Wilton Persian carpet.

54. Susan Borchert et al., "Domestic Spaces" and "Gunston Hall Room Use Study." George Washington Parke Custis, *Recollections and Private Memoirs of Washington* (Washington, D.C.: William H. Moore, 1859), p. 163. The desk does not appear in George Washington's probate inventory, but the settee bedstead appears in the study and the shaving table is likely one of the dressing tables in the bed chambers. Christine Meadows, "The Belvoir Sale," in *The Mount Vernon Ladies' Association Annual Report* (1991): 35–38. "An Inventory &c of Articles at Mount Vernon with their Appraised Value annexed," Fairfax County Will Book J, fol. 326, Historic Records Center, Fairfax, Va.

55. George Washington's purchases at Belvoir are listed in two documents: "Accot. of Sales, August 15th, 1774 at Belvoir," Fairfax Family Papers; and "Inventory of House Furniture bought by Colo. George Washington at Colo Fairfax's Sale at Belvoir, 15th Augt. 1774," George Washington Collection. In the first document, Washington's purchases are listed with his account and the rest of the attendees, while in the second, only Washington's purchases are listed.

56. George William Fairfax to George Washington, March 2, 1775, PGW Digital. For more on the delivery of the chintz curtains, see Samuel Athawes to George William Fairfax, August 14, 1775, FCM. Samuel Athawes wrote, "The Curtains I have sent to my upholsterers to be cleand & repaird" before sending them to Fairfax. Thompson, "George William Fairfax."

57. George William Fairfax to George Washington, June 23, 1785, PGW Digital. George Washington to George William Fairfax, June 30, 1786, PGW Digital. George Washington kept a careful accounting for Fairfax on two manuscript pages. They are: "The Honble. Geo. Wm. Fairfax, Esq in acct with Geo. Washington, October 1773–April 1774," MSS, Washington Library; and "The Honble. Geo. Wm. Fairfax Esqr. in acct with Geo[rge] Washington, 1774 June–December," original MSS owned by Dewitt Wallace Library, Macalester College, Saint Paul, Minn., photocopy on file at Washington Library.

58. George Washington commissioned John Rawlins to execute the ceiling in the front parlor in February 1786, and the work was complete by April 1787. See articles of agreement between George Washington and John Rawlins, February 25, 1788, PGW Digital; and George Washington to John Rawlins, April 13, 1787, PGW Digital. Susan Buck, "Cross-Section Paint Microscopy Report Interior Paint Study of the West Parlor Draft Two" (report prepared for Thomas Reinhart, Deputy Director for Architecture, Mount Vernon Estate and Gardens by Susan L. Buck, Ph.D., March 5, 2016). For more on the New Room, see Thomas A. Reinhart and Susan P. Schoelwer, "'Distinguished by the Name of the New Room': Reinvestigation and Reinterpretation of George Washington's Grandest Space," in *Stewards of Memory: The Past, Present, and Future of Historic Preservation at George Washington's Mount Vernon*, edited by Carol Borchert Cadou (Charlottesville: University of Virginia Press, 2018), pp. 41–69.

59. By 1790 the upholstery of the Fairfax suite appears to have come apart at the seams, much of the quilting in the back seems to have broken, and many of the brass nails had disappeared. George Washington made purchases from local firms Thomas Vowell, Patton and Butcher, and Hodgson and Nicholson to make the repairs. To repair the seams, Washington purchased "3 oz. of Silk for sewing the [show] Covers of the parlor Chairs and settee" as well as brass thimbles and "1 doz. Needles" for doing the work. He also purchased "2M tacks" to retack some of the hidden upholstery. To repair the quilting, Washington purchased "3 hanks of cord for the Chairs & Settee in the parlour," "blue Silk Cord for drawing the backs of [the Chairs and Settee]," and "1 large needle for running the silk Cord through the backs of the chairs." Lastly, he purchased "3M princes Mettal Nails . . . for the parlour Chairs," suggesting that he had all of the brass nails replaced on the chairs. While it would seem that George Washington should have simply reupholstered the chairs, there is no evidence that he purchased the textiles needed, and this period is particularly well documented in his account books. George Washington Ledger Book B, 1772–1793, p. 318, Papers of George Washington. Thompson, "George William Fairfax." George Washington to George William Fairfax, February 27, 1785, PGW Digital. George Washington purchased the Wilton carpet from the blue Dressing Room at the auction. The carpet was listed as "1 Large Carpet in the blue room" purchased for £11 in "Sales of Furniture at Belvoir, August 15th, 1774." George Washington to Tobias Lear, March 10, 1797, PGW Digital. This letter indicates that George Washington continued to use the furniture during the remainder his life. He requested a carpet for his "blue Parlour" and suggested "it ought to have a good deal of blue in it . . . that it may accord with the furniture." This quote led previous scholars to paint the front parlor blue after finding a layer of that color; however, Washington meant that the furniture coverings were blue rather than the walls. He clarified his statement in George Washington to Tobias Lear, March 12, 1797, [PGW Digital], when he wrote: "as the furniture was blue, the ground or principal flowers in it ought to be blue."

Appendix

Goods bought of Willm Gomm & Son and Company
in Clerkenwell Close, London, March 31, 1763
William and George William Fairfax Account Book
Fred W. Smith Library for the Study of George Washington
Mount Vernon, Virginia

The left column indicates packing crate numbers.

Crate	Description	£	s	d
No. 1 & 2	A mah^y. 3 ft. 9 In.s Double Chest of Drawers with Square Ends....¬	8	10	—
3 & 4	2 Mah^y. 3 ft. Single Chest of Drawers	9	10	—
5	A fine Mah^y. 3 ft. 6 In.^{s} Oblong Dining Table one for the flaps to take of..	3	15	—
6	A Mahy. Pembrook Table	1	10	
	A Strong fine Mah^y. Spider Leg Table	2	5	
	A folding fire Skreen lined wth. yellow Cany	1	1	
	A Cutwork D^o. Lined with India paper	2	—	—
7	A fine Mah^y. 5 f^t. Side board Table with fretwork upon the Edge of the Top Astragal Moulds & Brackets	5	5	—
8	1 p^r. of Mah^y. 3 f^t. Square Card Tables lind wth. Green Cloth Astragal mouldings & open Brackets	5	5	—
	An Ovall Bottle Cistern on a Frame	2	17	—
	A knife Tray	—	6	—
Pack.^{d} in no. 6	A Scollopt Mah^y Voider	—	14	—
	2 Dish Trays @ 16/	1	12	—
	A Neat Large Mah^y cutrim Tea Tray	1	10	—
	2 Sqr.^{e} Mah^y. Bason Stands 17/	1	14	—
9 to 13	5 Compass Deal Toilett Tables. @ 10/6	2	12	6
14	1 Hanging Glass Globe wth. Brass frame & Shade wth. Ballance weight Line & Double Brass pully	2	4	—
15	1 Large Sconce Glass the frame Carvd & Gilt in Burnish'd Gold	15	—	—
16	1 Large Ovall Glass in appeer Mah^y. frame painted Lead white.	5	10	—
	1 Ditto in Burnish'd Gold	5	10	—

17	1 Sconce Glass in A Carvd & painted frame	3	15	—
	3 Dressing Glassis @ 18/	2	14	—
	1 Compass Japannd Dressing Glass	2	15	
18	A Mah[y]. Shaveing Table & Glass	3	3	—
19 & 20	A Mahy. 3 f[t]. 6 In.[s] Desk & Book Case wth pidement head & Gilt Ornaments upon the freeze & Doors the doors wired wth Green Silk behind	16	16	—
21 to 27	14 Mah[y]. Square Top Marlborough Chairs pin Seats Coverd wth figur'd Stowehair @18	12	12	—
28 & 29	4 D.[o] the seats finish'.[d] in Canvass 15/6	3	2	—
	4 Saxon Green half Inch Cheque Cases	—	8	—
30	2 Mah[y]. Hollow Stuff Back & seatarm Chairs Coverd wth. figured hair Bordered & Brass Naild…@52/6	5	5	—
31 & 32	4 Mah[y]. Chairs Lether H pin seats Coverd with Green morine 22/	4	8	—
	4 Saxon Green 1/2 In.[s] Chique Cases to D[o].	—	8	—
33 & 34	4 Chairs Coverd wth yellow morine 22/	4	4	—
	4 yellow 1/2 In.[s] Chiq Cases to d.[o] 2/	—	8	—
35:36	4 Mah[y]. Chairs Pincushion seats finishd in Canvass 21/	4	4	—
	4 Crimson Chiq. Cases to Ditto 2/	—	8	—
37 to 39	6 Mah[y]. Chairs Coverd over the rail wth figured Horse hair & Brass naild 25/	7	10	—
40 to 45	12 Mahy. Chairs Covd. wth. Crimson morine Brass Naild 29/	17	8	—
	12 Rich Crimson Chiq. Cases to d.[o] 2/6	1	10	—

		£	s	d
60	3 Drapery Pully window Laths & brackˢ. Collourd & pllished 3/6	—	10	6
	67 yds. of Superf.ᶜ Saxon Blew Mixd Damask for Curtains & to cover 8 Chairs & a Sopha 7/	23	9	—
	23 yards fine Blew Tamy for Lineing 1/7	1	16	5
	54 yd.ˢ of the best silk Coverd Lace 3 ½	—	15	9
	24 yd.ˢ of Braid	—	2	—
	38 yd of Silk & worsted Fringe…2/2	4	2	4
	6 Silk & worsted Tassells to each Curtain & lines to D.º …19/	2	17	—
	Brass Lacquird Rings & Cloak pins 4/	—	12	—
	Sewing silk thred Nails Tax & c. 4/ Buchram for the heads & Lead weights 4/	—	12	—
	Cuting out & makeing D.º 3 Curtains in the Neates & best manner to draw in Drapery…12/	1	16	—
46 & 47	8 Mahʸ. Marlboroug Stuff back Chairs Stuff'd in the best french manner Cush Borderd & wilted & coverd w.ᵗʰ the above Damask & brass naild w.ᵗʰ 2 Rows N.º 3	14	—	—
	1 Large Sopha to match w.ᵗʰ 3 Bolsters	8	10	—
	33 yds. of Supf.ᶜ Saxon Blew In.ˢ Chiq for Cases to Ditto…1/9	2	17	9
	Cuting out & making Do. Cases thd. & Tape	1	—	—
the bedst.ᵈ is in No. 52	A four post Bedstead w.ᵗʰ Mahʸ. fluted Pillows Castors Rod & sacking Testor & base Laths & brass Caps to the Screws	4	10	—

60	81 yd of fine Chintz Cotton for furnit.ᵉ to D.º 2 window Curtains 4 Chairs & 1 Counterpin Included A Nem.ᵗ that is pack'd up …4/9	19	4	9
	54 yd of white D.º for Lineing 1/8	4	10	—
	140 yd of the best mixd worsted & lace 2/2	1	9	2
	16 yd.ˢ Buckram & Hessings 1/2	—	18	8
	Lines Tassels to the Curtains & Bed	—	10	—
	Rings and Cloak pins to D.º	—	9	—
	Thr.ᵈ Tape studs Nails &c to the bed Curtains & Counterpin	—	10	6
	Cuting out and makeing the bed window Curtains & Counterpin in the Neatest & best manner to stud on all Over	2	16	–
49 & 50	4 Mahʸ. Stuff back Chairs Round stuffed & finished in Canvass 21	4	4	
	Cuting out & making light Cases to Dº. of the above Cotton 3/6	—	14	—
60	9 yd of Supf.ᶜ Saxon blew 1/2 In.ˢ Chiq for C.ˢ 1/9	—	15	9
	Cuting out and make d.º w.ᵗʰ th.ᵈ & Tape	—	6	—
	3 Supfe. Crimson Morine Drapery Curtains fring'd all round w.ᵗʰ Lines Tasˢ & C	11	5	—
The bedst.ᵈ No. 51	A four Post yellow morine Bed w.ᵗʰ Mahʸ. fluted Pilliars & carvd Cornices made in the neatest manner to stud on all over	13	13	—
The Rest 60	2 Supf.ᶜ yellow morine plain Fustin Window curtains made in the Neatest Manner w.ᵗʰ Lines Tassels & c…38	3	16	—
	A four post Crimson Chique Bed made in the Neatest & best manner to Stud on all over	10	—	—
	A plain fustin window Curtain to Do.	1	18	—
	A four post Saxon Green1/2 In.ˢ Chique bed made in the Neatest manner to stud on all over	8	—	—
	1 plain festoon window Curtain to d.º	1		15

No.	Item	£	s	d
55 & 56	A neat Mah.ʸ 3 f.ᵗ 6 In.ˢ S'ettea bedstead Coverd w.ᵗʰ Saxon green morine & brass Naild w.ᵗʰ morine Curtains head Cloth and Testor	7	10	—
	A Saxon green 1/2 In.ˢ Chiq.e Lase to Dᵒ	—	9	—
60	2 Supf. Saxon Green morine plain Drapery Curtains w.ᵗʰ Lines & Tassills & c made in the neatest and best mann.ʳ 4/	5	8	—
	2 Long Wilton bedside Carpets 10/6	1	1	—
	3 Small Wilt'on Pirsian D.ᵒ 36/			
	1 very Large D.ᵒ	9	15	—
	1 p.ʳ fine Blankets		15	—
	1 p.ʳ of D.ᵒ Larger	1	2	—
	1 p.ʳ of D.ᵒ Ditto	1	6	—
	5 p.ʳ of D.ᵒ Larger…@36/	9	—	
	2 p.ʳ of under Blankets…@15/	1	10	—
57	5 Large Rugs @13/	3	5	—
	1 small Supf.ᶜ Bedtick Bolster & one Pillow white Fustion	1	16	—
	1 D.ᵒ Larger w.ᵗʰ 2 pillows	2	8	—
	3 Supf.ᶜ d.ᵒ w.ᵗʰ Bolsters & 2 fine white fustion Pillows to Each…50/	7	10	—
	5 Common Strong bedticks Bolsters and Pillows 5 of the pillows packed in 61 & 62 28/	7	—	—
58 & 59	1 very Good Chique Mattrass Flocks	1	3	—
	1 D.ᵒ Larger Blew Inch Chique	2	—	—
	3 D.ᵒ Larger Ditto @45/	6	15	—
No. 60	Sundries as have been Specified			

Stores No. 61 & 62	5 Chique flock Mattress.s 25/	6	5	—
	5 p.ʳ Blanketts 15/	3	15	—
	10 ld. of the best stove dryed Goose feathers fill'd into 5 of the above pillows 2/2	1	1	8
	28 yd of blew & white Copper plate Cotton 3/	4	4	—
	36 yd of Lace to D.°…2/2	—	7	6
60	3 very Neat green Tricklesses all Compleat	4	14	6
	3 green Spring Curtains @ 25/	3	15	—
	2 Bells 5 doz Cranks with Triggers wire mouldings &c &c with 3 Gimblets	3	—	—
	1 yellow Canvass Skreen for Chairs	—	4	—

	Amt. Brot. Over	427	1	9
Packing				
	3 Cases for Glasses	1	2	—
	1 d.° pembrook Table	—	12	—
	1 d.° Card Tables &c	—	8	—
	2 d.° 8 Stuff Back Chairs 14/	1	8	—
	1 D.° Sopha	1	10	—
	2 D.° Globe & Shaving Tables	0	6	—
	1 D.° Book Case	0	12	—
	1 D.° Beding	0	16	—
	6 double matted parcels Chests & Desks 3/	0	18	—
	1 d.° wth. partly a case to a sideboard	—	8	—
	27 matted parsels Chairs 1/6	2	0	6
	4 D.° Bedsteads 1/6	0	6	—
	4 D.° Mattrasses 2/6	0	6	—
	2 d.° Doub.ᶜ matted Settea bed	0	6	—
	1 D.° w.ᵗʰ A wrapper N.° 57	0	10	6
	5 Toilett Tables not packd			
	62 Parcels	11	13	—
	[Total]	438	14	
	Shipping Charges	1	10	—

Sundries had before viz.

March 11	A cane fuled Tea Table	3	10	—
	Packing D.º in A case		6	—
[March] 21	A pair neat Mahʸ. Brackets		12	—
	Packing d.º in A case		1	6
	House Furniture amounts to	444	14	3

Rec.ᵈ Aprill the 9ᵗʰ 1763 of G.º Wᵐ. Fairfax Eqʳ. four Hundred & forty four Pounds & fourteen Shillings & thre pence in full for the Contents for this Bill and all Demands p.ʳ Wᵐ Gomm & Son & Self

440: 4:9	Draft on Miss.ʳˢ Russell
4: 9:6	draft on Waterman
444:14:3	& Molleson @ 12 months
	Frances Peter Mallet

George William Fairfax utilized the 1763 invoice from William Gomm & Son & Company to compile this list of furniture and corresponding prices. The original inventory is heavily deteriorated, and when necessary, the missing words have been supplemented with the corresponding entry on the previous invoice. The entries for "The Passage Below Stairs" and "The Lobby" were left blank in the original document.

Dining [Room]

1 Mah.ʸ 5 ft. Sideb[oard]	5	5	—
1 pʳ. Mah:ʸ Square [Dining Tables]	5	5	—
1 Oval Bottle Cistern	2	17	—
1 Knife Tray	—	6	—
1 Scollopt Mah.ʸ Vo[ider]	—	14	—
2 Dish Trays	1	12	—
1 Large Mahʸ. Cutr[im Tray]	1	10	—
1 Sconce Glass gilt in b[urnished gold]	15	—	—
12 Mahʸ. Chairs @19	17	8	—
12 Covers for Ditto @ 2/6	1	10	—
3 Crimson Morine Drapery Window Curtains @ 7/7	11	5	—
1 Large Wilton Persian Carpet	9	15	—
1 pʳ Tongs Shovel Dogs & fender	3	10	—
	75	17	—

1 Mahʸ. Table (dining) one flap to take off	3	15	—
1 Mahʸ. Spider leg Table	2	5	—
[Fol]ing fire Skreen lined with y[ellow]	1	1	—
2 [M]ahʸ. Arm Chairs covᵈ with figurd [hair]	5	5	—
6 [Ma]hʸ. Chairs coverd over the rail with hair	7	10	—
Chimney Glass	18	—	—

Parlor

[1 pr] Tongs Shovle & Fender	2	14	6
[Sa]xon green plain Drapery Curtains	5	8	—
	37	18	6

Colonel Fairfax's D[ressin]g Room

to be sent to Colo. Wash:ˢ

[1 Large Ovall Glass in bur]nished gold	[5]	[10]	[—]
1 Mahʸ. Shaveing Table	3	3	—
1 Mahʸ. Desk & Ca.	16	16	—
4 Chairs and Cover 22/	4	8	—
1 Mahʸ. Settea Bedstead saxon Green	7	18	—
Covers for Ditto	—	9	—
1 Mahʸ. Pembrook Table	1	18	—
Dogs Shovel Tongs & fender	1	13	—
	41	15	—

Mrs. Fairfax's Chamber

1 Mah^y. Chest of Draws	8	10	—
1 Bedstead & Curtains	8	—	—
Window Curtains	1	15	—
4 Chairs do @ 15/6	3	2	—
Covers for Do @ 2/	—	8	—
Dressing Table	10	—	—
1 p^r. Dogs Shovle & Tongs	1	3	—
	32	18	—

The Yellow Chamber

1 = 4 post Bedstead with Curtains	13	13	—
2 Window Curtains	3	16	—
1 Compass Table	—	10	6
1 Bason Stand	—	17	6
for Mrs. Bushrod { 4 Chairs with Covers	4	16	—
1 Dressing Glass	—	18	—
Dogs Shovle Tongs & fender	1	14	6
~~Shovle Tongs Dogs & fender~~	4	~~3~~	8
2 Bed side wilton Carpets @ 10/6	1	1	—
1 ~~H~~ small Wilton Pertian Carpet	1	16	—
	29	2	6

The Chintz Chamber

1 = 4 post Bedstead & Ca	4	10	—
81 y^{ds} Chintz Cotton in Curtains	19	4	9
54 yards of Lining for Ditto	4	10	—
140 yards Lace	1	9	2
16 yards of Buchram and	—	18	8
Lines & tassels to the Bed & Curtains	—	10	—
Rings & Cloak Pins to Ditto	—	9	—
Thread Tape Studs Nails & C^a. to the Bed window	—	10	6
Curtains & counterpin			
4 M[ahy.] Chairs	4	4	—
Cuting out & making Covers for D^o.	—	14	—
9 yards Saxon blue for cases to D^o.	—	15	9
Cuting out & making Ditto	—	6	—
One Compass Table	—	10	6
1 Mah^y. Chest of Dr[awers]	4	15	—
1 Small Wilton Car[pet]	1	16	—
2 Bedside Ditto 10/6	1	1	—
Dogs Shovel Tongs [& Fender]	2	3	—
	[48]	[7]	4

The Red Chamber

	£	s	d
1 four post Bedstead & Curtains	10	—	—
1 Window Curtain	1	18	—
1 Com[pass Deal] Toilett Table	—	10	6
4 Cha[irs with] Chintz Covers	4	12	—
1 D[ressing Glass]	—	18	—
Dogs [Shovel Tongs] Fender	1	18	9
1 Small [?]	1	16	—
	21	7	[15]

The Dressing Chamber

	£	s	d
67 yards saxon Blue Damask for Curtains, a Sopha & covers for 8 Chairs	20	9	—
23 yards Blue Tammy	1	16	5
54 yards best silk Covered lace	—	15	9
24 yards of Braid	—	2	—
38 yards of silk worsted fringe	4	2	4
6 silk and worsted Tassells to each curt^n	2	17	—
Brass Lacquered Rings & Cloak Pins	—	12	—
Sewing silk thread Nails tax &C^a. Buckram for the heads & Lead w^{ts}.	—	12	—
Cuting out & making D^o 3 Curtains in the neatest manner to draw up in Drapery	1	16	—
1 p^r. Bellows 5/6	—	5	6
8 Mah^y. Chairs	14	—	—
1 Sopha	8	10	—
33 yards of Saxon blue In^s. Cheque for Cases	2	17	9
Cuting out making D^o. with th^d. & tape	1	—	—
A large Oval glass	1	—	—
1 Compass Dressing Glass	2	15	—
1 fine India Skreen	2	—	—
1 Large Carpet	12	—	—
Dogs Shovle Tongs & fender	4	3	8
	87	4	7

The Passage Below Stairs

The Lobby

Account of Sales at Belvoir, August 15, 1774
Virginia Historical Society, Richmond, Virginia

Richard Brandt D[r].

1774 Aug.[t] 16	To 1 dressing table, a looking Glass & 3 watring Potts	I	15	—
	By Thomas Willis Jur[n]. for Bal.[a]	I	15	—
	Cash D.[r]			
	2 butter Potts 2/3, 12 D[o] 3/	—	5	3
	18 quart Bottles	—	1	72
	1 bread baskett, 3 bottles & 1 Cork	—	—	72
	1 doz wine 12/ 1 broad sword 8/	I	—	—
	1 Copper kettle & wine pipes	—	4	—
	1 Lot of Lumber 2/ 2 Grid irons 21/6	I	6	6
	3 Pewter plates 6/6, 3 flat irons 12/6	—	19	—
	1 Landau box 1/ 1 tea tree 10/	—	11	—
	1 Card table 80/ 2 Japan tea treas 21/	5	1	—
	1 boot Jack 8[d], 1 ratt trap 4/	—	4	8
	To Miles Richardson	—	7	—
	To Gilbert Simpson	—	7	6
	To George Mason	—	17	6
		II	5	8
	By paid J Lomax y[r] lawyer	—	12	—
	By 5 Gallons Rum 5/	—	1	15
	By Miles Richardson for his assistance	—	15	—
	By Francis Willis Jun[r]. for Balance which he has Credited in G. W. Fairfax's Accot. Curren[t] with him	8	13	8
		II	5	8

Colo. John Carlyle D[r]

1774 Aug[t] 15	To 1 bedstead, Curtain, & window Curtains	7	—	—

Doct James Craik D[r]

1774 Aug[t] 15	To 1 Large Carpett	8	10	—

John Parke Custis Esq— D[r]

1774 Aug[t] 15	To 1 India Skreen	3	—	—
	1 mahogo[y] wash stand	4	—	—
		7	—	—

Joshua Gore Loudoun D[r]

1774 Aug[t]	To 1 bed, bedstead, 1 p[r] blanketts, 1 bolster & 2 pillows	8	15	—

Wm Keaton, Augustus Donell Severly

1774	To 1 feather bed bolster & pillow	6	3	—
Augt 15	By their Bond payable in 12 mo^s for Balance	6	3	—

Adam Lynn in Alex^a D^r.

1774	1 doz Wine 8/ 1 doz wine D^o 10/	—	18	—
Augt 15	To a parcell of old Copper	—	7	—

George Mason Lin D^r.

1774	To 6 quart Bottles 1/3, 6 d^o 1/ 6 d^o 1/	—	3	3
Augt 15	" 6 pictures 4/6, 1 desk 2/6	—	7	—
	" 1 Desk & book Case	—	15	—
	" 1 bed, 1 p^r Blanketts, 1 Counterpane 1 bolster & 2 pillows	9	10	—
		10	15	3
	By Cash	—	17	6
	By the bed	9	10	—
	By pictures & bottles D^o	—	7	9

Cleon Moore D^r.

1774	To 1 mahog^y Chest of drawers	6	15	—
Augt 15	1 matrass	1	1	6
	2 Candlesticks & 2 Extinguishers	—	14	9
	By Cleon Moore & To Willis Junr.	8	11	3
	P^r their bond for Bal^{ce}			

Lawson Parker D^r.

1774	To 4 butter Potts	—	4	—
Augt 15	1 Chest of Pine	—	7	6
		—	11	6
	By George Washington Esqr.	—	2	—
			9	6
	By Harriot work for Balance		9	6

Miles Richardson D^r.

1774	To 2 flatt Irons	—	7	—
Augt 15	By Cash for Balance	—	7	—

Gilbert Simpson D^r.

1774	To 9 butter potts	—	15	—
Augt 15	By Col^o. G Washington	—	7	6
		—	7	6
	By Cash in full	—	7	6

Daniel Stone D^r.

1774	To 1 Grid iron, 2 frames & 3 boxes	—	6	6
Augt 15	2 <tratts>	2	5	—
		2	11	6
	By Bal.^{ce} Charged ag^t your last Years wages w^h Col^o F desired FW to pay	2	11	6

Josias Shaw D^r.

1774	To 1 Mahogy Table	4	2	6
Augt 15	1 D^o D^o	2	16	—
	By Jonas Shaw & Richard Brandt Pr Bond for balance	6	18	6

Colo George Washington Dr.

		£	s	d
1774	To 6 Butter Potts	—	4	6
Augt 15	To G. Simpson 5 Do	—	7	6
	To Lawson Parker 2 Do	—	2	—
	" 2 doz wine	1	4	—
	" 4 Glasses & frames 12/6 irons for boat 12/6	1	5	—
	" 10 water palates	1	6	—
	1 Mahogy Shavg Disk	4	—	—
	1 Sittel bed wt furniture	13	—	—
	4 Mahogy Chairs	4	—	—
	1 Chamber Carpett	1	1	—
	1 oval Glass & Guilt frame	4	5	—
	1 Mahogy Chest wt Drawers	12	10	—
	1 bed, 1 pr. blanketts &ca	11	—	—
	1 Cistern & stand	4	—	—
	1 Sideboard	12	5	—
	1 Mahogy Voider, a dish trea & knife trea	1	10	—
	1 Card table	4	—	—
	1 Japan bread trea	—	7	—
	12 Chairs & 3 Windw Curtains	31	—	—
	1 Looking Glass	13	5	—
	2 Candlesticks & a bust of Shakespr.	1	6	—
	1 Carpett	11	—	—
	3 Carpetts	3	5	—
	1 wash stand & bottle &ca	1	2	6
	1 Mahog.y Close Stool	1	10	—
	2 mattrass's	4	11	—
	1 pr End irons, tongs fender &ca	3	10	—
	1 Sett Do	3	17	6
	1 Sett Do	1	17	6
	1 pair Dogs	3	—	—
	1 pott rack	4	—	—
	1 roasting fork	—	2	6
	1 plate basket	—	3	—
	1 spider leg'd table	1	11	—
	1 Skreen	—	10	—
	1 Carpett	2	15	—
	1 pair bellows & broom	—	11	—
	2 window Curtains	2	—	—
	1 marble mortar	1	1	—
	1 Celler pot rack	1	7	6
		169	12	6

William Lyles D^r.

1774	To 1 Mahog^y dress^g table	13	—	—
Augt 15	To 2 dish treas	1	6	—
	" 1 bed, 1 pr. Blanketts, 1 Coverlaid, 1 p^r. pillows & 1 bolster	11	6	—
	4 Mahog^y Chairs	4	12	6
	1 small sett of End irons	1	5	—
	1 d^o d^o	1	15	—
	1 mahog^y table	4	2	6
	2 mahog^y table	9	2	6
	1 small mortar	—	5	±
		46	14	6

Mr Francis Willis Junr D^r.

	To 1 large bottle 3/6 quart D^o 2/	—	5	—
	3 bread baskets	—	1	—
	10 Pictures 9/ 3 Spotts 6/	—	15	—
	1 bedstead Curtains & wind^w Curtains	11	12	—
	1 bed, 1 pr blankets, & c^a	8	10	—
	1 bedside Carpett	1	—	—
	1 pair bellows & 1 broom	—	9	—
	1 warming pan	—	6	—
	1 Cooler 2/2,^d 4 Chairs 70/	3	16	2
	1 p^r Shoe & knee buckles	—	2	—
	1 p^r End irons	—	10	—
	1 Coffee mill	—	9	—
	1 Glass Lanthorne	1	10	0
		29	5	2
	To Richard Brandt p^r acco^t	1	15	—
		31	0	2

Account of Sales at Belvoir, December 5, 1774
Virginia Historical Society, Richmond, Virginia

1 Case & a dozen bottles	1	16	—
1 pair Garden Shears, 1 Snuffer stand, a brush, 1 pʳ. butt 4	—	1	3
2 flint Decanters 2/, an old pine desk 16/6	—	18	6
a large Pot & an old lanthorne 6/ a lot of queens China 30/	1	16	—
9 knives & 10 forks 12/ Glass 2/6, 1 pʳ end irons 5/	—	19	6
1 pʳ scales & 5 weights 10/ & 2 pair Stilyards 12/	1	2	—
2 brass Candlesticks 9/ 2 Copper Stewpans 6/6	—	15	6
1 Copper fish kettle 18/ 4 dᵒ. Stewpans wᵗ. Cover 16/	1	14	—
3 d.ᵒ Saucepans 5/ 4 Ditto kettles 10/	—	15	—
1 tea kettle 2 Cannisters & an Oven 15/ a Pestal mortar &ca/ 12/6	1	7	6
a lot of Housings 2/6, 5 pieces of mattings 20/	1	2	6
a Fishing Seene Ropes & cᵃ. 15/	—	15	—
a Waggon wᵗ. Swingletrees £9.7.6—a Ditto wᵗ. 1 Ditto £9	18	7	6
A Ditto wᵗ. Ditto £8	8	—	—
a black mare named Sprightly branded F. x	16	12	6
a bay horse, Ranger £5.5—a bay Colt £6.2.6	11	7	6
a bay mare, Fly £10.10—a bay horse, Wanton £8	18	10	—
a Gray Colt, silver Eye £10—2 old flour searches 72	10	—	72
2 doz & 9 quart bottles 7/6, 4 maps 7/6, 10 Candle moulds 18/	1	13	—
1 Cutlast 4/ seene Ropes 5/6, 2 bell borers 1/6	—	11	—
a hoop & cᵃ. 2/ a butter pott 72ᵈ, 1 pʳ old Cart wheels 21/	1	3	72
1 hand Mill 30/, 1 80 Gallon Copper kettle 75/	5	5	—
1 large iron Pot 20/, 1 bread toaster 1/3ᵈ	1	1	3
12 Ewes £7.10—8 Lambs £4.12—12 Ewes & a Ram £7.2.6	19	4	6
3 Cow Yearlings, 3 Steers & a bull Ditto	8	5	—
4 Cows & 3 Calves £12.5.0 1 large brown Steer £6.10	18	15	—
1 dark brown Stear £5.12.6, 1 Small fried Dᵒ. £5	10	12	6
1 large fried Do. £7—12 Shotes 48/	9	8	—
13 Shotes 49/ Corn blades 2 Stacks 31/	4	—	—
80 feet of fodder, Shocks & ca	3	—	—
1 hand mill 12/ 3 Cows 3 Calves & a bull £10	10	12	—
60 barrells of Corn—a 10/ pʳ. bance	30	—	—
	219	11	9

The Revᵈ. Andrew Morton, a Lease of the mansion house, Plantation & ca. at £100.5—pʳ. Year for 7 years——

Richard Newman—Lease of The Plantation call'd Frederick quarter £12.5 for 1 Year

Amy Hudson Henderson

French & Fashionable: The Search for George and Martha Washington's Presidential Furniture

▼ ABIGAIL ADAMS LIKELY DETERMINED the fate and historical fortunes of the French furniture suite that once graced George and Martha Washington's presidential drawing room when, as the incoming first lady, she declared to her husband in February 1797: "I want not a stick of it at the close of the term" (fig. 1). Resolved that Congress—and not she and John—should pay to refurnish the president's residence after the Washingtons retired to Mount Vernon that spring, Abigail instructed her husband to turn down George Washington's offer to purchase the fine French chairs and settee the Washingtons had assembled during George's presidency. As John informed his wife, the president personally owned the furniture in the drawing room, besides many items throughout the house, and now "all the Glasses, ornaments, kitchen furniture, the best Chairs, settees, Plateaus &c." had to be replaced. The Adamses, however, were determined to live modestly and within the allowance Congress provided for household furnishings and expenses—even if it meant, as John put it, they "shall be put to great difficulty to live and that in not one third the Style of Washington." As a result, they declined to purchase the "Articles in the Green Drawing Room" proffered by Washington. The Adamses' decision thus set in motion the first auction of presidential furniture and, ultimately, the widespread dispersal of what would become the famed—and elusive—drawing room suite.[1]

More than 200 years after the Adamses' decision, historians continue to search for those auctioned chairs and settee in the French taste, as they unquestionably give insight into the Washingtons and their carefully considered furnishing choices. Just as pertinent, however, is what this famous suite reveals about the material and philosophical decisions many members of the founding generation faced when they set out collectively to build their new republic. In essence, the story of a few chairs brings attention to several key questions these men and women faced as they transitioned from a confederation to a more mature nation. For instance, would the leaders of this new nation follow the materials and manners of Britain and Europe, or would they embark on something entirely new? How would they define moderation and simplicity as well as extravagance and superfluity? And, how would these concepts impact the development of a cohesive national identity? Scholars seek to identify and authenticate the pieces in this drawing room suite because their journey from an upholsterer's workshop in Paris to a workshop in New York (after being damaged in the Atlantic crossing), their service in the elevated salons of a French ambassador and then an American president, and finally their legacy as souvenirs after that 1797 auction, attest to—and visually document—the emerging and competing values that profoundly shaped Federal America.[2]

Today there is considerable confusion about what the Washingtons' French furnishings looked like since there are multiple contenders that vary in style, materials, and provenance. New research into written records and the physical evidence of extant pieces now allows scholars to clarify several misattributions and to state with greater authority which of these pieces were once part of the set. According to historical records, the core of the suite comprised twelve armchairs, six side chairs, and a sofa—all uphol-stered in a green, flowered silk damask and made in Paris by Jean-Baptist Lelarge—and imported into the United States by then-French ambassador the cômte de Moustier. Washington purchased the suite in 1790 and three years later commissioned Georges Bertault, a French émigré upholsterer in Philadelphia, to make an additional six side chairs and two stools in a matching green silk. Ever since the twenty-four green chairs and a sofa were purportedly sold at auction in 1797, there has been tremendous interest in the pieces as relics of Washington, his presidency, and the style of his and Martha's republican court. There has also been uncertainty as to which "rel-ics" are authentic.[3]

This article relates a broad story about the Washingtons and how they came to be interested in, and have access to, a wide array of French decorative objects. The narrative explores how the Washingtons navigated the changing perceptions of what kinds of material display were appropriate, desirable, and even necessary, in a nascent republic; the role of American diplomats and tourists in introducing the French taste to their countrymen; the French craftsmen responsible for their suite of furniture and shopping practices in ancien régime Paris; and finally, what the green drawing room in the Presi-dent's House in Philadelphia looked like during the Washingtons' tenure. By contextualizing the suite in terms of its style, function, and evolution in the salons of Paris, New York, and Philadelphia, we can analyze more deeply the cultural and political vision the Washingtons and their contemporaries shared for their country.

The story of the Washingtons and their consumption of French fashions should rightly begin at the close of the Revolution, when Americans were seeking ways to rebuild their communities and homes after seven long years of war. It was in the early 1780s when the Washingtons were introduced to the elegant manufactures of Paris and had their first taste of what the luxury capital of Europe had to offer. Through the friendships they formed with French officers serving in the war, they were exposed to French aristocratic manners. In 1782 Martha received a "Present of Elegant China" from a titled French officer, Adam-Philip, comte de Coustine, in appreciation for a din-ner he attended at Mount Vernon (fig. 2). The tea and coffee service was likely a sampler set since each piece is enameled with a different combination of ribbons, swags, garlands, bands, and scrolls yet linked by the monogram "GW." In one gesture, the comte de Coustine demonstrated his admiration for Gen. Washington and his family while simultaneously advertising the

Figure 2 Dessert service, Niderviller, France, ca. 1782. Porcelain (hard-paste). (Courtesy, Mount Vernon Ladies' Association; photo, Gavin Ashworth.)

wares of the Niderviller porcelain factory, of which he was the principal owner. In return, the Washingtons joined a select community of Americans with access to the products of France. Equally important, they now had friends with knowledge of, and a taste for, such refined wares.[4]

The following year, as the war ended and Gen. Washington prepared to return to Mount Vernon and resume life as a private citizen, he initiated a plan to enhance the French porcelain service with a collection of new furniture, dinner china, and silver wares. Accordingly, he did what he had often done in the past: he sought out trusted friends and family members for advice on shopping. "There is another thing likewise which I wish to know," he wrote to his nephew Bushrod Washington from his encampment at Rocky Hill, New Jersey,

> & that is, whether French plate is fashionable & much used in genteel houses in France & England; and whether, as we have heard, the quantity in Philadelphia is large—of what pieces it consists, & whether among them, there are tea urns, Coffee pots, Tea pots, & the other equipage for a tea table, with a tea board, Candlesticks & waiters large & small, with the prices of each.

Figure 3 Adolf Ullrik Wertmüller (1751–1811), *George Washington,* United States, 1795. Oil on canvas. 25½" x 20¹³⁄₁₆". (Courtesy, Nationalmuseum, Stockholm, Sweden; photo, Nationalmuseum, CC BY-SA.)

Bushrod was then studying law in Philadelphia and a frequent guest in the home of Samuel and Elizabeth Willing Powel, among the city's more esteemed and wealthy citizens and dear friends to the Washingtons. One presumes Bushrod was happy to share his observations on what was fashionable in the homes of the city's genteel families, many of whom he met through the Powels. Furthermore, he may have been able to visit shops along High Street to enquire about availability. Although there is no record of Bushrod's response to his uncle, he likely wrote that yes, such items were fashionable, but no, not readily available in post-war Philadelphia, because the next letter Washington composed on the subject was to his French brother-in-arms, the marquis de Lafayette, requesting his assistance in procuring "everything proper for a tea table" in silver plate.[5]

Like so many of their colonial peers, the Washingtons (figs. 3, 4) were long used to Great Britain serving as their guide in all things cultural and material. In fact, prior to the war, few Americans had access (through either commercial or personal ties) to household goods that did not originate within the British Empire. All of this changed when the Confederation Congress dispatched diplomats to the courts of Europe; word of fashions on the Continent began to trickle home, first in personal correspondence and then when the goods themselves eventually arrived as gifts or prized possessions. Upon the signing of the Treaty of Paris in 1783, trade with foreign nations was legalized, and Americans eagerly turned to France to see what she had to offer in the domestic line. Indeed, post-war negotiations among the British, French, and Americans were barely over before Washington initiated his correspondence with Lafayette.[6]

Washington could not have selected a better friend than Lafayette to help him with his shopping, for the marquis had returned to France during the treaty negotiations with the view of being an unofficial American representative at the court of Louis XVI. Lafayette's passion for the well-being of both countries led him to believe that a policy of open markets was in the best interests of both nations. In his view, this was the only viable way for America to rebuild its commerce and thus repay its debt to France. Ideally, the French would provide a market for America's raw materials in exchange for manufactured goods, and if France acted quickly to open her markets, there was the added benefit of financially cutting off the British from her former colonies. Lafayette surely recognized that there could be no better way to show off the variety and beauty of French wares than by sending examples to the Washingtons at Mount Vernon.[7]

Washington knew his friend well and understood that he would be delighted to serve as a proxy shopper. Yet Washington still felt the need to justify the commission, assigning the following reasons for recruiting Lafayette as his delegate:

> 1st. then, because I do not incline to send to England (from whence formerly I had all my goods) for any thing I can get upon tolerable terms elsewhere.

> 2nd. Because I have no correspondence with an[y] Merchants or artisans in France.

Figure 4 James Peale (1749–1831), portrait miniature of Martha Washington, United States, 1796. Watercolor on ivory. H. 1⅛", W. 1¼". (Courtesy, Mount Vernon Ladies' Association; photo, Paul Kennedy.)

3d. If I had, I might not be able to explain so well to them, as to you, my wants, who know our customs, taste & manner of living in America. and 4th Because I should rely much more upon your judgment and endeavors to prevent impositions upon me, both in the price & workmanship, than on those of a stranger.

It is hard to know which of the reasons was most important—breaking ties with England, getting the best price, or having a friend with good judgment to serve as a style guide—yet the last may well have been uppermost in Washington's mind. At the start of the letter he also noted that "as I am not much of a connoisseur in, & trouble my head very little about these matters, you may add anything else of the like kind which may be thought useful & ornamental." Washington was looking for guidance on what was fashionable and appropriate and evidently ready to put himself in the hands of the marquis for his first commission of French wares.[8]

The memorandum Washington included at the end of the letter documents an extensive order, and one wonders what role Martha played in the process, especially in light of Washington's admission that he thought little upon these matters. "A List of Plated Ware to be Sent to General Washington, by the Marq.s de la Fayette," with the following descriptions, could very well be imagined as Martha communicating with Lafayette's wife, Adrienne, who likely assisted her husband with the shopping:

> Everything proper for a tea-table, & these it is supposed may consist of the following Articles: A Large Tea salver, square or round as shall be most fashionable; to stand on the Tea table for the purpose of holding the Urn, teapot, Coffee pot, cream pot, China cups and saucers &ca.
>
> A large Tea-Urn, or receptacle for the water which is to supply the tea pot, *at the table*. 2 large Tea pots, and stands for Ditto, 1 Coffee Pot and stand, 1 Cream Pot, 1 Boat or Tray, for the Tea spoons, 1 Tea-chest, such as usually appertains to tea or breakfast tables, the inner part of which, to have three departments, two for tea's of different kinds, the other for Sugar. If any thing else should be judged necessary it may be added, although it is not enumerated.
>
> Also, Two large Salvers, sufficient to hold twelve common wine glasses, each.
>
> Two smaller size Do for 6 wine glasses, each.
> Two Bread baskets, middle size.
> A Sett of Casters, for holding, oil, Vinegar, Mustard &ca.
> A Cross or Stand for the centre of the Dining table.
> 12 Salts, with glasses in them.
> Eight Bottle sliders.
> Six large Goblets, for Costers.
> Twelve Candlesticks. Three pair of snuffers, and stands for them.
>
> And anything else which may be deemed necessary, in this way. If this kind of plated Ware will bear engraving, I should be glad to have my arms thereon, the size of which will, it is to be presumed be large or small in proportion to the piece on which it is engraved.

The marquis and marquise de Lafayette were pleased to help the Washingtons establish connections with Parisian silver merchants, and by the spring of 1784 the Lafayettes had done their best to fulfill the order.

Surviving pieces include a pierced, oval bread basket with engraved leaves, wheelwork flowers, and swags, as well as a similarly decorated bottle slider, or coaster, both done in the delicate neoclassical style then taking over cosmopolitan Europe (figs. 5, 6). With these wares as exemplars, the Washingtons and Lafayettes began to ponder the many commercial advantages that could result from a strong Franco-American trade relationship.[9]

The Washingtons were hardly alone in turning to France for commercial and cultural opportunities. By the time the Treaty of Paris was ratified on September 3, 1783, an influential band of American diplomats, businessmen, and tourists had gathered in the French capital and were becoming acquainted with Paris and her material world first hand, an experience that would profoundly impact them and their country's future. The list of Americans in Paris after the war is long and distinguished and includes such individuals as Benjamin Franklin, John and Sarah Livingston Jay, John and Abigail Adams and their children (John Quincy, Charles, and Nabby), Thomas Jefferson, William and Anne Willing Bingham, Alice DeLancey Izard, Gouverneur Morris, Abraham Swan, Henry Laurens, and Matthew and Anne Richardson Ridley. This expatriate group used diplomatic channels and ties with French officers and ministers, forged during the war, to gain entrée into the elite levels of French society. It was there—in the salons of French hostesses, along the paths of the Tuileries gardens, shopping in the Palais Royal, or visiting the theater—that they carefully observed French manners, hospitality, and style of living. It was also in Paris that these Americans began to form opinions about which (if any) French manners, and what material goods that supported politeness and sociability, would be best suited in a republic back home. A deeper look at their experience in Paris is therefore fundamental to the story of the Washingtons' drawing room chairs. Collectively, the Lafayettes and expatriate friends helped the Washingtons develop an appreciation for French decorative arts as well as the art of polite sociability, which consequently influenced the appearance of, and protocols in, the president's house.[10]

One could argue that among the many lessons Americans learned during their years in Paris was how to recognize the invisible ties among the French drawing room, worldly sociability, and the Enlightenment. As historian Antoine Lilti explores in his study of eighteenth-century Paris, behaviors in the drawing room had much to do with evolving notions of status, since men of noble birth could no longer rely on military valor or their membership in the nobility to solidify their high place in society. Rather, aristocratic prestige rested on being a *l'homme du monde* or "man of the world," capable of demonstrating mastery of the cultural practices of polite society. In salons—the *appartements de societé* or the room in a Paris townhouse where hosts received guests—men and women could practice, perfect, and demonstrate their worldly sociability and lay claim to this prestige. Moreover, in contrast to the French royal court, salons were spaces in which individuals of varied backgrounds (aristocrats, men of letters, patrons of the arts and belle lettres, diplomats, members of government, financiers, and foreign visitors) could assemble and converse on a wide range of topics, all

the while exhibiting wit, knowledge, and generosity to others. The salon was ultimately both a physical space and a society composed of men and women, based in private homes and often orchestrated by women, where individuals made (or lost) their reputations for gentility and civility.[11]

Tastefully decorated salons were integral to the demonstration of prestige and worldly hospitality; elegant furnishings not only signaled a host's financial resources but also his or her commitment to what was known as *l'art de vivre*. Historian Joan DeJean has shown how this concept, the art of living, grew out of Greek Stoic philosophy and by the late eighteenth century could be linked directly to the decorative arts and manufactures of France. Drawing on related strands of Enlightenment thought, DeJean argues that when civilizations began to measure themselves by their degree of material, social, and cultural advance, then enhancements in architecture and household furnishings—such as improved seating furniture, more efficient lighting, or the convenience of indoor plumbing—were an indication of rational thought and a society's ability to make continual progress. She sees the French as taking this idea one step further and states "it was only in a comfortable environment that individuals could use rational thinking (as opposed to religious faith) to transform their way of life." The relationship then, among French furniture design, materials, and use at the end of the ancien régime is clear: the French style came to be synonymous not just with quality, beauty, and comfort but also with rational thinking and worldly sociability.[12]

Letters and journal entries by Abigail and Nabby Adams, John and Sarah Jay, Thomas Jefferson, and Gouverneur Morris all attest to the importance—and indeed brilliance—of this salon culture in 1780s Paris. As members of the diplomatic corps, they received their education in French man-

Figure 7   Grand Salon from the Hôtel de Tessé, by Nicolas Huyot; carved by Pierre Fixon and (or) his son Louis-Pierre Fixon, Paris, ca. 1768–1772. (Courtesy, Metropolitan Museum of Art, gift of Mrs. Herbert N. Straus, 1942, acc.42.203.1.)

ners in the afternoon salons and evening dinner parties of some of America's greatest champions, including the marquis and marquise de Lafayette, the marquis and marquise de Chastellux, the duchesse de Mazarin, monsieur and madame Necker, madame de Genlis, madame de Ségur, madame de Helvetius, and madame de Tesse. In these elaborately decorated rooms, such as the grand salon from the Hôtel de Tesse (fig. 7), the Americans observed how to blend politics and politeness. They discovered which decorative furnishings lent support to their hosts' efforts to create spaces of distinction and comfort, on the one hand, and how those furnishings were best arranged to facilitate rational conversation and entertainment on the other.[13]

Those lessons in decorating revealed the importance of creating visual and social harmony throughout the salon. By the 1780s the soft, curvaceous rococo style popular under Louis XV had given way to the geometry and motifs of the classical world favored by Louis XVI and his court. Well-appointed social spaces were filled with groups of objects that matched and were designed to work as a whole. New, specialized furniture forms—sofas, and chairs of varying shapes and sizes; tea, card, and pier tables; looking glasses and picture frames—coordinated with one another in materials, ornamentation, color, and texture as well as with the architectural fixtures, as demonstrated in the elevation by François-Joseph Bélanger for the salon of the duchesse de Mazarin illustrated in figure 8. Upholstery on chairs

Figure 8 François-Joseph Bélanger, elevation of a wall in the salon of the duchesse de Mazarin, Paris, ca. 1780. Pen, ink, and watercolor on paper. 16⅟₁₆" x 10⅞". (Copyright, Victoria and Albert Museum, London.)

matched the window treatments. Both were likewise in accord with the color of the walls, whether they be covered with paint or wallpaper. Of all the objects in the salon, seating furniture was paramount. Chairs in this period were designed for a multitude of functions and consisted of two ranks: armchairs and side chairs. Large armchairs and sofas with flat backs (called *sieges meublant*) were placed along the walls around the room, while side chairs and lighter cabriolet armchairs (or *sieges courants*) were positioned either in a U or circular fashion to facilitate group conversation or in small clusters for games and private discourse (figs. 9–11). By some accounts, the formal etiquette of the French salon dictated that guests did not sit in the *sieges meublant* around the perimeter of the room but only in the *sieges courants*, and that the host and hostess reserved for themselves yet another form of armchair, the *bergère*, which was stationed on either side of the hearth, the place of honor. Symmetry, hierarchy, and harmony were the underlying principles in this French neoclassical decorating scheme.[14]

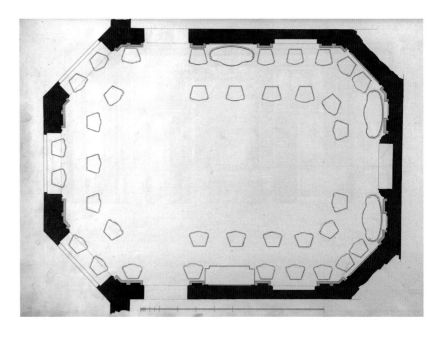

Figure 9 Erik Palmstedt, floor plan of the Hôtel du Châtelet, Paris, 1778–1780. Pen and ink on paper, 20¼" x 13¾". (Courtesy, Kungliga Akademien för de fria konsterna/Royal Academy of Fine Arts, Stockholm.) This plan shows the two-row circular configuration of seating with *sieges meublants* on the outside and *sieges courants* on the inside.

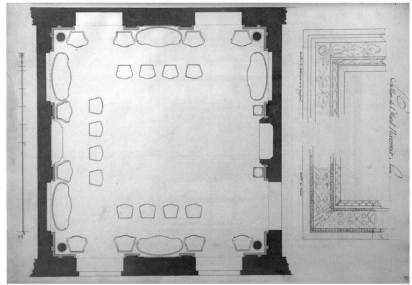

Figure 10 Erik Palmstedt, floor plan of the Hôtel du Nivernai, Paris, 1778–1780. Pen and ink on paper, 10¹⁄₁₆" x 14³⁄₁₆". (Courtesy, Kungliga Akademien för de fria konsterna/Royal Academy of Fine Arts, Stockholm.) This plan shows the U-shaped grouping of side chairs in the center and the larger armchairs and sofas along the perimeter.

There was never any question in the minds of American diplomats that their world was quite different from the one they found in these aristocratic townhouses, yet they also realized that many aspects were adaptable and transferable. Subsequently, when they furnished their own homes in Paris to receive guests as part of their diplomatic obligations, they gave careful consideration to which furnishings they might bring home after their mission. It is interesting to note that among their first considerations was whether to buy French or British furnishings; both were available in 1780s Paris due to the Anglomania sweeping through many aristocratic households. Indeed, there was an equal degree of Francomania in London as British tourists, artists, and diplomats had likewise flocked to Paris at the close of the war intent on experiencing *l'art de vivre* and bringing home to England that quintessential French style.

Cross-pollination and exchange between the two countries was evident in everything from furniture, silks, and silver wares to garden design, scientific equipment, and porcelain. Nabby Adams, for instance, enjoyed two visits to the Paris home of the duc de Chartres—one of the more notable collectors

Figure 11 François Dequevauviller, after Niklas Lafrensen II, *L'assemblé au salon (Gathering in a Salon)*, Paris, 1783–1784. Engraving and etching. 15⅞" x 19¾". (Copyright, Victoria and Albert Museum.) The chairs have been arranged in small, informal groups for a variety of activities.

of things English—and commented how "The Duke has built, finished, and furnished the house in the English style," and she found the rooms "truly elegant." And in London, cabinetmakers were heeding the advice of George Hepplewhite and Thomas Sheraton and making delicate, neoclassical drawing room chairs in the French taste: lightweight, upholstered in silk, and painted. The lesson learned from these examples was that sometimes the French, and sometimes the British, did things "better," and it was the responsibility of savvy American consumers to decide which country's manufactures suited their lifestyle.[15]

Gouverneur Morris nicely articulated the process Americans went through to find the right balance between the manufactures of France and England. In a 1792 letter to Thomas Pinckney, who was then serving as U.S. ambassador to Great Britain, Morris offered this advice:

> In respect to Furniture there is no doubt but that rich and elegant Furniture can be had in this Town [Paris] for much less than London, but plain and neat Furniture can be had rather cheaper and a great deal better with you. The Stile of living in the two Countries is so different that I have found myself as it were oblig'd to lay out a great Deal of money in Furniture which I should hardly know what to do with in America, Whereas you can in London get Articles which will answer well to take with you.

Morris was not alone in his assessment. A popular travel journal aimed at advising German tourists similarly instructed readers intent on buying goods abroad: "English furniture is almost without exception solid and practical; French furniture is less solid, more contrived and more ostentatious." And even the Frenchman and social observer Louis-Sébastien Mercier wrote: "England may seem to have more to offer in the way of peacefulness and the decent conduct of domestic life; but then, what prevents the Frenchmen from enjoying these blessings? They might be his if he would choose comfort and commodity rather than his present silly luxury, which kills true happiness and wastes energy and money." Despite such a chorus of criticism, Paris remained *the* shopping destination for wealthy tourists, especially those making the Grand Tour, as it was the fashion center of Europe; and for every warning against buying French, there was an equally happy shopper who did so. The Baroness d'Obkirche, for instance, confided in her diary, "We did not know where to put all our purchases, which accumulate, one scarcely knows how, in a city like Paris." So, shop in Paris these Americans did.[16]

Morris may have warned Pinckney away from investing in French goods, but he, like his predecessors Thomas Jefferson and Abigail Adams, was a seasoned shopper in Paris and knew what was available and at what price. They all spent time visiting the *marchands merciers* in the Palais Royal and along the rues Saint Honoré and Saint Martin, the heart of the high-end trade in new and used luxury goods, as well as the *marchands de meubles* (cabinetmakers), *tapissier* (upholsterers), and wallpaper and porcelain manufactories scattered throughout the city and surrounding villages (fig. 12). They visited shops for the social experience as well as for purchasing much needed household furnishings. Jefferson, it seems, furnished his Paris town-

Figure 12 Robert Bénard, after Radel, *Tapissier.
Intérieur d'une boutique et différens ouvrages*,
plate 1, *Encyclopédie, planches, sur les sciences, les
arts libéraux, et les arts méchaniques, avec leur
explication*, vol. 9, edited by Denis Diderot et al.
(Paris: Chez Briasson, 1762-1772). Engraving.
18⁴⁵⁄₆₄" x 13³¹⁄₃₂". (Courtesy, Kislak Center for
Special Collections, Rare Books and Manuscripts,
University of Pennsylvania.)

house top to bottom in the French style, while Abigail Adams just rented furniture and used her resources selectively to purchase table and bed linens, tea and dinner china, glass, and plate (fig. 13). Abigail complained about prices and that "Everything which will bear the name of elegant, is imported from England, and, if you will have it, you must pay for it, duties and all." But Paris shops were renowned for both the quality and novelty of their wares. Indeed, there was a strong second-hand market that kept prices accessible for non-aristocrats. Ultimately, each of these Americans learned how to compare style, quality, cost, and suitability and to weigh their options with an eye both to their immediate needs in Paris and their future interests back home.[17]

Over the course of the next several years these American diplomats and travelers gradually made their way back to Massachusetts, New York, Pennsylvania, Virginia, and South Carolina, their minds filled with ideas and their trunks laden with goods. One cannot pass on the opportunity to reflect on the sheer amount of furnishings Jefferson shipped home in 1790: eighty-six crates filled with bedsteads, tables and chairs; paintings, looking glasses, wallpaper, and window curtains; silverware utensils and serving pieces, and a silver-plated plateau; dinner china, tea china, and decorative porcelain figurines for the table; clocks, watches, scientific instruments; and myriad other goods such as the Brescia marble table illustrated in figure 14. Philadelphians William and Anne Bingham, who completed a Grand Tour between 1783 and 1786, similarly returned with enough furnishings from Paris and London to outfit their 18,000-square foot mansion on South Third Street, then the largest townhouse in America. So notable was their taste that a visiting Frenchman remarked that the Binghams "displayed a luxury and a magnificence that could not be more French. He has built a very beautiful house that he is furnishing with the greatest elegance."

Whether on a small or grand scale, these diplomatic families shipped home enough French goods (and British-made goods in the French style) for themselves, their families, and their friends to make a statement about their newly acquired taste (fig. 15).[18]

Material souvenirs were only part of the imports, for these well-traveled Americans also returned with an acute awareness of French manners and the rituals of hospitality. Nabby Adams, who carefully chronicled the individuals she met while living in Paris, London, and New York—and was therefore well versed in behaviors at home and abroad—could appreciate a woman such as Anne Bingham for having mastered the art of conversation, or Sarah Jay in her pleasures of the French table. "Mrs. B. gains my love

Figure 15 Side chair, France, ca. 1780–1790. Beech. H. 37½", W. 17", D. 16". (Courtesy, John Jay Homestead State Historic Site, Katonah, New York, New York State Office of Parks, Recreation and Historic Preservation; photo, Gavin Ashworth.) In the fall of 1783, Parisians were captivated by the recent invention of the hot-air balloon. Sarah Livingston Jay witnessed several ascents, including the first hydrogen-powered balloon flight by Jacques Charles and Nicolas Robert. Many French craftsmen translated the popular balloon shape into furniture, jewels, and clocks. The Jays brought two such souvenir chairs back to the United States upon their return in 1784.

and admiration, more and more every time I see her," Nabby confided in her journal:

> she is possessed of more ease and politeness in her behavior than any person I have seen. She joins in every conversation in company; and when engaged herself in a conversation with you, she will, by joining directly in another chit chat with another party, convince you, that she is all attention to everyone.

The ability to converse freely, draw others into the conversation, and make everyone feel special was considered one of the highest accomplishments of the Parisian *salonnière*. Anne Bingham would show her friends in Philadelphia how it was done.[19]

In New York, Sarah Jay likewise introduced French customs. Nabby noted that when the Jays hosted a party for the diplomatic corps in the late 1780s, "the dinner was à la *Française* and exhibited more of the European taste than I expected to find." These little insights on conversational style and how a table was set reveal the quiet way some of the wealthier, more influential families in the United States were adopting French customs. Before long, these were the families who would be shaping the political discourse during the Constitutional Convention and the creation of the federal government, and their time in Paris would be felt. Abigail Adams, who forever despaired at the costs tied to hospitality, never underestimated its worth. She saw clearly how all the lessons learned in the Paris salon—polite sociability, civility, and harmony—were put to use for diplomacy: "More is to be performed by way of negotiation, many times, at one of these entertainments, than at twenty serious conversations." These Americans who ventured across the Atlantic to secure independence came home with the materials and manners of polite sociability that they would use—just as much as the trade agreements—to build and define their new republic.[20]

This interest in French manufactures and the French style remained steady in the years following the American Revolution. Many Americans saw the fine examples brought back by the diplomats, but they increasingly also had the opportunity to purchase French goods themselves. Importation statistics indicate that Great Britain continued to dominate the post-war American commercial market, but French furnishings did find their way into ever greater numbers of American homes. Few families, of course, spent time personally shopping in Paris and London or, as the Binghams had, turned their homes into showpieces of European elegance and style. Yet some did have friends abroad who served as proxy shoppers. Robert and Mary White Morris, Samuel and Elizabeth Powel, and James and Dolley Todd Madison relied variously on Gouverneur Morris, Sarah Jay, and James and Elizabeth Kortright Monroe to fulfill commissions, just as the Lafayettes had for the Washingtons. In this way Americans at home acquired French seating and case pieces (bedsteads, chairs, commodes, and tables); lighting devices (silver-plated candlesticks and Argand lamps); looking glasses; porcelain dinner and tea china; decorative *plateaux* with porcelain figurines, vases, and flowers; silk (damask and velvet for seating upholstery and plain silk for window treatments); and clocks.[21]

Finally, for those families with no international ties, there were always local shopkeepers and émigré craftsmen eager and willing to introduce them to the French taste. By 1787 cabinetmaker and carver William Long, recently arrived from London, advertised that he made "French Sophas in the modern taste" and had "Cabriole and French Chairs on reasonable terms." In 1790 upholsterer Francis De L'Orme, lately from Paris, began boasting that he made furniture in "the most fashionable Taste, . . . all in the English or French style" and that he had an "assortment of Handsome Paper-Hangings from Paris." Craftsmen's advertisements suggest that by the 1780s, furniture and housewares in the United States were readily distinguishable by country of origin and that there was a French versus a British style on this side of the Atlantic Ocean. Consumers were therefore increasingly faced with a choice: how did they want their American homes to look? Further, what were they signaling if they invested in one style over another, or between things made in Europe versus in America? As the United States was moving closer to reorganizing itself as a more unified, federal body, what would it mean for its founders to embrace the French *art de vivre*?[22]

George Washington could very well have been mulling over such questions following the summer of 1787, when he resided in Philadelphia during the Constitutional Convention and was a daily witness to the fine French furnishings his friends the Binghams, Morrises, and Powels were displaying in their townhouses. With the aid of such companions as the comte de Coustine and the marquis de Lafayette, Washington had already been introduced to French manners and select examples of porcelain and silver table wares; but one can imagine the Binghams' home was an entirely new experience for him (fig. 16). Polish statesman Julian Ursyn Niemcewicz left this account of visiting the Binghams' grand house on South Third Street:

> One mounts a staircase of white native marble. One enters an immense room with a sculptured fireplace, painted ceiling, magnificent rug, curtains, armchairs, sofas in Gobelins of France. The dinner is brought on by a French cook; the servants are in livery, the food served in silver dishes, the dessert on Sèvres porcelain. The mistress of the house is tall, beautiful, perfectly dressed and has copied, one could not want for better, the tone and carriage of a European lady . . . . In a word, I thought myself in Europe. This house, as opulent as it is, would never be pointed out in the big cities of Europe, but here it attracts attention, criticism and envy; and woe for the country if it ceases to astonish, if it ceases to be pointed out.

Although Washington did not leave a similar account of his impressions (indeed, all he noted on his first visit in May 1787 was "Dined, and drank Tea at Mr. Binghams in great Splender"), he surely understood that the Binghams and their French taste represented an entirely new commitment to the cosmopolitan manners of Paris. Is it possible that the Binghams' ostentation and obsession with Europe could have caused him to reconsider what place French-made things should have in the nascent republic?[23]

As the months ticked by and the delegates to the Constitutional Convention re-settled themselves in at home and waited for the states to ratify the constitution, Washington began to put into words his evolving thoughts about how much Americans should look to France for models of taste.

Figure 16 William Birch and Son, "View in
Third Street, from Spruce Street, Philadelphia,"
Philadelphia, 1800. Hand colored engraving on
paper, 13" x 16". (Courtesy, Library Company
of Philadelphia.) This view shows the William
Bingham Mansion.

Perhaps in anticipation of the coming election (in which he knew, whether he wanted to admit it openly or not, that he would be elected the first president), Washington spent time reflecting on American manners and the influence the new executive would have in shaping them. In response to a letter from his friend Annis Boudinot Stockton, in which she had congratulated him on the likely passage of the constitution, he returned the compliment by observing that while American women had been essential to the colonies in securing independence from Great Britain, they could now have an even more important role in the creation of the federal government. "I think the Ladies are in the number of the best Patriots America can boast," he shared in August of 1788:

> And now that I am speaking of your Sex, I will ask whether they are not capable of doing something towards introducing federal fashions and national manners? A good general government, without good morals and good habits, will not make us a happy People; and we shall deceive ourselves if we think it will. A good government will, unquestionably, tend to foster and confirm those qualities, on which public happiness must be engrafted. Is it not shameful that we should be the sport of European whims and caprices? Should we not blush to discourage our own industry and ingenuity; by purchasing foreign superfluities and adopting fantastic fashions, which are, at best, ill suited to our stage of Society?

Throughout his life Washington repeatedly embraced the principles of balance, and it would seem he thought the ladies of America were the best individuals to show the nation how to find balance in their manners and their homes. Within eight months Washington would rise to the presidency and need the aid of everyone—and especially women—to help him steer this infant nation down the right path, presumably away from "foreign superfluities" and "fantastic fashions" and toward republican simplicity.[24]

If Washington thought it would be easy to define republican simplicity as president, he would discover within days of arriving in New York City for his inauguration the inherent challenges in modeling such an ambiguous concept. This would prove especially difficult when he and Martha assumed the management of the first presidential household, a physical embodiment of the executive branch. The Washingtons may have wanted to encourage their countrywomen to furnish their homes with (and display on their bodies) American products that represented a national ingenuity and taste—and also spur on manufacturing and commerce—but in those early days of the federal government, the couple was unable to make that commitment. In 1783 buying French goods had helped Washington symbolically break with Great Britain, and six years later it would help him prove that the reconstituted United States was ready to be a player in the Atlantic world. He quickly realized that to secure his (and his country's) place on the international stage, he would first have to demonstrate that he was an *homme du monde*, and he recognized that American manufactures were not quite ready for this task. So, with the help of America's diplomatic families, the Washingtons would learn how to gain power and prestige by following the rules of civility and blending polite sociability with American politics. It is undoubtedly this recognition that led the Washingtons to buy the cômte de Moustier's furnishings and chart a new path for republican simplicity, one that found inspiration in—but was never a slavish imitation of—French manners and materials.[25]

The story of the French furniture suite thus picks up again on the eve of Washington's inauguration on April 30, 1789. In the frenzied days prior to the president-elect's arrival in New York (by himself, as Martha remained in Mount Vernon for an additional two weeks to ready their household for the transition), Congress rented a house for the president at 3 Cherry Street and commissioned two local businessmen, Samuel Osgood and William Duer, to furnish the dwelling, top to bottom, in eight days (fig. 17). According to Osgood's niece, Sarah Robinson, the gentlemen quickly recognized the monumental scope of this commission, so they "pitched on their wives" for help as the ladies were "likely to do it better." Catherine Alexander Duer and Maria Franklin Osgood, evidently seasoned shoppers, "spared no pains nor expense" and acquired for every room the "best of furniture" available on short notice. Indeed, the ladies knew which craftsmen, merchants, and shopkeepers had ready-made furniture on hand and could supply such a

Figure 17 G. Hayward, "No. 3 Cherry Street, First Presidential Residence," New York, 1853. Lithograph published in *Valentine's Manual* [*Manual of the Corporation of the City of New York*, edited by D. T. Valentine]. (Courtesy, New-York Historical Society.)

substantial order. New York cabinetmaker Thomas Burling alone provided 125 pieces of furniture, from tables and sideboards to wash stands, beds, and seventy-three chairs. In Sarah's estimation, the completed house did "honors" to her aunt and Catherine Duer. Shortly after being furnished, the house was being described as the "palace."[26]

Despite the ladies' every effort, opinions varied on whether or not they had succeeded in creating a home fit for the leader of the new nation. Martha Washington observed that the house was "a very good one and is handsomely furnished all new for the General;" but the French ambassador, the cômte de Moustier, used the word *chétive* to describe it, and this has been translated as both "humble" and "squalid." To visitors like Moustier— seasoned diplomats and foreign dignitaries with an appreciation for the importance of image in the world of international politics—the house did not measure up. Later inventories of the presidential furnishings, coupled with a surviving example of a Burling chair with a Washington provenance (fig. 18), suggest that the ladies purchased items in a provincial, less fashion-

Figure 18 Armchair (one of a pair), attributed to Thomas Burling, New York City, ca. 1790. Mahogany with oak; haircloth. H. 40", W. 28", D. 17". (Courtesy, Division of Cultural and Community Life, National Museum of American History, Smithsonian Institution.)

able style. To Moustier, coming from Paris where furniture styles changed on average every six years and a sophisticated neoclassicism was all the rage, the house at 3 Cherry Street must have seemed inelegant indeed. Based on Washington's own reaction to his accommodations, the president likely felt the same way. While the couple wanted to promote American manufactures, they decided soon after settling into their new house—which they called the President's House—that it would not be prudent to avoid *all* the fripperies and fantastic fashions of Europe.[27]

This recognition that the President's House needed more elegant furnishings was undoubtedly informed by the social events that the Washingtons hosted from the earliest days of the presidency. Prior to his inauguration, George had determined that he and Martha would interact carefully with the public in such a way as to avoid showing preference to any single private citizen. Once they arrived in New York, however, they quickly discovered that some form of structure was essential to manage the numerous visitors who sought them out on both official and unofficial business at all hours of the day. As a result, George enacted a set of protocols designed to construct a social environment for the leaders of the new country. The solution was a combination of formal and informal events, called "levees" and "Drawing Rooms," hosted respectively by the president and the first lady. On Tuesday afternoons between 3:00 and 4:00, upon the close of Congress, Washington held his levee, and on Friday evenings between 7:00 and 10:00, Martha hosted her reception in the drawing room. Additionally, on Thursday evenings they jointly hosted state dinners for members of the president's cabinet and Congress, foreign diplomats, and their wives. All visitors, as long as they wore formal attire, were welcome at these events.

Abigail Adams wrote that Martha Washington's drawing rooms were "usually very full of the well born and well bred. Sometimes it is as full as her Brittanick Majesties Room, and with quite as handsome ladies, and as polite courtier." From the very beginning of George Washington's administration, he and Martha turned to the European patterns of polite sociability to cope with the crowds and to bring dignity to their new roles. Other leading families immediately joined them in opening their drawing rooms on different nights of the week, and an official salon culture—just as in Paris and London—was born. First in New York, and then in Philadelphia once the capital was relocated, genteel Americans perfected the art of worldly hospitality. Over tea, dinner, and rounds of cards, they discussed literature and the theater, horticulture and politics, all the while performing their version of sociability. Historians in the nineteenth century would dub this social and political whirl the Washingtons' "republican court," a nice turn of phrase that suggests they could at once blend republican principles with the aristocratic aura of nobility.[28]

Washington's first steps in ameliorating the look and feel of the President's House came just two weeks after Martha joined him in New York and took charge of housekeeping. As frequent guests in the homes of leading families in Philadelphia and New York, the Washingtons were already well aware how the strategic placement of decorative objects in the French style could transform a room from pedestrian to prominent. They likely observed in these same houses that a new taste for the classical world was spreading, advocated by such designers as Thomas Sheraton, who advised his readers that anyone wanting a drawing room to "admit of the highest taste and elegance" would naturally turn to the neoclassical style. Once again, Washington relied on his instincts and past practices: he reached out to friends to help him buy more fashionable French and neoclassical pieces to supplement the furnishings provided by Congress. One can only assume that the president and the first lady believed they could remedy the situation with the addition of a few decorative accents in their public rooms.[29]

On June 8, 1789, secretary Tobias Lear wrote to Clement Biddle in Philadelphia on Washington's behalf:

> The President is desireous of getting a sett of those waiters, salvers, or whatever they are called, which are set in the middle of a dining table to ornament it—and to occupy the place which must otherwise be filled with dishes of meat, which are seldom or never touched. Mr. Morris & Mr. Bingham have them, and the French & Spanish Ministers here, but I know of no one else who has—I am informed that they are most likely to be got at French Stores as they are made in France;—we can find none in this place, and the Presid.t will thank you to enquire if a sett can be procured in Philada. And if it can, to procure it for him.

One wonders if Washington persuaded himself he needed a *plateau de dessert* after dining at the French minister's residence, which he had done just a few weeks previously on May 14. According to the *Gazette of the United States,* that evening had been "uncommonly elegant, in respect both to the company and the plan of the entertainment;" another eyewitness reported how "three rooms were filled [for dancing], and the fourth most elegantly set off as a place for refreshment." It could very well have been on these tables that Washington spied the silver and porcelain ornaments and decided they could provide that all important touch of *l'art de vivre*.[30]

Unfortunately, no *plateau* matching Lear's description was to be found in Philadelphia, so the president wrote next to Gouverneur Morris, then in Paris and always a willing proxy shopper. Washington commissioned Morris to find "mirrors for a table, with neat and fashionable but not expensive ornaments for them—such as will do credit to your taste," and to refer to the *plateau* on Robert and Mary Morris's table as a model. After describing the general parameters of his request and giving Morris leeway to shop in either London or Paris—wherever he could get the best terms—Washington stressed yet again the importance of financial restraint. "One idea however I must impress you with," he confided, "and that is in whole or part to avoid extravagance. For extravagance would not comport with my own inclination, nor with the example which ought to be set."[31]

Gratified to render his friend this service, Morris promptly filled the order for the *plateau* and figurines (fig. 19). With his knowledge of the fickleness of French fashions, Morris recognized that the style of these pieces was essential: if he sent less expensive, but what he called a more *au courant* design, the president's table would resemble "the style of a petite Maitresse of this city," which was most assuredly not the style they would want. If, on the

Figure 19 Presidential table wares, including
the *plateau*, figural group of Venus and cupids
and La Peinture, and Sèvres dinner service.
(Courtesy, Mount Vernon Ladies' Association;
photo, Gavin Ashworth.)

other hand, the Washingtons were willing to invest a reasonable amount of money, they could be assured that their ornaments would be fashionable (as well as valuable) for years to come and, perhaps most importantly, they would exude a "noble Simplicity." Morris could not refrain from reminding the president that at this point in the nation's development it was essential "to fix the Taste of our Country properly," and that his example alone would "go very far in that Respect." Morris thus explained:

> It is therefore my Wish that every Thing about you should be *substantially good* and *majestically plain*; made to endure. Nothing is so extravagant in the Event as those Buildings and Carriages and Furnitures and Dresses and Ornaments which want continual Renovation. Where a Taste of this kind prevails, each Generation has to provide for itself whereas in the other there is a vast Accumulation of real Wealth in the Space of half a Century.

Morris selected a *plateau* in the neoclassical style together with two vases and fifteen biscuit-porcelain figurines representing characters from classical mythology that would, he believed, allow the Washingtons to signal their politeness without triggering a fear of luxury. These visual allusions to the classical world—columns, swags, chitons, the pure white of marble, and Venus, the mother of Rome herself—referenced the political ideals of ancient Greece and Rome and reminded viewers that America was founded on these same principles (figs. 20–22). Through this commission, Morris instructed the Washingtons how to use French fashions to signal their confidence that America could be—indeed would be—the next great civilization.[32]

Relating this whole exchange on the *plateau* is instructive in illustrating how the Washingtons (with the help of their proxy friends) were consciously and conscientiously crafting a persona for the presidential family through mate-

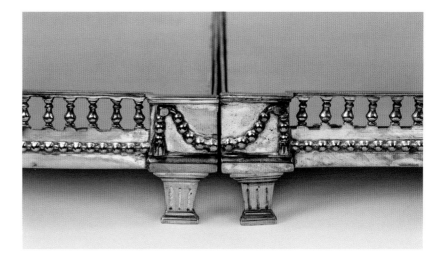

Figure 20   Plateau, France, ca. 1789. Silvered brass, mirrored glass, unidentified wood. H. 2⅞", W. 17⅜", L. 24". (Courtesy, Mount Vernon Ladies' Association; photo, Gavin Ashworth.)

Figure 22 *La Peinture*, Duc d'Angoulême's porcelain factory, France, ca. 1790. Biscuit porcelain (hard-paste). H. 11¼", W. 5", D. 3½". (Courtesy, Stephen L. Zabriskie; photo, Gavin Ashworth.)

rial choices. They understood the political and personal risks the president was taking with each purchase, and Washington communicated as much to his acquaintance, British historian Catherine Macaulay Graham. "In our progress toward political happiness my station is new; and I may use the expression, I walk on untrodden ground," he began. "There is scarcely any action, whose moves may not be subject to a double interpretation. There is scarcely any part of my conduct which may not hereafter be drawn into precedent." Washington wrote this letter in January 1790, the same month when Morris completed the commission in Paris and Washington himself was contemplating additional changes to the President's House. Washington was keenly aware that he would be criticized for being aristocratic if he surrounded himself with expensive (but equally beautiful, convenient, and elegant) foreign imports on the one hand, and uncivilized if he did not invest in the tools and activities of polite sociability on the other. As a result, he attempted to steer a narrow path between the two extremes. Judicious purchases of French furnishings would, he hoped, show him to be a man not only of republican virtue but also of cosmopolitan taste.[33]

Desirous of finding that middle ground between aristocratic pretension and republican austerity, the Washingtons might have contented themselves with adding those few, select table decorations Morris shipped to the President's House and considered the business done. However, an unlooked-for opportunity to buy French furnishings en suite arose when the French ambassador, Élénor-Francois Élie, Comte de Moustier, was recalled to Paris in October 1789 and chose to sell his household goods instead of shipping them home. This was the same minister who had fêted Washington in grand style the previous May and had worked hard to cultivate a relationship with the new president since his arrival in January 1788. As the Cherry Street house selected by Congress proved rather inconvenient for the Washingtons in terms of size and location, the first couple opted to take over the lease of 39 Broadway from the French legation (fig. 23). This house was newer,

Figure 23   Charles Burton, "Bunker's Mansion House, Broadway, New York City: Study for Plate 5A of 'Bourne's Views of New York,'" (39–41 Broadway), New York, ca. 1831. Brown ink and wash, gray wash, and graphite on paper. H. 2⅝", W. 3½". (Courtesy, New-York Historical Society, bequest of Stephen Whitney Phoenix, 1881.10.)

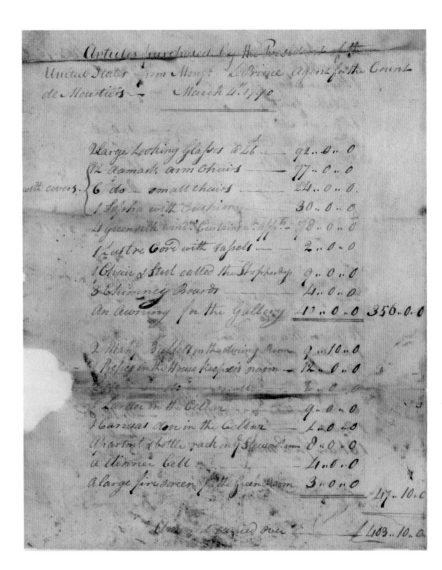

Figure 24 "Articles purchased by the President of the United States from Mons. Le Prince agent for the Count de Moustiers, March 4, 1790." (Courtesy, Mount Vernon Ladies' Association.)

larger, and better situated to the work of Congress in Federal Hall in the lower Broadway; and, most importantly, it was decorated in the French taste. Using £665 of their personal money, the Washingtons purchased the ambassador's furnishings and were thereby able to infuse their public rooms with the lightness and sophistication of French neoclassicism without the added expense and delays associated with proxy shopping abroad (fig. 24).[34]

Among the many benefits to the Washingtons in securing such a large collection of furnishings was that these items had been pre-selected and assembled by fashionable Parisians who understood worldly hospitality. While the practice may seem strange to modern sensibilities, buying and selling second-hand luxury and semi-luxury goods was quite common in Paris. It offered aristocrats an outlet for the items they no longer needed (because of rapidly changing fashions or excessive debts), and it made high-end fashions available to individuals who could otherwise not afford them new. Such furnishings were desirable not only because they were often of excellent quality and design (and had a discounted price), but also because they gave purchasers a connection to the original owners. By moving into 39 Broadway and stepping into the furnished spaces orchestrated by Moustier and his traveling companion, his sister-in-law Anne-Flore Millet, marquise de Bréhan, the Washingtons were taking advantage of Moustier and Bréhan's collective skills setting up houses intended for the work of diplomacy.[35]

Moustier was an experienced ambassador by the time of his arrival in the United States, having worked his way up through the diplomatic service with postings to Lisbon, London, Naples, and Coblenz, and he certainly knew the role polite sociability and hospitality could play in forging strong diplomatic relations between the two countries. Indeed, this awareness may be the reason the widowed minister invited his sister-in-law to accompany him and serve as his hostess in this prominent posting. Thomas Jefferson (then still in Paris) certainly believed that together the pair were imminently suited for the new position and would serve as welcome models of European politeness. In his letters of introduction to both Madison and Jay, Jefferson sang Moustier and Bréhan's praises, declaring his countrymen would find in the new minister a man "simple in his manners, and a declared enemy to ostentation and luxury." Moreover, he continued, they could not find a "better woman, more amiable, more modest, more simple in her manners, dress, and way of thinking" than madame de Bréhan (fig. 25). Jefferson in fact saw such promise in the pair that his parting words to the minister upon his departure for New York were "Mr. Jefferson . . . considers the Count de Moustier as forming, with himself, the two end links of that chain which holds the two nations together;" and he cautioned Bréhan that although the "imitation of European manners, which you will find in our town, will, I fear, be little pleasing," he hoped she would continue to practice her own, "which will furnish them a model of what is perfect." Arbiters of taste, manners, and (Jefferson hoped as well) French policy, Moustier and Bréhan came with all the essential housewares they needed to entertain on a grand scale and share their culture with the new nation (fig. 26).[36]

Figure 25 Ignazio Pio Vittoriano Campana, *Marquise Jean-François-René-Almaire de Bréhan (Anne-Flore Millet)*, 1777. Watercolor on ivory. H. 2¹¹⁄₁₆". (Courtesy, Nationalmuseum, Stockholm, Sweden; photo, Nationalmuseum, CC BY-SA.)

Figure 26 Marquise Jean-Françoise-René-Almaire de Bréhan (Anne-Flore Millet), *George Washington*, France, 1789. Watercolor on ivory. H. 2 ¾". (Courtesy, Yale University Art Gallery.) Madame de Bréhan was an accomplished pastelist and noted for the artistic decorations she created and displayed during lavish events at the minister's residence. She made two miniatures of George Washington: the first shortly after her visit to Mount Vernon in the spring of 1788; and this one after her return to Paris in 1789.

One can assume that when the Washingtons moved into 39 Broadway on February 23, 1790, they anticipated that the elegance and comfort of their French furnishings would lend prestige to their weekly social and political gatherings. They could replace the less fashionable items purchased by Congress for their public rooms and use instead the coordinated suite of drawing room seating furniture with matching window treatments, fire screens, mahogany buffets, looking glasses, and lamps. They also now had a desk, dressing table, bidet, and clothes presses for the private rooms, and a dinner service of white and gold Sèvres porcelain for their public events (a welcome upgrade from the everyday Queen's Ware they had been using) (figs. 27–30). Visually, the new pieces spoke a different stylistic language

Figure 27 Victor-Jean-Gabriel Chavigneau, lady's writing table, France, ca. 1787–1789. Mahogany and mahogany veneer with white oak; marble, brass, silvered brass, leather, gold leaf. H. 41½", W. 28¼", D. 19". (Courtesy, Mount Vernon Ladies' Association; photo, Gavin Ashworth.)

than the ones made locally, as can be seen by comparing them with furniture made in Thomas Burling's workshop. Burling was a well-respected cabinetmaker in New York when he received this important commission for the President's House, and his surviving furniture indicates he was aware of the latest taste for neoclassicism. Like so many of his contemporaries,

Figure 28 Dressing table, France, ca. 1760–1780. Mahogany with fir; marble, glass. H. 29", W. 37⅝", D. 21". (Courtesy, Mount Vernon Ladies' Association; photo, Gavin Ashworth.)

Figure 29 Bidet, France, ca. 1790. Mahogany; leather, brass. H. 15½", W. 18¼", D. 8⅞". (Courtesy, Joseph James Ryan; photo, Gavin Ashworth.)

Figure 30 Dinner service, Sèvres factory, France, ca. 1780. Porcelain (hard-paste). (Courtesy, Mount Vernon Ladies' Association; photo, Gavin Ashworth.)

Figure 31 Abraham Godwin, label of Thomas Burling, New York, ca. 1786–1793. Engraving on paper. Dimensions not recorded. (Courtesy, Collection of the Museum of Early Southern Decorative Arts, Old Salem Museum and Gardens, Winston-Salem, North Carolina.)

Burling began to embrace the so-called Federal style during the 1780s, but it is impossible to determine if the Cherry Street furnishings were in that mode or were more indicative of New York furniture made just prior to or during the Revolutionary War (fig. 31). It is likely, however, that the chairs he provided Congress represented an intermediate step between the two styles and could thus have been deemed less fashionable.[37]

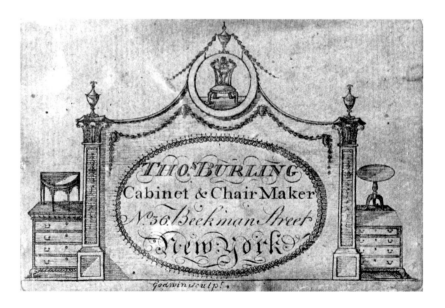

Characterized as "plain" or "carved" in period inventories, Burling's mahogany chairs derived inspiration from British seating. Although surviving chairs from the Duer-Osgood decorating campaign can no longer be attributed reliably to Burling, an armchair reputedly purchased by Washington from Burling in 1790 provides some suggestion of what the other chairs might have looked like (fig. 18). This shield-back chair, with a feather-motif splat design popularized by the British firm Gillow and Company, has reeded arm supports and reeded legs that terminate in spade feet. It is decidedly British in its aesthetic and contrasts greatly with the painted French chairs (see fig. 1). The former appears heavy and at times awkward in its execution with thick legs and feet, whereas the latter's molded stretchers, tapered, straight, and fluted legs, with neatly carved rosettes set in the corner blocks, lend it a more refined and delicate aspect. These are certainly unequal interpretations of the neoclassical—one provincial, the other cosmopolitan—and that distinction could have highlighted their juxtaposition in the same house. The visual comparison of the chairs shows how the Washingtons aligned themselves more than ever before with the materials and manners of French sociability. With the purchase of the Moustier suite they silently acknowledged that the products of France offered a roadmap to civility and, thereby, a path to a strong and enlightened federal government.[38]

When the government relocated to Philadelphia nine months later, the entire contents of 39 Broadway were carefully packed up, shipped south, and reinstalled in 190 High Street, the home Congress rented from Robert and Mary Morris to serve as the third President's House (fig. 32). With

Figure 32 W. L. Breton, "Residence of Washington in High Street, Philadelphia," Philadelphia, ca. 1828-1830. Watercolor on paper. 9¹³⁄₁₆" x 7½". (Courtesy, Historical Society of Pennsylvania.)

secretary Tobias Lear's able assistance (and likely also Mary Morris's since Washington reminded Lear to seek her advice, too), each and every piece of presidential furniture was strategically placed to create, once again, that sense of distinction in the public rooms. George Washington hosted his levees now in the dining room, located on the ground floor, while Martha held her formal drawing rooms in the large, second-floor parlor, officially known as the "Green Drawing Room" because of the coordinating upholstery in their beautiful French suite (figs. 33, 34). On the whole, it seems likely the new drawing room was arranged much like it had been established by Moustier and Bréhan in New York, although the Washingtons did make a few changes. They installed a new carpet, which had been ordered from London and intended for 39 Broadway but had not arrived before the relocation; acquired additional mirrors and lighting devices; and enlarged the suite of chairs from eighteen to twenty-four. After settling into a routine, one presumes the Washingtons recognized a need for additional side chairs, and George paid French émigré upholsterer Georges Bertault for "six chairs, 2 stools G[reen] Drwg" in January 1793.[39]

Knowing the precedents for furnishing salons in Paris, a picture of the Washingtons' famed state drawing room increasingly comes into focus (fig. 35). The painted walls and woodwork provided an elegant architectural backdrop for the furnishings. Although the exact nature of the woodwork cannot be determined, it is possible the walls were finished with pedestal-

Figure 35 Conceptual sketch of the Green Drawing Room, President's House, 190 High Street, Philadelphia. (Artwork by Wynne Patterson.) This is a visual interpretation that relies on such evidence as a fire insurance survey from 1773, Edward Lawler Jr.'s conjectural reconstruction of the floor plans, Washington's inventory of the drawing room in 1797, personal correspondence of the president and his aides, as well as extant furnishings and architectural trimmings.

Figure 36 Mantelpiece, Philadelphia, ca. 1781. Wood; paint. H. 56½", W. 79½", D. 8½". (Courtesy, Philadelphia History Museum at the Atwater Kent, Historical Society of Pennsylvania Collection; photo, Gavin Ashworth.) This mantelpiece was salvaged from the yellow drawing room in the President's House prior to the building's demolition in 1832, and the pulvinated frieze of banded foliage may represent the style of the woodwork on the mantel wall and above the doors in the green drawing room.

Figure 38 Looking glass, attributed to James Reynolds, Philadelphia, 1791–1797. Yellow poplar with Atlantic white cedar; gesso, gold leaf, glass. H. 50", W. 16½". (Courtesy, Mount Vernon Ladies' Association; photo, Gavin Ashworth.)

Figure 37 Looking glass, probably France, ca. 1788. Basswood; gesso, gold leaf, glass. H. 81¼", W. 43". (Courtesy, Mount Vernon Ladies' Association; photo, Gavin Ashworth.)

Figure 40 Argand wall lamp, probably England, ca. 1790–1797. Silver-plated copper, brass, tin, glass. H. 16⅛", W. 7¾", D. 4". (Courtesy, Mount Vernon Ladies' Association; photo, Gavin Ashworth.) This lamp was retailed by Joseph Anthony.

Figure 39 Wall bracket, attributed to James Reynolds, Philadelphia, ca. 1791. White pine; gesso, gold leaf, wire, iron. H. 15¾", W. 12¼", D. 9". (Courtesy, Mount Vernon Ladies' Association; photo, Gavin Ashworth.)

high wainscoting and a fretwork cornice, and that the chimney wall and door pediments were set off with a more elaborate pulvinated frieze of banded oak foliage (fig. 36). The paint could have been cream-colored, as was then the fashion, giving the room a light, airy aspect. The inventory Washington completed in 1797 indicates the walls were adorned with a combination of gilt mirrors, framed pictures, and lighting devices. The two rectangular looking glasses purchased from Moustier could have hung on the northern, eastern, or western walls, but it is more likely they were displayed as a pair, bracketing either the doors or the mantle and arranged in such a way as to maximize the sense of light and space (fig. 37). Complementing these large looking glasses were four oval mirrors with brackets (figs. 38, 39). Also in the neoclassical style, these pieces were made in Philadelphia by carver and gilder James Reynolds. Hanging nearby were two matching, urn-shaped patent lamps with delicately engraved floral garlands that echoed details on the mirrors (fig. 40). Washington listed two landscape views as part of the wall furnishings, *The Great Falls of the Potomac* and *The Passage of the Potomac*, both by George Beck (figs. 41, 42). The final piece of fixed decoration was a lustre of eight lights, with carved and gilt flowers and tassels, suspended from the center of the ceiling.[40]

These bright and elegantly decorated walls played a supporting role to the seating furniture, which continued to be the main attraction of the green

Figure 41   George Beck, *The Great Falls of the Potomac*, United States, 1797. Oil on canvas. 44" x 55¼". (Courtesy, Mount Vernon Ladies' Association; photo, Gavin Ashworth.)

Figure 42   George Beck, *The Passage of the Pato'k thro' the blew mountain, at the confluence of that River with the Shan'h*, United States, 1797. Oil on canvas. 39" x 49⅝". (Courtesy, Mount Vernon Ladies' Association; photo, Gavin Ashworth.)

drawing room. The matching sofa, twelve armchairs, twelve side chairs, and two stools, which were all covered in green upholstery, probably sat around the perimeter of the room until needed. One cannot overstate the importance of balance and harmony—among the individual pieces in the suite, the window treatments, and the carpeting—because it was this unifying effect of color, materials, and the large number of chairs that lent the room such distinction. The standard collection of seating furniture in the French *appartement de société* most often included an even number of chairs that were purchased in matching sets, a fact commonly misunderstood since complete sets rarely survive intact. The Washingtons' drawing room should thus have had a proper combination of the *sieges meublants* and the *sieges courants*, arm and side chairs that matched in their color treatment, carving detail, and upholstery fabric. Surviving chairs indicate this assortment is exactly what they did have. The upholstery—a green flowered, silk damask—accorded with the green silk of the three curtains set in the bow window, and the variations in seating forms—sofa, armchair, *bèrgere*, side chair, and stool—allowed for a range of social activities. In effect, the visual and spatial balance and harmony created by the furnishings were intended to infuse the Washingtons' social gatherings with the same balance and harmony. These furnishings allowed the Washingtons to show a nation that beauty, politeness, and hospitality were fundamental elements to ruling a strong, unified republic.[41]

No period accounts of the furnishings in the Washingtons' drawing room are known, but surviving descriptions of events held there provide insight into how Martha Washington used that space and the adjoining rooms. Abigail Adams observed the first lady's receptions in all three of the President's Houses:

> August 1789
> The form of Reception is this, the servants announce & col. Humphries or Mr. Lear, receives every Lady at the door, & Hands her up to Mrs. Washington to whom she makes a most Respectful courtesy and then is seated without noticeing any of the rest of the company. The Pressident then comes up and speaks to the Lady, which he does with a grace dignity & ease, that leaves Royal George far behind him. The company are entertained with Ice creems & lemonade, and retire at their pleasure performing the same ceremony when they quit the Room.

> January 1790
> In the Evening I attended the drawing Room, it being Mrs. W[ashington']s publick day. It was as much crowded as a Birth Night at St. James, and with company as Briliantly drest, diamonds & great hoops excepted. My station is always at the right hand of Mrs. W.; through want of knowing what is right I find it sometimes occupied, but on such an occasion the President never fails of seeing that it is relinquished for me, and having removed Ladies several times, they have now learnt to rise & give it me, but this between our selves, as *all distinction* you know is unpopular.

> July 1709
> tho if one was to Credit the Clamours of the Boston papers we should imagine that there was nothing going forward but dissipation, instead of which, there is nothing which wears the least appearance of it, unless they term the Pressidents Levee of a tuesday and Mrs. Washingtons drawing room of a fryday such. One last[s] two & the other perhaps three hours.

She gives Tea, Coffe, Cake, Lemonade & Ice Creams in summer. All other Ladies who have publick Evenings give Tea, Coffe & Lemonade, but one only who introduces cards, and she is frequently put to difficulty to make up one table at whist.

February 1791
here the company are entertained with Coffe Tea cake Ice creams Lemonade &c. [T]hey chat with each other walk about, fine Ladies shew themselves, and as candle Light is a great improver of Beauty, they appear to great advantage; this shew lasts from seven, till Nine oclock comeing & going during those hours, as it is not Etiquette for any person to stay Long. on other days any Lady who is in habits of intimacy may visit mrs Washington with the same freedom & take Tea with her as unceremoniously as my good Aunt.

Notable is the fact that Martha Washington seems to be sitting as she received guests; visitors are shown a seat after their presentation; gentlemen (here, it is the president) walk around and converse with the seated ladies; and finally, there are variations on this arrangement in that, in the later years at least (suggesting an evolution in practice), women also walked around and did not simply sit. Adams thus painted a picture of a salon where the seating furniture brings structure, predictability, and even stature into Martha Washington's gathering. One can envision Martha sitting in the *bèrgere* placed on one side of the mantle (or perhaps in the bow window, another space of honor), with Abigail—the vice president's lady and therefore second in prestige—nearby in another armchair. Whether the chairs were either in a tight circle or U shape around Martha, or dispersed along the perimeter of the room, this configuration reinforced the notion that the president's wife, the central figure and model of civility, was the hostess not just of a single salon but of an entire nation.[42]

With the exception of serving refreshments—coffee, tea, lemonade, cake, and ice cream—the Washingtons followed much of the etiquette of European salons. Hosts and hostesses in Paris never offered food or drink during their salons; consequently, there were rarely tables or buffets in the *appartements de société*. The Washingtons did, however, use the adjoining parlor for this purpose, and it was in the yellow drawing room that they placed the two sideboards purchased from Moustier, presumably to display and serve food. It was also in the yellow drawing room that Martha Washington hosted less formal gatherings, such as taking tea with her smaller circle of friends and family. With three sofas, ten side chairs, and two armchairs covered in yellow silk, this front parlor likely functioned as an extension of the green drawing room and offered guests the opportunity to move around (or show themselves to advantage, as Adams posited), change their seats, and possibly also switch conversational partners. Certainly, by offering refreshments—and not cards—the Washingtons focused their guests' attentions on polite conversation and set the stage for an even greater demonstration of hospitality.[43]

Over the course of eight years, the Washingtons learned to appreciate the social and political advantages an elegant collection of French furnishings would bestow on them as the leaders of the new nation. They trusted friends who had greater knowledge of, and access to, the chairs, mirrors, *plateaux*, and porcelains of Paris to guide their buying choices; and then they adapted the lessons of the French salon to suit their political agenda. Although their budding patriotic impulse may have been to decorate the President's House exclusively with American-made furniture, they acknowledged that this was an impracticality for a young nation just finding its footing on the international stage. Instead, they showed their contemporaries and fellow founding families a way to invest time and money in both domestic and French wares—how to supplement the solid, neat furniture made locally with the elegance, whimsy, and classicism of French accents. They did their very best to introduce their countrymen and women to things that were substantially good and majestically plain so that together they could lay the foundation for an enduring republic.

Within days of his inauguration, Washington recognized the need for a shared space where he and Martha could interact with the American public in a controlled manner, and the levees and drawing rooms presented the perfect solution. As hosted in the President's House, these events made the Washingtons at once visible and accessible, but on terms that allowed them to present a carefully constructed persona. Surrounded by the beauty and comfort of the green drawing room furnishings, for instance, they were able to create opportunities for enlightened conversation and entertainment—for men and women to discuss science, history, literature, music, and fashion, but also national and international politics. This was a space for deal-making *and* dancing. The green drawing room furniture—which was still rare, expensive, and exotic in this foundling republic—defined the president and first lady as genteel and polite, and it showed them as being in tune with the manners and traditions of European civility. It would not be an exaggeration to say that these chairs supported the making of the United States, for it was in these seats that the leaders of the new nation debated who they were as a people and what kind of country they might become. One can only imagine that as symbols of worldly hospitality and the Enlightenment, these chairs presaged a bright future, a vision that George and Martha Washington animated through their attention to all that was French and fashionable.[44]

Coda: The Green Drawing Room Suite Puzzle
On April 27, 1856, Elizabeth Lawrence inscribed these words on a label and affixed it to a French-style chair:

> When Gen Washington left Philadelphia to reside in Washington City— all his Furniture was sold in Phil.a Many persons were desirous of having some relics of their belov'd Genl and his drawing room chairs, were sold separately (2 dozens). Dr. Tho Redman purchased *this chair*, and gave it to his Sister, Mrs. Rebecca Lawrence—it descended to me at her death and I now give it to my ever kind & affec.e friend Lieut Foxhall A. Parker with the hope that it may descend to his children—Eliza Lawrence[.]

Such was the presumed fate of the Washingtons' drawing room furniture when Tobias Lear supervised its sale on March 10, 1797: that the twelve armchairs, twelve side chairs, two stools, a sofa, and three curtains in matching green silk were auctioned off to the highest bidder and began a new chapter in the homes of admiring Americans (fig. 43). There are, unfortunately, no known official records of the Washington sale to confirm Lawrence's account. Lear left one brief description, when he wrote to Washington on March 15:

> The furniture of the Green Drawing Room & other Articles sold at Auction went off very low indeed. The numbers attending the Auction was considerable; but they were disappointed in an expectation which they had formed that the Painting, P[r]ints &c. were to have been sold. The Lustres—Stoves & other fixtures in the House will be taken by the President [Adams] at a cost or a fair valuation.

The exact contents of the auction, its attenders, and its purchasers have long remained obscure, and so there has been much confusion about what happened to the green drawing room suite after the Washingtons retired from the scene.[45]

Today, there are twenty-one contenders for Washington-owned French-made and French-style furniture with purported ties to the presidential years in both private and public collections. Yet inconsistencies among these objects make some of the associations problematic. In 2012 curators at Montpelier conducted a study of six Louis XVI-style side chairs with a Madison provenance and significantly narrowed the field by suggesting a link between James and Dolley and the 1797 auction. Since 2015, with the support of curators at Mount Vernon who commissioned paint studies on an additional armchair and a stool with unparalleled Washington provenance, the author has built on this Madison-Washington connection and solidified the Washington associations. It is now possible to present an updated inventory of the Washingtons' French seating furniture and offer a new explanation of its history from the moment Abigail Adams refused to buy it in 1797.[46]

At the outset, it is instructive to understand why the Washingtons chose to part with the suite, especially since its role within their presidential drawing room had brought them much esteem. That the Washingtons chose not to take their beautiful French furniture suite home to Virginia can be explained by a number of circumstances. Perhaps first and foremost, they did not perceive a need for high-style chairs designed for formal entertaining at Mount Vernon. One must presume they remained content with the suite of chairs they had purchased from George William and Sally Cary Fairfax for the front parlor and could not anticipate using the green drawing room furniture in other rooms. Although the Washingtons did need chairs for their "New Room" (the two-story room they built on the north side of the house during the Revolution and had completed at the start of the presidency), they intended to use this space for dining, which required a different kind of chair (fig. 44). As George Hepplewhite explained to his readers, seating furniture in dining rooms should be "plain and neat," whereas chairs in the drawing room "should possess all the elegance embellishments can give" due to their location in the most public room of the house. For the

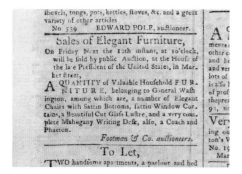

Figure 43 "Sales of Elegant Furniture," advertisement in *Claypoole's American Daily Advertiser*, Philadelphia, March 8, 1797. (Courtesy, Historical Society of Pennsylvania.)

New Room, the Washingtons purchased twenty-four mahogany dining chairs and two inlaid sideboards in the neoclassical style from Philadelphia cabinetmaker John Aitken (figs. 45, 46).[47]

Trained in London or Edinburgh, Aitken made furniture that closely resembles designs in Thomas Sheraton's *The Cabinet-Maker and Upholsterer's Drawing Book* (1st edition, 1791). His work was quite British in style. Although it can often be difficult to pinpoint the differences between "plain" and "neat" or "rich" and "elegant"—recalling Gouverneur Morris's descrip-

Figure 44 New Room, Mount Vernon, Mount Vernon, Virginia. (Courtesy, Mount Vernon Ladies' Association; photo, Gavin Ashworth.)

tions of British versus French furniture—it seems likely the Washingtons perceived Aitken's chairs as plain and neat and, accordingly, perfect for their dining room. In 1797 George was eager to return to his country house and resume life as a gentleman farmer. He thus chose furnishings for a more casual lifestyle, one that demanded solid and practical furniture over delicacy and ostentation. Retiring from the presidency and the formalities of a public life, the Washingtons elected to buy British once again (if only in style) as it best fit their vision of themselves quietly residing at Mount Vernon.[48]

Stylistic and functional considerations aside, John and Abigail Adams also influenced the dispersal of the suite at the 1797 auction. Between January and March of that year, the president-elect and his wife were preoccupied with the location of the presidential residence, how and by whom it was to be furnished, and the high cost of housekeeping. Having witnessed daily the public events their predecessors had hosted, the Adamses realized how challenging and expensive it would be to follow in the Washingtons' hospitable footsteps. In essence, they agonized over the real costs of political sociability, leading John to exclaim: "In Short all Levees and Drawing Rooms and Dinners must be laid aside and I am glad of it. I will entertain my friends, and Such as I please and no more." Washington only learned of their decision not to buy the Moustier suite after he had departed Philadel-

Figure 45 Side chair, attributed to John Aitken, Philadelphia, ca. 1797. Mahogany and light wood inlay with unidentified secondary wood. H. 37⁷⁄₁₆", W. 20⅝", D. 18¾". (Courtesy, Mount Vernon Ladies' Association; photo, Gavin Ashworth.)

phia on May 9, and the delay may have caused further confusion about how to dispose of the French furnishings. As Washington explained to Mary Morris later that spring, he had been told that if Adams rented 190 High Street, "he wou'd be glad (in case I was disposed to part with it) to take the

Figure 46 Sideboard, attributed to John Aitken, Philadelphia, ca. 1797. Mahogany, mahogany veneer, and light and dark wood inlays with white pine, tulip poplar, and unidentified softwood. H. 37⅝", W. 71⅞", D. 26¹¹⁄₁₆". (Courtesy, Mount Vernon Ladies' Association; photo, Gavin Ashworth.)

Furniture of the two largest Rooms also." These were the green drawing room and the state dining room below, where the majority of the French furnishings were in use. Evidently, Washington was disposed to part with it. He had designated some of those furnishings for "other purposes" and some for the auction block; but, he continued:

> to cull the best, and offer him [Adams] the rest, I conceived would be indelicate, & therefore with the exception of the Pictures, all of which were fancy pieces of my own chusing, I made a tender of the whole; at such reduced prices as he, or any other, should adjudge them to be the worse for wear. The expectation of his taking them, and the pressure of many matters previous to my departure, caused me to leave the City without giving precise directions relative to the disposition of the furniture of these Rooms, beyond the offer that had been made of them to the President; of course, when in the last moment, he declined taking them, it rested on the judgment of Mr Lear & Mr Dandridge to dispose of them in the manner they conceived best.

Eliza Lawrence's chair label intimates that twenty-four French chairs were auctioned off *and* purchased on March 10; yet Washington's letter to Morris suggests the strong possibility that Lear and Dandridge packed up at least some of the seating furniture and shipped it home to Virginia.[49]

George and Martha Washington's estate papers reveal that the couple did in fact bring home many of the French furnishings they had acquired in New York and Philadelphia. The entire collection of Sèvres dinner china found its way to Mount Vernon, as did the writing desk, dressing table, bidet, large gilt looking glasses, many of the lamps, silver-plated *plateau*, and some of the porcelain figurines. In addition, there are several chairs and stools listed in three separate documents that may refer to the Moustier pieces. Among George Washington's probate inventory (December 1799), Martha Washington's last will and testament (March 1802), and the account of sales for Martha Washington's personal estate (July 1802), one finds the following: two round stools in the New Room; a writing table paired with a seat in Martha's room; an "easy chair" and a "great chair" (the first listed in 1799, the second in 1802, so presumably the same chair), also in Martha's room; and three chairs with either a high value ("1 chair" for $20) or distinctive colors ("1 Green bottom chair" for $10.00 and "1 White arm [chair]" for $2.50). Granddaughters acquired most of those pieces: Martha Parke Custis Peter inherited the French writing table and seat; Eleanor Parke Custis Lewis inherited the "great chair" and purchased the two colorful chairs; and Eliza Parke Custis Law purchased the very expensive $20.00 chair. Two *bergères*, one round stool, and one square stool, all in the French style, were passed down through the years by descendants of the three granddaughters and thus offer the first pieces to this presidential puzzle. For the sake of clarity, this article will refer to these four pieces as the Law *bergère* (fig. 47), the Peter *bergère* (not illustrated), the round stool (fig. 48), and the square stool (fig. 49). The next question is how to determine which of the remain-

Figure 47 *Bergère*, attributed to Jean-Baptiste Lelarge, Paris, ca. 1780. Beech; paint, brass. H. 35⅛", W. 25½", D. 22⅜". (Courtesy, Mount Vernon Ladies' Association; photo, Gavin Ashworth.)

Figure 48 Footstool, attributed to Georges
Bertault, Philadelphia, ca. 1793. Ash with sweet
gum and beech; silk, flannel, haircloth. H. 18",
D. 16¾". (Courtesy, Tudor Place Historic House
and Garden; photo, Gavin Ashworth.)

Figure 49 Footstool, attributed to Georges
Bertault, United States, ca. 1788–1790.
Mahogany, walnut, and pine; leather. H. 12",
W. 23", D. 23". (Courtesy, Mount Vernon Ladies'
Association; photo, Gavin Ashworth.)

ing nine armchairs, seven side chairs, stool and sofa, all of which allegedly descend from the green drawing room suite, were actually used in Philadelphia by the president and first lady.[50]

The claims of authenticity for many of these other pieces are compelling, and several of them have labels like the one on Eliza Lawrence's chair or affidavits intended to substantiate their legitimacy. Such labels were often affixed to objects with a Washington association and used to document (or fabricate) the chain of descent from Washington, as well as to highlight the current owner's relationship to the first president (figs. 50, 51). Beyond the labels, common features among this group of armchairs tie them to the

Figure 50 Armchair, France or United States, ca. 1790–1795. Unidentified woods; paint, silk. H. 34½", W. 24", D. 21½". (Courtesy, Museum of the American Revolution; photo, Gavin Ashworth.)

Figure 51 Detail showing the plaque on the armchair illustrated in fig. 50. (Photo, Gavin Ashworth.) The inscription reads: "Presented after Washington's death, by the members of his Family to Gen. Sam Smith, after Gen. Smith's death, purchased by Jno. B. Cannon, Baltimore, Md."

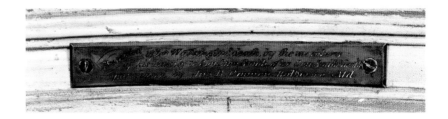

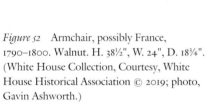

Figure 52 Armchair, possibly France, 1790–1800. Walnut. H. 38½", W. 24", D. 18¾". (White House Collection, Courtesy, White House Historical Association © 2019; photo, Gavin Ashworth.)

Figure 53 Armchair, France or United States, 1790–1795. Beech; paint. H. 31¾", W. 23⅜", D. 20¼". (Courtesy, Mount Vernon Ladies' Association; photo, Gavin Ashworth.)

Figure 54   Sofa, probably France, ca. 1795–
1800. European walnut; paint, silk. H. 39⅞",
W. 70", D. 23½". (Private collection; photo,
Gavin Ashworth.)

Figure 55 Details of the arm terminals of the chairs and sofa illustrated in (from left to right) figs. 50, 54, 53, 52. (Photos, Gavin Ashworth.)

French style and thus the Washingtons' green drawing room suite: they are all upholstered and, with two exceptions, appear originally to have been painted. Moreover, in several instances there are corresponding ornamental details carved onto the crest rails, arm supports, and legs, which suggest that certain pieces may have been part of a matching set. Three chairs (figs. 50, 52, 53) and a sofa (fig. 54) have very similar arm supports that end in a distinctive cylindrical, reeded terminal topped with a carved rosette (fig. 55); they also share fluted and reeded baluster-turned supports set above ribbed blocks (fig. 56). But for all the similarities between two or three chairs, there are also profound differences in style, form, materials, and execution across the entire group.[51]

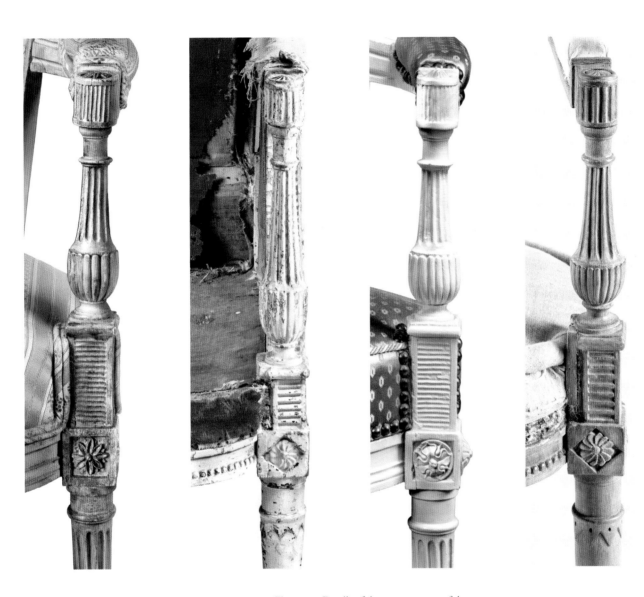

Figure 56 Details of the arm supports of the
chairs and sofa illustrated in (from left to right)
figs. 50, 54, 53, 52. (Photos, Gavin Ashworth.)

Figure 57 Armchair, probably France, 1785–1790. Beech; silk. H. 38½", W. 24", D. 18¾". (Courtesy, Mount Vernon Ladies' Association; photo, Gavin Ashworth.)

Figure 58 Armchair, possibly United States, ca. 1790–1810. Ash; paint, gold leaf, silk. H. 35½", W. 21", D. 20". (Courtesy, Delaware Historical Society; photo, Gavin Ashworth.)

Figure 59 Armchair, France or United States, ca. 1785–1797. Beech; silk, linen, haircloth, paint, gold leaf. H. 34¼", W. 22³⁄₁₆", D. 22". (Courtesy, Connecticut Historical Society, lent by Mrs. Arnold G. Dana, 1983.57.0.)

The lessons of the French salon dictate there must be visual and material harmony among the pieces of a set, and there is no reason to doubt that Moustier and Bréhan imported a fully matching collection of drawing room furniture. It is therefore highly unlikely that their set could be composed of an assortment of forms: arched, or horseshoe, backs (fig. 57); rectangular backs with a *chapeau de gendarme* top rail and fluted finials (fig. 52); backs with an open lyre motif (fig. 58); or scrolled-back crest rails (fig. 59). Moreover, such variations in form and carving indicate that several of these pieces were made after 1790, precluding their arrival (see fig. 52) with the ambassador. The leg and arm supports of at least two of the chairs are made of a single piece of wood, a construction technique not found in Paris until the early to mid-1790s; thus the likely date of manufacture for this set is after 1795. Although the nine armchairs are all *fauteuil*, meaning they have open sides and upholstered arms, the differences are just too great to believe they were ever used together in a single salon. One would expect to find a combination of arm and side chairs (*bergère*, *fauteuil*, and *chaise*) with unifying details, such as pieces by Jean-Baptist Lelarge that are illustrated in figures 60–62, now in the collection of Versailles.[52]

Finally, and perhaps most importantly, none of these nine armchairs matches the four pieces that descended in the families of Martha's granddaughters. The stylistic similarities among the Law *bergère*, the round stool,

Figure 60 Jean-Baptiste Lelarge III, *bergère*, Paris, ca. 1780. Beech; paint, silk. H. 39⅜", W. 28½", D. 26½". (Courtesy, Chateaux de Versailles et de Trianon, Versailles, France. Copyright, RMN-Grand-Palais/Art Resource, NY ; photo, Christophe Fouin.)

Figure 61 Jean-Baptiste Lelarge III, *fauteuil*, Paris, ca. 1780. Beech; paint, silk. H. 38³⁄₁₆", W. 26⁷⁄₃₂", D. 23¹⁵⁄₆₄". (Courtesy, Chateaux de Versailles et de Trianon, Versailles, France. Copyright, RMN-Grand-Palais/Art Resource, NY; photo, Christophe Fouin.)

Figure 62 *Chaise*, Paris, ca. 1809. Beech ; paint, silk. H. 36²⁹⁄₆₄", W. 19¹¹⁄₁₆", D. 18⁴⁵⁄₆₄". (Courtesy, Chateaux de Versailles et de Trianon, Versailles, France. Copyright, RMN-Grand-Palais/Art Resource, NY; photo, Franck Raux.)

Figure 63 Frontal views of (from left to right) two of the side chairs attributed to the Paris workshop of Jean-Baptiste Lelarge and the side chair attributed to the Philadelphia workshop of Georges Bertault. Side chair (left), see fig. 1. Side chair (center), attributed to Jean-Baptist Lelarge III, Paris, ca. 1780. Beechwood. H. 34¾", W. 17¾", D. 16". (Courtesy, National Trust for Historic Preservation and Montpelier Foundation; photo, Gavin Ashworth.) Side chair (right), attributed to Georges Bertault, Philadelphia, 1793. Beechwood, oak (rear corner blocks), paint. H. 35⅛", W. 18½", D. 16⅛". (Courtesy, Mount Vernon Ladies' Association; photo, Gavin Ashworth.)

and several of the surviving side chairs exclude all nine armchairs from being part of the Washingtons' suite. This conclusion is further supported by the Montpelier and Mount Vernon studies, which show that four surviving side chairs (see fig. 63) have the same paint history as the Law *bergère* and round stool. Moreover, the Montpelier study strongly suggests that the Madisons purchased at least four chairs from the Washington auction and brought them back to Virginia. When the physical evidence of paint layers is coupled with the oral and documentary histories of the six pieces—all of which descended through families with close personal ties to the Washingtons—it becomes apparent that they alone survive from the green drawing room suite.[53]

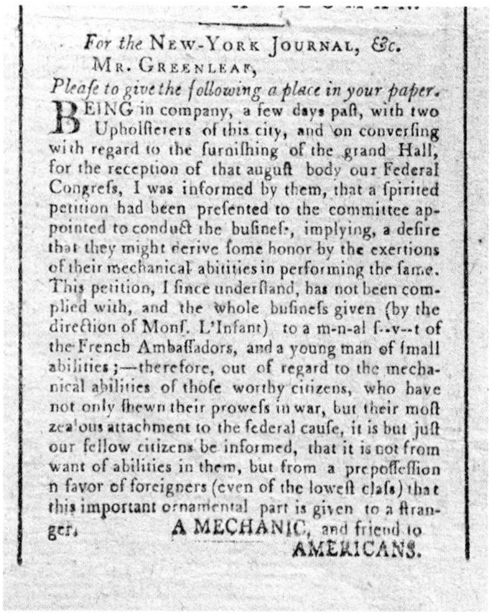

This new evidence suggests an alternative narrative for the collection of French furnishings that George and Martha Washington assembled during the presidential years. When Moustier and Brèhan arrived in New York City aboard the ship *L'Aigrette* in January 18, 1788, they received news that a significant portion of their household furnishings had been damaged in the ocean crossing. As conservator Ron Blank has discovered in the course of his research on the Washington suite, Moustier submitted to the French government a petition for compensation to cover the costs of damaged furniture. After his return to Paris, Moustier wrote: "On the crossing from Brest to New York, he suffered losses to part of his furniture due to the effects of rough weather estimated at 10,000 francs which he had to replace." This letter raises new questions regarding the history of the chairs, most importantly about when upholsterer Georges Bertault may have entered the scene and commenced work enlarging the suite. A revised narrative could account for two things: first, the multiple number of early paint layers on the six surviving pieces; and second, how the two additional French-style pieces with a strong oral tradition of belonging to the Moustier purchase—the Peter *bergère* and square stool—came into the Washington family.[54]

Beyond Moustier's claim, we know nothing about what happened during the crossing or what, specifically, was harmed. Whether Moustier paid to repair or replace items is also unclear, but it is important to note the value. Exchange rates in 1788 varied from 21½ to 24 livres per pound sterling, so if Moustier submitted a claim for 10,000 francs, that was approximately £440, almost equal to the £463 Congress paid cabinetmaker Thomas Burling for all the mahogany furniture—125 pieces—in the Cherry Street house. At that price, it is reasonable to theorize that Moustier paid for repairs to some of his costlier furnishings, such as upholstery or upholstered items, since fabric was the single most expensive element in household furniture. The question then arises: could Moustier have engaged an upholsterer in New York, one either familiar with French techniques or trained in Paris, to repair or replace any of the seating furniture? And the answer to that is a speculative "yes."[55]

Historian Travis Bowman has recently uncovered an article published on March 26, 1789, in the *New York Journal* revealing that Moustier had a relationship with a French upholsterer (fig. 64). As Bowman relates, Pierre Charles L'Enfant, the French military engineer who served under Lafayette during the Revolution and worked as an architect in the United States fol-

Figure 64   Editorial, *New York Journal*, March 28, 1788. (Courtesy, Library of Congress; photo, author.)

lowing the war, was in charge of renovating Federal Hall for the use of the Congress. Sometime between October 1788 and March 1789, L'Enfant hired a Frenchman to make new furniture for the Senate chamber. In protest, several American upholsterers applied to the committee overseeing the renovation to request that they—men who had served during the war and were zealously attached to the federal cause—also be given an opportunity to work on the project. When they were denied employment, the author of the article—"A MECHANIC, and friend to AMERICANS"—declared the process suspect and pointed out that L'Enfant had awarded the whole business "to a [manual servant] of the French Ambassadors, and a young man of small abilities," because of a "prepossession in favor of foreigners (even of the lowest class)." Evidently, Moustier's connection to this French upholsterer was well enough known to be dragged into the press as an example of national nepotism during a heated debate on whether American or foreign craftsmen should have been given the honor of furnishing the new halls of Congress.[56]

Scholars have yet to determine when Georges Bertault arrived in the United States, but it is certainly plausible that he was the "manual servant" mentioned in the 1789 article and that he started his career in New York under the patronage of either Moustier or L'Enfant. Delving into the Paris archives, furniture historian Xavier Bonnet was able to identify a Jacques Georges Bertault, born in 1762 and the son of Parisian master upholsterer Georges Bertault (b. 1733); at age twenty-six he could certainly have qualified as "young" and inexperienced. The elder Bertault completed a six-year apprenticeship in Paris under Jean-Baptiste Solleilac and became a master upholsterer in 1760. He opened his first shop in the rue Saint-Anne, and then a second in the rue Saint-Honoré, before being listed as among the forty most important upholsterers in the *Almanach Dauphin* of 1772. Although he seems to have belonged in the same league as such acclaimed upholsterers as Georges Jacob, Jean-Baptiste Lelarge, and Jean-Baptiste-Claude Sené, his success did not endure; he declared bankruptcy in 1776. The elder Bertault was still active as an upholsterer in Paris in 1791, and it is possible the father's financial instability led the son to pursue a career in the United States.[57]

If Bertault was indeed in New York when Moustier arrived with a collection of damaged furniture, it is reasonable to assume that the ambassador would hire this French émigré upholsterer, who had ties to a well-respected Parisian *tappisier* in Paris, to fix the pieces that could be repaired and to replace those that were unsalvageable. One can also posit that the Georges Bertault who later enlarged the Moustier suite for the Washingtons in 1793 was the same upholsterer recommended by Moustier for the Federal Hall chair commission; that Moustier referred Bertault because of his work on the ambassador's French suite; and that the Washingtons learned of Bertault's expertise through his work for Moustier. The visual similarities between one of the side chairs Bertault made for the Washingtons in 1793 and a Federal Hall armchair are compelling and support the notion that Bertault helped introduce French neoclassicism in New York (fig. 65). That work may have facilitated in turn his rise within the craftsman community and positioned him to become a leading upholsterer in the new nation. With such aristocratic (and eventually presidential) backing, this recent émigré would have offered stiff competition to native craftsmen.

It is plausible that Moustier sold Washington seating furniture that was made by Jean-Baptiste Lelarge in Paris and subsequently repainted, reupholstered, and partially replaced by Georges Bertault in New York. This

Figure 65 Armchair, New York, ca. 1788.
Mahogany. H. 36", W. 23½", D. 20".
(Courtesy, New-York Historical Society.)

scenario could account for why the imported chairs have two generations of paint—a light grey followed by a cream layer—under a coat of light grey that matches the paint on the six side chairs and two stools Bertault made for the Washingtons in 1793. Further, Bertault could have used that opportunity to demonstrate to Moustier (as well as to the larger commercial community) that his skills went far beyond paint and repairs; that he was indeed a *tapissier* capable of producing replica seating in the elegant style of Lelarge. One must therefore consider whether Bertault made new side and armchairs to replace any from the drawing room suite that were unsalvageable or perhaps made a *bergère* and stool for another room. The final two pieces of furniture that descended with Martha Washington's granddaughters may add another important clue.

Figure 66 Armchair, attributed to Georges Bertault and Adam Hains, Philadelphia, 1793. Mahogany, ash. H. 35", W. 23", D. 19¾". (Courtesy, Longfellow House-Washington's Headquarters, National Park Service; photo, Andrew Davis.)

The March 4, 1790, inventory of the Moustier sale refers to one other piece of seating furniture pertinent to this study: "1 Chair & Stool called the Shepherdess," listed just under the green chairs, sofa, and curtains and valued at £9. It has long been assumed that the Law *bergère* was this Shepherdess chair and that the stool had been lost (fig. 47). Yet there is a second *bergère* that survives, the Peter *bergère*, and it has an oral tradition of being a gift from Martha Washington to her granddaughter Martha Peter upon the birth of her first child in the 1790s. But is this possible? Martha Peter gave birth to her daughter in January of 1796, well before the Washingtons were ready to dispose of their French furniture. Moreover, the Shepherdess and stool show up again in the 1797 inventory, indicating that they remained in the capital through Washington's presidency.

There is, however, an alternative possibility for when this chair came into Martha Peter's family. In her will, Martha Washington gives her granddaughter the "writing table and the seat to it standing in my Chamber." That desk was the lady's writing table originally owned by madame de Bréhan, and it seems plausible the bespoke chair was the French-style Peter *bergère* and its matching square stool (fig. 49). "Shepherdess" is simply a fanciful name for the enclosed, upholstered *bergère*; and although one associates the *bergère* with the chair of honor in the French salon, it was also sometimes paired with desks in private spaces. Given that the Peter *bergère* and square stool are simplified, unpainted versions of the neoclassicism exhibited in the other chairs, they could be early examples of Bertault's collaborative work with cabinetmakers in the United States. When the Law and Peter *bergères* are studied side by side, certain details stand out. Although they have a similar scroll on the arm support and carved rosettes in the corner blocks, the forms are not identical in shape (square versus rounded back), and they have different crest rails (straight versus elliptical), suggesting they never formed part of a set. Additionally, the lack of paint on the mahogany Peter *bergère* and square stool may indicate that Bertault made them to replace a pair always intended for the privacy of a bedchamber and not the public display of the drawing room. These pieces, then, could have formed part of the Moustier purchase even if they were never part of the green drawing room suite.[58]

Bertault made chairs with a number of slight variations in the 1790s. Several surviving sets, which are visually comparable to the Peter *bergère*, support the suggestion that Bertault was indeed the principal craftsman for Moustier's Shepherdess chair and stool. After relocating to Philadelphia (presumably to follow wealthy clients tied to the federal government), Bertault completed at least four sets of open armchairs and settees remarkably similar to the Peter *bergère*. Several of these sets are well documented and reveal that Bertault contracted with local cabinetmaker Adam Hains for the mahogany frames. Although none of these sets was ever painted, their forms and carved details are based closely on French precedents, and one wonders if Bertault supplied Hains with a model or design. In the spring of 1792, after completing a large renovation on his house, Massachusetts financier Andrew Craigie placed an order with Bertault; a year later (shortly

Figure 67   Detail showing the stamp on the side illustrated on the far left in fig. 63.

after Craigie's marriage to Elizabeth Shaw), he received twelve mahogany armchairs and two settees, plus four curtains, all in a green and white silk damask (in addition to slipcovers in a "fancy chintz") for his home in Cambridge (fig. 66). Related sets of surviving chairs are also tied to some of Craigie's business partners and social acquaintances, including Alexander and Elizabeth Schyler Hamilton of New York, Christopher and Rebecca Gore of Boston, and Theodore and Lydia Williams Lyman of Waltham, Massachusetts. By the time the Washingtons commissioned Bertault to enlarge the green drawing room suite in 1793, the French upholsterer was already well on his way to supplying chairs in the fashionable French taste for an ever growing network of families with ties to the president and the rounds of political sociability defining the nation's capital.[59]

Recent scholarship makes it increasingly possible to answer the driving question behind this investigation: what did the Washingtons' suite of green drawing room chairs and sofa really look like? The physical and documentary evidence, combined with a better understanding of decorating practices in the Paris salon, suggest that each piece in the suite looked like the four surviving chairs that originated in the workshop of Jean-Baptiste Lelarge in Paris and the side chair and round stool that were copied by Georges Bertault in Philadelphia (figs. 67, 68). The Law *bergère* is one of the twelve armchairs listed in Moustier's sale inventory and likely had a partner. The remaining ten "arm chairs" in the 1790 sale list were other forms, such as *cabriolet* or *fauteuil à la reine*, as it was common to have one or two *bergères* and then six to ten open side chairs. Ever keen observers of their friends with taste for and knowledge of fashions, the Washingtons understood the rules of harmony and matching sets. Thus they assembled a blended collection that adhered to these principles. Until other chairs or the sofa in this style are found, these six pieces will serve to represent the French, cosmopolitan character of George and Martha Washington's presidential drawing room. They alone tell the tale of how the Washingtons, who by embracing the rules of polite sociability emanating from the salons of Paris, created a space of visual and social harmony that could support the rituals of worldly hospitality for Americans and their guests.[60]

Figure 68   Five of the six surviving pieces from George and Martha Washington's Green Drawing Room suite.

ACKNOWLEDGMENTS For assistance with this article, the author thanks Marc Anderson, Zara Anishanslin, Gavin Ashworth, Luke Beckerdite, Travis Bowman, Douglas Bradburn, Lydia Mattice Brandt, Susan Buck, Elizabeth Chew, Kenneth Cohen, Alexander Dubois, Diane Ehrenpreis, François Furstenberg, John H. Fuson, Amanda Isaac, Catherine E. Kelly, Meg Kennedy, Cornelia King, Alexandra A. Kirtley, Carrie Landfried, Josh Lane, Edward Lawler Jr., Rebecca L. Martin, Philip C. Mead, D. Doug Mooberry, Michelle Moskal, Melissa Naulin, Wynne Patterson, Jennifer Potts, Grant Quartermous, Susan P. Schoewler, Samantha Snyder, K. Allison Wickens, and the private collectors. Special thanks go to Adam Erby for lending me his connoisseur's eye, deep knowledge of Mount Vernon, and insight into the lives of George and Martha Washington; he was a true collaborator who made it delightful piecing together this presidential puzzle.

1. A Fred W. Smith National Library for the Study of George Washington Fellowship at Mount Vernon in 2015 provided invaluable financial assistance for this research. Abigail Adams to John Adams, Quincy, February 19, 1797; and John Adams to Abigail Adams, Philadelphia, February 4, 1797, *Adams Family Papers: An Electronic Archive*, Massachusetts Historical Society, http://www.masshist.org/digitaladams/ (hereafter AEA). For specific reference to outfitting the house, see John Adams to Abigail Adams, January 28, February 4 and 9, March 3, 9, 17, and 22, and April 11, 1797; and Abigail Adams to John Adams, January 15 and 30, February 19, and March 18, 1797 (AEA). As John Adams was preparing to assume the presidency, Abigail suggested someone take an inventory to determine which furnishings belonged to the United States and which belonged to the Washingtons. A manuscript in George Washington's hand, "Inventory of Goods in President's House, February 1797," is likely the response; and it is here that Washington catalogued some of the furnishings as "Articles in the Green Drawing Room." The Papers of George Washington, *Founders Online*, National Archives and Records Administration, Washington, D.C. (hereafter PGW Digital).

2. The earliest references to the Washingtons' French drawing room furniture are found in private correspondence and labels affixed to the chairs with a purported Washington provenance. See endnotes 45 and 46 for the relevant literature.

3. Conservation studies, coupled with extensive provenance research, on the existing Washington chairs have been the most productive in identifying the authentic pieces. See Travis M. Bowman, "Federal Hall Chairs at John Jay State Historic Site" (report prepared for the New York State Office of Parks, Recreation and Historic Preservation, Waterford, N.Y., 2018); Susan L. Buck, "Analysis of the Paints on the Tudor Place Stool 4005.01" (report prepared for George Washington's Mount Vernon, Mount Vernon, Va., 2018); Susan L. Buck, "French Armchair (*Bergère*) W877, Paint Analysis" (report prepared for George Washington's Mount Vernon, Mount Vernon, Va., 2015); Susan L. Buck, "Cross-Section Paint Microscopy Report, Six Madison Upholstered Side Chairs" (report prepared for the Montpelier Foundation, Orange, Va., 2010); Thomas A. Snyder, "A Comparative Analysis of Six Louis XVI-Style Chairs" (report prepared for the Montpelier Foundation, Orange, Va., 2012); Grant Quartermous, "Summary of French Chair Research" (report prepared for the Montpelier Foundation, Orange, Va., 2009); Ron Blank, "French Furniture in the American President's House: Documenting a Tabouret Purchased by George Washington" (master's thesis, Smithsonian Institution, Furniture Conservation Training Program, 2002); and Ron Blank, "Did George Washington Sit Here? French Furniture in the American President's House," WAG Postprints, Philadelphia, Pa., 2000, http://www.wag-aic.org/2000/WAG_00_blank.pdf, accessed on February 27, 2019. The author would like to thank Meg Kennedy and Grant Quartermous for making available their extensive and significant Montpelier study materials, and Travis M. Bowman for graciously sharing his report and ideas on New York furniture makers.

4. Susan Gray Detweiler, *George Washington's Chinaware* (New York: Harry N. Abrams, Inc., 1982), pp. 67–76; Aileen Dawson, *French Porcelain: A Catalogue of the British Museum Collection* (London: British Museum Press, 1994), pp. 283–90.

5. George Washington to Bushrod Washington, Rocky Hill, N.J., September 22, 1783, PGW

Digital. George Washington to Marie-Joseph-Paul-Yves-Roch-Gilbert du Motier, marquis de Lafayette, Princeton, N.J., October 30, 1783, PGW Digital.

6. For the most comprehensive study on this shift in allegiance from British to French culture and commerce, see François Furstenberg, *When the United States Spoke French: Five Refugees Who Shaped a Nation* (New York: Penguin Press, 2014), especially pp. 98–101, 129–36. For examples of the diplomatic families' sending fashion advice and articles home, see *Selected Letters of John Jay and Sarah Livingston Jay*, compiled and edited by Linda M. Freeman, Louise V. North, and Janet M. Wedge (Jefferson, N.C.: McFarland and Company Press, 2015), pp. 122–23, 125, 138. For American diplomats Gouverneur Morris and James Monroe serving as proxy shoppers in Paris, see Amy H. Henderson, "Furnishing the Republican Court: Building and Decorating Philadelphia Homes, 1790–1800" (Ph.D. diss., University of Delaware, 2008), ch. 2, 5.

7. Laura Auricchio, *The Marquis: Lafayette Reconsidered* (New York: Alfred A. Knopf, 2014), ch. 8; Stanely Izdera et al., *Lafayette in the Age of the American Revolution: Selected Letters and Papers, 1776–1790*, 5 vols. (Ithaca, N.Y.: Cornell University Press, 1977–83), 5: ch. 12; Louis Gottschalk, *Lafayette Between the American and French Revolution* (Chicago: University of Chicago Press, 1950), ch. 3. In his effort to expand trade between the two countries, Lafayette had support from American diplomats and businessmen who also assessed French wares for quality and suitability. For instance, John Jay noted during a trip to Rouen: "Their manufactures are very considerable & very proper for our Country, with whom they will certainly have a great Trade unless it be fettered & embarrassed with superfluous Regulations and ill-judged Restrictions." John Jay to Sarah Jay, Rouen, January 18, 1783, in *Selected Letters of John Jay and Sarah Livingston Jay*, p. 130.

8. George Washington to Lafayette, Princeton, N.J., October 30, 1783, PGW Digital. For a detailed description of proxy shopping in the eighteenth-century Atlantic world, see Henderson, "Furnishing the Republican Court," ch. 3.

9. George Washington to Lafayette, Princeton, N.J., October 30, 1783, George Washington Papers, Series 2, Letterbooks 1754 to 1799: Letterbook 11, Feb. 28, 1778–Feb. 5, 1785, Manuscript/Mixed Material, Library of Congress, https://www.loc.gov/item/mgw2.011/. For the full correspondence on the order, see George Washington to Lafayette, New York, December 4, 1783; Mount Vernon, February 1, 1784; Mount Vernon, April 4, 1784; and Lafayette to George Washington, Paris, March 9, 1784, PGW Digital. According to Washington's payment to Lafayette on August 21, 1784, the cost for the silver-plated wares came to 2,214 *livres*, or £120.7.6 (George Washington Papers, Series 5, General Ledger B, 1772–1793, p. 199, Library of Congress; Carol Borchert Cadou, *The George Washington Collection: Fine and Decorative Arts at Mount Vernon* [Manchester, Vt: Hudson Hills Press, 2002], pp.114–15).

10. For a history of polite sociability, see Dena Goodman, *The Republic of Letters: A Cultural History of the French Enlightenment* (Ithaca, N.Y.: Cornell University Press, 1994), p. 4; and Antoine Lilti, *The World of the Salons: Sociability and Worldliness in Eighteenth-Century Paris*, translated by Lydia G. Cochrane (2005; reprinted, New York: Oxford University Press, 2015). For the author's use of the term in the context of late eighteenth-century material culture in the early republic, see Henderson, "Furnishing the Republican Court," especially ch. 1.

11. Lilti, *The World of the Salons*, pp. 8, 42.

12. Joan DeJean, *The Age of Comfort: When Paris Discovered Casual—and the Modern Home Began* (New York: Bloomsbury, 2009), pp. 229–32.

13. On the role furniture played in supporting polite sociability, see Mimi Hellman, "Furniture, Sociability, and the Work of Leisure in Eighteenth-Century France," *Eighteenth-Century Studies* 32, no. 4 (1999): 415–45. For the practices and routines of sociability in the French salon, see Lilti, *The World of the Salons*.

14. Mimi Hellman, "The Joy of Sets: The Uses of Seriality in the French Interior," in *Furnishing the Eighteenth Century: What Furniture Can Tell Us about the European and American Past*, edited by Dena Goodman and Kathryn Norbert (New York: Routledge, 2007), p. 130; Florence de Dampierre, *The Best of Painted Furniture* (New York: Rizzoli, 1987), p. 21; DeJean, *The Age of Comfort*, p. 106; and Martin Chapman et al., *The Salon Doré from the Hotel de la Trémoille* (San Francisco: Fine Arts Museums of San Francisco, 2014), pp. 9, 38–39.

15. On the cultural and artistic exchange between England and France following the cessation of the Seven Years' War and the American Revolution, see Lilti, *The World of the Salons*, p. 65; Carolyn Sargentson, *Merchants and Luxury Markets: The Marchands Merciers of Eighteenth-Century Paris* (London: Victoria and Albert Museum in association with the J. Paul Getty Museum, 1996), ch. 6; Charles Saumarez Smith, *Eighteenth-Century Decoration: Design and the Domestic Interior in England* (New York: Harry N. Abrams, Inc., 1993), p. 307; Alden Gordon

and Maurice Déchery, "The Marquis de Marigny's Purchase of English Furniture and Objects," *Furniture History* 25 (1989): 86–108; and Peter Thornton, *Authentic Décor: The Domestic Interior, 1620–1920* (1984; reprinted, London: Seven Dials, 2000), p. 140. The cross-pollination between the two countries can also be observed in the advice George Hepplewhite and Thomas Sheraton gave their readers about drawing room chairs. In effect, they encouraged patrons to decorate their drawing rooms with chairs in the French style—elegantly painted cabriole and side chairs with silk upholstered backs and seats, which were light in both color and weight and therefore less massive than traditional British, mahogany chairs. George Hepplewhite, *The Cabinet-Maker and Upholsterer's Guide* (1794; reprinted, New York: Dover Publications, 1969), p. 2; and Thomas Sheraton, *The Cabinet-Maker and Upholsterer's Drawing Book* (1793; reprinted, New York: Dover Publications, 1972), pp. 85, 139, 155. The fashion for English goods was readily supplied by a number of *marchands merciers* who specialized in British imports, such as Le Petit Dunkerque, on the quai de Conti at the foot of the Pont Neuf. For more on this shop, see Dena Goodman, *Becoming a Woman in the Age of Letters* (Ithaca: Cornell University Press, 2009), pp. 172–74. Abigail Adams Smith, entry for October 7,1784, *Journal and Correspondence of Miss Adams, Daughter of John Adams, Second President of the United States. Written in France and England, in 1785*, edited by Caroline Amelia Smith De Windt (New York: Wiley and Putnam, 1841), p. 21.

16. Gouverneur Morris Letter Book, August 23, 1792, Gouverneur Morris Papers, Manuscript Division, Library of Congress, as cited in Julie B. Chase, "Keeping up Appearances: Furnishings of American Embassies in Europe, 1778–1825" (master's thesis, University of Delaware, 1996), p. 36. *Journal des Luxus und der Modern* (1786), as cited in Thornton, *Authentic Décor*, p. 140. Louis-Sébastien Mercier, *Panorama of Paris, Selections from Le Tableau de Paris*, based on the translation by Helen Simpson, edited and with a new preface and translations of additional articles by Jeremy D. Popkins (University Park, Pa.: Pennsylvania University Press, 1999), p. 157. For Paris as fashion capital, see Natacha Coquery, "Luxury and Shopping in the Eighteenth-Century Paris, Capital of Luxury" (paper presented at the conference Creating the Europe 1600–1815 Galleries, Victoria and Albert Museum, London, April 8, 2016), p. 1; and Coquery, "The Language of Success: Marketing and Distributing Semi-Luxury Goods in Eighteenth-Century Paris," *Journal of Design History* 17, no. 1 (2004): 77. Henriette-Louise de Waldner de Freundstein, baronne d'Oberkirch, entry for June 18, *Memoirs of the Baroness D'Oberkirch, Countess de Montbrison*, edited by the Count de Montbrison, 3 vols. (London: Colburn and Co., 1852), 2: 47.

17. Valuable insight on Morris's shopping experience can be found in his diary entries for March 31, 1789; January 6, 11, 13, 15, 18, 20, and 21, 1790; November 11, 12, and 14, 1790; August 27, 1791; and May 11, 1792 (*A Diary of the French Revolution by Gouverneur Morris 1752–1816, Minister to France During the Terror*, edited by Beatrix Cary Davenport, 2 vols. [Boston: Houghton Mifflin Company, 1939]). For Jefferson's shopping, see Susan R. Stein, *The Worlds of Thomas Jefferson at Monticello* (New York: Harry N. Abrams, Inc., 1993), pp. 18–34; Howard C. Rich Jr., *Thomas Jefferson's Paris* (Princeton, N.J.: Princeton University Press, 1976), p. 23; and for the details of his purchases, see Thomas Jefferson, "Memorandum Books," 1784–1789, The Papers of Thomas Jefferson, *Founders Online*, National Archives (hereafter PTJ Digital). For descriptions of Abigail Adams's shopping for household furnishings, see Abigail Adams, *The Adams Family in Auteuil, 1784–1785, as Told in the Letters of Abigail Adams*, with an introduction and notes by Howard C. Rice Jr. (Boston: Massachusetts Historical Society, 1956), pp. 10–11, 21, 30. For Nabby Adams's visit to the Palais Royal, see the entry for January 3, 1783 (Smith, *Journal and Correspondence of Miss Adams*, p. 31). On the geographic distribution of the *marchands merciers*, see Natacha Coquery, "Shopping Streets in Eighteenth-Century Paris: A Landscape Shaped by Historical, Economic and Social Forces," in *The Landscape of Consumption: Shopping Streets and Cultures in Western Europe, 1600–1900*, edited by Jan Hein Furné and Clé Lesger (New York: Palgrave Macmillan, 2014), pp. 57–77; for the luxury and semi-luxury trades in Paris, see Coquery, "The Language of Success" and "Luxury and Shopping;" Natacha Coquery, "The Social Circulation of Luxury and Second-Hand Goods in Eighteenth-Century Parisian Shops," in *The Afterlife of Used Things: Recycling in the Long Eighteenth Century*, edited by Ariane Fennetaux, Amélie Junqua, and Sophie Vasset (New York: Routledge, 2015), pp. 13–24; and Sargentson, *Merchants and Luxury Markets*.

18. Stein, *The Worlds of Thomas Jefferson*, pp. 23–34. Monticello Assistant Curator Diane C. Ehrenpreis identified the commission of the Brescia marble table in Jefferson's receipt books and its subsequent importation to Monticello in his packing lists (conversation with the author, April 18, 2019). Henderson, "Furnishing the Republican Court," ch. 2, 3. Victor du Pont,

"Journal of a visit to Philadelphia," April–May 1788, Papers of Victor du Pont, group 3, series B, box 19, W3-3542 and 3543, Hagley Library and Museum, Wilmington, Del.; translation by Carrie Landfried.

19. Abigail Adams, October 26, 1784 (Smith, *Journal and Correspondence of Miss Adams*, p. 28). Lilti, *The World of the Salons*, p. 42. Even John Adams came to admire Anne Bingham for this characteristic: "I Yesterday dined at Mr. Binghams and Sitting next to Madam at Table, had Something like a political Conversation with her. She has more ideas of the Subject than I Suspected: and a corrector Judgement. She gave me the Characters of Several of the notable Foreigners, and I find has the Same Jealousies of them, which I have entertained. Talleyrand, Liancourt, Volney, Caznove &c. Noailles is the only one, that She thinks has much Friendship for America. She Says that Noailles declares to them all that he has renounced France forever, that he never will return, in any change of affairs, unless as a Traveller or Visitor and that if France Should make War on America he would take Arms in her Defence. Talleyran since his return to France has been very bitter against Us, she says. Liancourt has become very violent and is negotiating his return. Volney she Says professes Friendship and a good opinion, but is so proud a Man and has such Principles that she can have no confidence. Caznove from a high Government Man has become an inveterate Democrat. She considers them all Spies upon Us, and wishes them all away. This is confidential, and I would not be the occasion of any Misunderstanding between her and these Gentlemen but I was highly pleased with her Attachment to her County" (John Adams to Abigail Adams, Philadelphia, December 20, 1796, AEA).

20. À la *Française* referred to dishes being placed on the table all at once, as opposed to being served in courses; Abigail Adams Smith to Abigail Adams, New York (no date given), cited in Louise V. North, "Sarah Jay's Invitations to Dinner/Supper, 1787–1788," *Hudson River Valley Review* 21, no. 2 (Spring 2005): 76. Abigail Adams to Mary Smith Cranch, Auteuil, France, September 5, 1784 (Rice, *The Adams Family in Auteuil*, p. 11).

21. Determined to regain a commercial dominance over their former colonies, British merchants flooded the American market with the goods they had stockpiled during the war; to re-energize trade they were willing to take significant losses by offering credit and low prices. On buying British, see Kariann Akemi Yokota, *Unbecomming British: How Revolutionary America Became a Postcolonial Nation* (New York: Oxford University Press, 2011), p. 99. This account of French goods is gleaned from household inventories. See the 1805 inventory of the Binghams' household furnishings in Robert C. Alberts, *The Golden Voyage: The Life and Times of William Bingham, 1752–1804* (Boston: Houghton Mifflin, 1969), appendix 4; and 1797 inventory of Robert and Mary Morris's household furnishings in "List of furniture sold by Robert Morris to Thomas FitzSimons, Esq., May 19, 1797," Thomas FitzSimons Papers, McAllister Collection, Library Company of Philadelphia, Philadelphia, Pa. For the Morrises's engagement with French architecture, see Ryan K. Smith, *Robert Morris's Folly: The Architectural and Financial Failures of an American Founder* (New Haven: Yale University Press, 2014). For the proxy shopping relationships of these individuals, see Henderson, "Furnishing the Republican Court," ch. 2, 3, 5.

22. William Long, *Pennsylvania Packet*, July 11, 1788; and Francis De L'Orme, *General Advertiser*, November 18, 1790, reprinted in *The Arts and Crafts in Philadelphia, Maryland, and South Carolina, 1786–1800*, compiled by Alfred Coxe Prime, 2 vols. (Topsfield, Mass.: Walpole Society, 1932), 2: 188, 219.

23. Julian Ursyn Niemcewicz, *Under Their Vine and Fig Tree: Travels through America in 1797–1799, 1805*, translated and edited by Metchie J. E. Budka [Collections of the New Jersey Historical Society at Newark, vol. 16] (Elizabeth, N.J.: Grassman Publishing Co., 1965), p. 37. George Washington, May 21, 1787, *The Diaries of George Washington*, edited by Donald Jackson and Dorothy Twohig (Charlottesville: University Press of Virginia, 1976), pdf https://www.loc.gov/item/75041365/.

24. George Washington to Annis Boudinot Stockton, Mount Vernon, August 31, 1788, PGW Digital.

25. One of Washington's greatest challenges in forging the role of president was creating a strong executive without abusing his authority. Many Americans were understandably suspicious of a single executive and were watching for any visual signs or social indications that Washington would assume the role of a king. Washington's concerns about public opinion and the appropriate style of living for the president are covered in Melissa C. Naulin, "'The style proper for the chief magistrate to live in': Furnishing the First President's Homes in New York City" (paper presented at the Material Culture of Colonial and Early Federal New York Symposium, Yale University, New Haven, Conn., 2001). She cites Washington's "wish

& intention to conform to the public desire and expectation, with respect to the style proper for the Chief Magistrate to live in;" George Washington to James Madison, Mount Vernon, March 30, 1789, PGW Digital.

26. Martha traveled with several members of her household, including: her grandchildren Eleanor (Nelly) Custis and George Washington Parke Custis; nephew Bob Lewis (who would serve as secretary to the president); and six enslaved servants. They left Mount Vernon on May 16 and arrived in New York City on May 27, 1789. For Martha's journey to the capital, see Patricia Brady, *Martha Washington: An American Life* (New York: Penguin Books, 2005), p. 163. Congress authorized prominent local businessmen Duer and Osgood to furnish 3 Cherry Street on April 15, 1789; the task was apparently completed by April 22, when the Osgoods' niece, Robinson, visited the furnished house. Sarah Franklin Robinson to Kitty Franklin Wistar, New York, April 30, 1789, Benjamin Pickman Papers, Peabody Essex Museum, Salem, Mass. For a transcription, see Mary Robinson Hunter, "The Franklin Family," *New York Genealogical and Biographical Record* 23, no. 3 (1892): 130. Naulin, "The Style Proper," p. 6. In addition to making new furniture, Burling also sold second-hand furnishings and carried an extensive inventory of furniture made by other craftsmen. For an account of his workshop and the chairs he supplied the President's House, see Margaret Van Cott, "Thomas Burling of New York City, Exponent of the New Republic Style," *Furniture History* 37 (2001): 32–50; and Cadou, *The George Washington Collection*, pp. 136–39; 284, n. 40. Cott notes that Maria Osgood was Thomas Burling's cousin, which might account for his receiving such an important commission. For the architecture of the President's House in New York, see Patrick Phillips-Schrock, *The White House: An Illustrated Architectural History* (Jefferson, N.C.: McFarland and Company, Inc., 2013), pp. 5–9; and Henry B. Hoffman, "President Washington's Cherry Street Residence," *New York Historical Society Quarterly Bulletin* 32, no. 1 (January 1939): 90–101.

27. Martha Washington to Fanny Bassett, New York, June 8, 1789, quoted in Stephen Decatur, *Private Affairs of George Washington from the Records and Accounts of Tobias Lear* (Boston: Houghton Mifflin, 1933), p. 21. Blank notes the different translations in "French Furniture in the American President's House," pp. 18-–9: Decatur, *Private Affairs of George Washington*, p. 4, translated Moustier's letter to the comte de Montmorin: "I descended from the carriage and accompanied him [Washington] up to the humble house which has been provided as his residence," whereas Douglas Southall Freeman translated *chétive* as squalid in his *George Washington: A Biography*, 6 vols. (New York: Charles Scribner's Sons, 1948–1954), 6: 182. Susan Gray Detweiler observed the use of "plain," "carved," and "inlaid" in Osgood's receipts for the Burling purchases and concluded they referred both to older and newer styles. For instance, "inlaid" breakfast, card, and tea tables likely refer to neoclassical details, and "circular" side boards may also refer to a newer, neoclassical form. None of the chairs provided by Burling is described as other than "plain" or "carved." See Detweiler, "Two Philadelphia Side Chairs from President Washington's Official Residence in Philadelphia" (report prepared for the Barra Foundation, Inc., 1993), Mount Vernon Curatorial Files, Mount Vernon, Mount Vernon, Va.; "List of Articles furnished the Household of the President of the United States," vol. 138, pp. 316–24, Records of the Register's Office, Record Group #53, National Archives; and "Inventory of Goods in President's House, February 1797," PGW Digital. The rococo style, although still popular in the 1780s, was gradually being supplanted by the Adam style. For a detailed analysis of these furnishings, see Naulin, "The Style Proper," pp. 5–9; for chairs belonging to this group of seventy-three, see Cadou, *The George Washingotn Collection*, pp. 136–39; and Betty C. Monkman, *The White House: Its Historic Furnishings & First Families* (New York: Abbeville Press, 2000), p. 20. Mercier observed: "The greatest expense nowadays is in furnishings, which must be changed every six years to keep up with the fashion" (Mercier, *Panorama of Paris*, p. 70).

28. For these presidential protocols and the evolution of the Washingtons' republican court, see David S. Shields and Fredrika J. Teute's "The Republican Court and the Historiography of Women's Domain in the Public Sphere," "The Meschianza: Sum of All Fêtes," "The Confederation Court," "The Court of Abigail Adams," and "Jefferson in Washington: Domesticating Manners in the Republican Court," all in *Journal of the Early Republic* 35, no. 2 (Summer 2015): 165–262; and Henderson, "Furnishing the Republican Court," ch. 2. Abigail Adams to Cotton Tufts, Philadelphia, February 6, 1791, The Adams Papers, *Founders Online*, National Archives.

29. Sheraton, *The Cabinet-Maker and Upholsterer's Drawing Book*, p. 139.

30. Tobias Lear to Clement Biddle, New York, June 8, 1789, in "Selections from the Correspondence of Colonel Clement Biddle," *Pennsylvania Magazine of History and Biography* 43, no. 1 (January 1919): 66. *Gazette of the United States*, New York, May 13–16, 1789, no. 10, p. 39;

as cited in Detweiler, *George Washington's Chinaware*, p. 119. The eyewitness was Elias Boudinot, who sent a detailed account of the evening to his wife; as cited in Rufus W. Griswold, *The Republican Court, or, American Society in the Days of Washington* (1855; reprinted, New York: D. Appleton and Co., 1867), p. 158.

31. George Washington to Gouverneur Morris, New York, October 13, 1789, PGW Digital.

32. Gouverneur Morris to George Washington, Paris, January 24, 1790, PGW Digital. Morris identified different levels of French decorations: less expensive "pretty trifles" that were popular with the "petite Maitresses" of Paris (presumably the fashionable society women who had reputations for late nights, gambling, and dissipation), and slightly more expensive, better quality decorations in tune with classical antiquity. Morris purchased an ensemble of biscuit-porcelain figures at the Angoulême factory of Christophe Dihl and Antoine Guérnhard on the boulevard du Temple in Paris. The collection included three groups, two vases, and twelve individual figures. Today, there are two surviving pieces at Mount Vernon: one of the figural groups, "Venus and Cupids," an allegory of love and youth, which was intended to sit at one of the two rounded ends of the *plateau*; and one of the single figures, "La Peinture." The largest group, described by Washington as "Apollo instructing the Shepherds," may have been the same as the group in the Museo Arqueológico Nacional in Madrid. The recent discovery of "La Peinture" (which was likely purchased at the 1802 Martha Washington estate sale and descended in the family of William Costin, a free African American man who had close ties to the Custis family) has brought into question whether or not the other surviving porcelain figurines with a Washington provenance were once part of the 1790 Morris commission. It is more likely they were purchased by the Washingtons in New York and Philadelphia at different times during the 1790s. "La Peinture" is currently on loan to Mount Vernon by Stephen L. Zabriskie. For a history of these pieces, see Adam Erby, "Rediscovering a Bisque Porcelain Figure," *Mount Vernon Magazine* (Winter 2018): 10–11; Detweiler, *George Washington's Chinaware*, pp. 107–18; and Cadou, *The George Washington Collection*, pp. 142–43.

33. George Washington to Catharine Sawbridge Macauley Graham, New York, January 9, 1790, PGW Digital. For an example of this criticism, see the June 15, 1789, issue of the *Daily Advertiser* (New York), as cited in Blank, "French Furniture in the American President's House," p. 20: "We also find Levees, Drawing-rooms, &c. are not such strange, incomprehensible distant things as we have imagined; and I suppose, that in a few years, we shall have all the paraphernalia yet wanting to give the superb finish to the grandeur of our AMERICAN COURT!"

34. For the full list of furnishings, see "Articles purchased by the President of the United States from Monsr. Le Prince Agent for the Count de Moustier," , Mount Vernon Ladies' Association Archives, Mount Vernon, Va.; this invoice, written on March 4, 1790, is also in *The Papers of George Washington*, Presidential Series, edited by Dorothy Twohig, 19 vols. (Charlottesville, Va.: University of Virginia Press, 1987–), 5: 70–72.

35. On the second-hand goods market in Paris, see Coquery, "The Language of Success," p. 84. Jon Stobart discusses the different values buyers assumed when acquiring used goods at British country house sales. He suggests buyers could "capture value" (discounted price) and "capture difference" (ownership of unusual, harder-to-find objects), and that capturing difference also implied the chance to share in the elevated life and material world of the original owner. Stobart, "Luxury and Country House Sales in England, c. 1760–1830," in *The Afterlife of Used Things: Recycling in the Long Eighteenth Century*, edited by Ariane Fennetaux, Amélie Junqua, and Sophie Vasset (New York: Routledge, 2015), pp. 26–31.

36. Élénore-François-Élie, compte de Moustier (1751–1817) was appointed by Louis XVI and served as French minister plenipotentiary to the United States between September 1787 and October 1788. Anne-Flore Millet, marquise de Bréhan (1749–1826) was the sister of his deceased wife and accompanied Moustier with her son Amand-Louis-Fidèle (1770–1828). Moustier also had in his entourage a young secretary, Victor Marie du Pont (1767–1827), the son of Pierre Samuel du Pont de Nemours (1737–1817) and brother to Eleuthère Irénée du Pont (1771–1834). For Jefferson's letters of recommendation, see Thomas Jefferson to John Jay, Paris, October 8, 1787; and Thomas Jefferson to James Madison, Paris, October 8, 1787, PTJ Digital; for Jefferson's parting advice to Moustier and Bréhan, see Thomas Jefferson to Moustier, Paris, October 9, 1787; and Thomas Jefferson to madame de Bréhan, Paris, October 9, 1787, PTJ Digital. For Bréhan's miniature of Washington, see Kevin M. Murphy, *American Encounters: Anglo-American Portraiture in an Era of Revolution* (Bentonville, Ark.: Crystal Bridges Museum of American Art, 2013), p. 44; and Robin Jaffee Frank, *Love and Loss: American Portrait and Mourning Miniatures* (New Haven, Conn.: Yale University Press, 2000), pp. 100–104. Although the Washingtons maintained cordial relations with Moustier and Bréhan,

the two failed to earn the respect of other influential American statesmen and their wives, a situation that compromised Moustier's ability to serve a longer term as French ambassador. Both James Madison and John Jay reported to Jefferson that Moustier and Bréhan were in a romantic relationship, which was deemed immoral by the Americans in their circle. As a result, Bréhan found herself socially shunned and excluded from the households of prominent New Yorkers, a factor that contributed to Moustier's early recall to Paris. For contemporary views on the French couple, see Frank, *Love and Loss*, p. 100; and Jonathan Daniels, *Ordeal of Ambition: Jefferson, Hamilton, Burr* (Garden City, N.Y.: Doubleday and Company, 1970), pp. 15–18.

37. Cott, "Thomas Burling," p. 35.

38. Cott, "Thomas Burling," p. 37. For additional information on the two armchairs Washington purchased from Burling, see Charles F. Montgomery, *American Furniture: The Federal Period* (Wilmington, Del.: Winterthur Museum, 2001), p. 110; and Stein, *The Worlds of Thomas Jefferson*, pp. 270–71. Two chairs at Mount Vernon have long been identified as part of the Burling purchase (W-4116 and W-259). However, curators at the museum now speculate that the chairs were made in Philadelphia (author's conversation with Adam Erby, March 6, 2019).

39. Congress rented 190 High Street (today Market Street) from Robert Morris, who moved next door to 192 High Street with his family. The best architectural history of the house remains Edward Lawler Jr., "The President's House in Philadelphia: The Rediscovery of a Lost Landmark," *Pennsylvania Magazine of History and Biography* 126, no. 1 (January 2002): 5–96, and Lawler, "The President's House Revisited," *Pennsylvania Magazine of History and Biography* 129, no. 4 (October 2005): 371–410, both available online (http://www.ushistory.org/presidentshouse/index.php). For Lear and Washington's collaboration on setting up the new house, see their correspondence during the fall of 1790, particularly October 27, 28, 31, and November 4, 5, 7, and 14, PGW Digital. It is likely that Mary Morris assisted Lear in determining the placement of some of the furnishings. The best account of upholsterer Georges Bertault is in Blank, "French Furniture in the American President's House," pp. 34–41, 93–96. It seems likely that Washington ordered the chairs in late 1792 since he paid Bertault £32.11 on January 24, 1793, for the six chairs and two stools and then £17.1 on April 8, 1793, for "Contg't Exp's, Dr to Cash, pd. Barteau in full of his Acct for Chairs &c." (Blank, "French Furniture in the American President's House," appendix A, p. 93). The drawing rooms in 39 Broadway and 190 High Street were approximately 32' x 22' After Washington ordered the addition of a bow along the southern wall, the Philadelphia room measured 34' x 21'. Lawler, "The President's House in Philadelphia," pp. 25, 33; Phillips-Schrock, *The White House*, p. 8.

40. The pedestal-high wainscoting and fretwork cornice are detailed in the insurance survey completed for Mary Masters, Philadelphia Contributionship, survey nos. 167-71, March 1, 1773, reproduced in Lawler, "The President's House in Philadelphia," p. 11. The exact nature of the woodwork cannot be determined, however, because the house experienced an extensive fire on January 2, 1780. No records survive indicating how the woodwork was replaced in the 1780s, and the fire insurance survey conducted in 1798 leaves out those details (Mutual Assurance Company, policy nos. 891-95, June 19, 1798, copy in the 500 Market Street/Washington Mansion file, Philadelphia Historical Commission). Based on the survival of the mantelpiece with the pulvinated frieze of banded foliage, which was salvaged in 1832 from the yellow drawing room by the last owner of the house, Nathaniel Burt, Lawler speculates that Robert and Mary Morris installed a matching mantelpiece in the green drawing room. Moreover, Lawler argues the doorways of the public rooms on this level could have had matching pulvinated friezes on their pediments, much as one finds in the library of John Penn Jr.'s country villa, The Solitude (1784–1785) (Lawler, "The President's House in Philadelphia," pp. 37-40; the pediments from The Solitude can be seen in the Historic American Buildings Survey, Library of Congress Prints and Photographs Division, HABS Pa, 51-PHILA, 30-18). The wall color is speculative, and it has recently come to the author's attention that the walls may have been decorated with Chinese wallpaper. In 1782, Catharine Livingston observed that Robert Morris installed two Chinese wallpapers in his newly refurbished house, and it is plausible one of these was in the green drawing room. Chinese wallpaper was still exceedingly expensive and rare in this period and likely displayed in the most public rooms. Livingston's description suggests the wallpaper was of the bird-and-flower type and that each panel exhibited a different native tree sprouting from a flower pot. Over the course of 15 "breaths" (perhaps panels), she noted a great variety of birds, butterflies, flowers, and fruits and that "the luxuriance & richness of the colors is beyond description" (Catharine W. Livingston to John Jay, Springestbury, August 12, 1782, in Richard B. Morris, ed., John Jay: The Winning of the Peace, Unpublished Letters 1780-1784, 2 volumes [New York: Harper & Row, 1980], 2: 459-60). On average, Chi-

nese wallpapers were produced in widths ranging from 32 to 47" and could be up to 12' in height, and the dimensions of the green drawing room allow for at least fifteen panels with such measurements. Although Washington enlarged the green drawing room with a bow in 1790, it is certainly possible he salvaged the wallpaper and had it reconfigured for the larger space. Washington was well aware of the value of such Chinese wallpapers as he, too, considered installing them at Mount Vernon. Indeed, following his three-month stay with Robert and Mary Morris in the summer of 1787 during the Constitutional Convention, Washington thanked Morris for his offer to import "India Papers" which he was tempted to use in his "new Room" (George Washington to Robert Morris, Mount Vernon, October 2, 1787, PGW Digital). The author thanks Ed Lawler for the citation on the Chinese wallpaper. Washington purchased "Brackets glasses etc." from James Reynolds on March 16, 1791, and the patent lamps on December 14, 1791, from Philadelphia silversmith Joseph Anthony, although they were likely made in England and imported ("Sundries bought on account of G.W." [1789–1796], Joseph Downs Collection of Manuscripts and Ephemera, Henry Francis du Pont Winterthur Museum and Library, Winterthur, Del.).

41. Although the exact color and type of the carpet is unknown, Washington attempted to acquire an example "of the best kind" with a "Pea-Green ground with white or light flowers or spots," so it is possible the ground cover was a shade of green that complemented the chairs. Tobias Lear to Clement Biddle, New York, February 10, 1790, Washington-Biddle Correspondence, Historical Society of Pennsylvania, Philadelphia, Pa., cited in Alexander Macomb to Tobias Lear, January 31, 1790, PGW Digital. The essential nature of matched sets of seating furniture was recently emphasized in the reinstallation of the Salon Doré at the Fine Arts Museums of San Francisco (Martin Chapman, "Introduction," in Chapman et al., *The Salon Doré*, p. 9. For general information on Lelarge (1743–1802), see F. J. B. Watson, *The Wrightsman Collection*, 2 vols. (New York: Metropolitan Museum of Art, 1966), 1: 39–40, 552.

42. Abigail Adams to Mary Smith Cranch, Richmond Hill, August 9, 1789, *New Letters of Abigail Adams, 1788–1801*, edited with an introduction by Steward Mitchell (Boston: Houghton Mifflin, 1947), p. 19. Abigail Adams to Mary Smith Cranch, [Richmond Hill], January 5, 1790, *New Letters of Abigail Adams*, p. 35. Abigail Adams to Mary Smith Cranch, Richmond Hill, July 27, 1790, *New Letters of Abigail Adams*, p. 55. Abigail Adams to Cotton Tufts, February 6, 1791, Adams Papers, *Founders Online*, National Archives. Martha Washington would have been following precedent had she received guests while seated near the mantle. Anne Bingham, for instance, was observed receiving guests in this fashion: "But instead of her being in a little room, as you have been told, till all her company arrived, she was seated at the head of the drawing-room, I should call it, or, in other words, on one side of the chimney, with three ladies only." Rebecca Lowndes Stoddart to her sister, January 23, 1799, in Kate Mason Rowland, "Philadelphia a Century Ago," *Lippincott's Monthly Magazine* 62 (July–December 1898): 815. Abigail Adams also seems to have continued this tradition as she described one of her days receiving guest: "The day is past, and a fatiguing one it has been. The Ladies of Foreign Ministers and the Ministers, with our own Secretaries & Ladies have visited me to day, and add to them, the whole Levee to day of senate & house. Strangers &c making near one Hundred asked permission to visit me, so that from half past 12 till near 4, I was rising & sitting down." Abigail Adams to Mary Smith Cranch, Philadelphia, May 16, 1797, *New Letters of Abigail Adams*, p. 91.

43. Alexandre Pradère, "Life in the Salon: Precedences, Customs, and Furnishings in the Appartement de Reception of Eighteenth-Century Parisian Hotels," in Chapman et al., *The Salon Doré*, p. 42. Not surprisingly, the front parlor gained the title "yellow drawing room" due to the coordinating yellow upholstery on its sofas, chairs, and window treatments. For the furnishings in the yellow drawing room, see Lawler, "The President's House in Philadelphia," pp. 40–41. Lawler speculates that some of the yellow chairs and sofas could have been placed as well in the hallway. Indeed, the account of one visitor on May 13, 1796, Thomas Twining, notes only one sofa in this room: "A middling-sized, well-furnished drawing room on the left of the passage. Nearly opposite the door was a fireplace, with a wood-fire in it. The floor was carpeted. On the left of the fireplace was a sofa, which sloped across the room. There were no pictures on the walls, no ornaments on the chimneypiece. Two windows on the right of the entrance looked into the street" (Thomas Twining, *Travels in India a Hundred Years Ago with a Visit to the United States* [London, 1893], pp. 419–20, cited in Lawler, "The President's House in Philadelphia," p. 41).

44. For Washington's decision to host the levees and drawing rooms, see George Washington to Madison, New York, May 12, 1789, PGW Digital; and William Maclay, diary entry, May 4,

1789, in *The Diary of William Maclay and Other Notes on Senate Debates*, edited by Kenneth R. Bowling and Helen E. Veit (Baltimore: Johns Hopkins University Press, 1988), p. 21.

45. Eliza Lawrence's label is cited in Sotheby Parke-Bernet, *The American Heritage Auction of Americana*, New York, January 23–29, 1982, lot 1094: "Extremely Rare and Important Federal Turned, Carved, Painted and Gilt Ash Open Armchair, once the property of George Washington, Philadelphia, 1785–90." Tobias Lear to George Washington, Philadelphia, March 15, 1797, PGW Digital. Once Tobias Lear had the Washingtons' personal belongings packed and the President's House prepared for the Adamses, he sent George Washington a bill of lading for the articles shipped to Virginia on the sloop *Salem*. Lear indicated that the ship was "entirely filled with your things; and a very few are yet remaining, which will be put on board a Vessel that sails for Alexandria this week." Unfortunately, the bill of lading has not been found. See Tobias Lear to Washington, Philadelphia, March 20, 1797, PGW Digital.

46. Nineteen pieces of French furniture with a Washington provenance are in private or museum collections: Mount Vernon (*bergère* W-877, side chair W-217A, side chair W-217B, square stool W-731, armchair W-30, armchair W-2545); James Madison's Montpelier (side chair NT1988.6); Connecticut Historical Society (armchair 1983.57.9, stool 1844.73.0); Tudor Place (stool 4005.01); White House (armchair 975.1182.1, armchair 962.401.1); Delaware Historical Society (armchair 1940.8); Philadelphia History Museum at the Atwater Kent (armchair X-17); Winterthur (side chair 1990.0025); Museum of the American Revolution, formerly of the Valley Forge Historical Society collection (armchair 2003.00.1501); private collection (Peter *bergère*); private collection (side chair); private collection (sofa); private collection (armchair). Three additional chairs have also been noted in the collections of the Valentine Museum, Richmond, Va., the Westmoreland County (Virginia) Historical Society, and a private collection (matching MVLA W-2545), but the author could not locate them. The literature on these pieces is vast, with the earliest reference dating to the 1850s. See *Tudor Place: America's Story Lies Here*, edited by Leslie Buhler (Washington, D.C.: White House Historical Association, 2016), p. 211; Phillips-Schrock, *The White House*, p. C1; Nancy Carlisle, *Cherished Possessions: A New England Legacy* (Boston: Antique Collector's Club for the Society for the Preservation of New England Antiquities, 2003), pp. 221–23; Cadou, *The George Washington Collection*, pp. 146–45; Monkman, *The White House*, pp. 22, 24; Naulin, "The Style Proper;" Andrew J. Brunk, "'To Fix the Taste of Our Country Properly': The French Style in Philadelphia Interiors, 1788–1800" (master's thesis, University of Delaware, 2000), pp. 92–97; Sotheby's, *Important American Furniture and Related Decorative Arts, Property of the Rosen Family*, New York, February 1, 1991, lot 812: "Extremely Rare and Important Federal Turned, Carved, Painted and Gilt Ash Open Armchair, once the property of George Washington, Philadelphia, 1785–90;" *An Albany Girlhood: Huybertie Pruyn Hamlin*, edited by Alice P. Kenney (Albany, N.Y.: Washington Park Press, 1990), p. 187; Deborah Dependahl Waters, *Delaware Collections in the Museum of the Historical Society of Delaware* (Wilmington: Historical Society of Delaware, 1984), pp. 28–29; Andrew Passeri and Robert Trent, "Some Amazing Washington Chairs! Or, White-and-Gold Paint and the Square Stitched Edge," *Maine Antiques Digest* (May 1983): pp. 1–3C; Sotheby Parke-Bernet, *The American Heritage Auction of Americana*, New York, January 27–30, 1982, lot 1094; Deborah I. Prosser, *Furniture from the Society's Collection: Late Seventeenth to Early Nineteenth Century* (Philadelphia: Historical Society of Pennsylvania, 1988), Helen Maggs Fede, *Washington Furniture at Mount Vernon* (Mount Vernon, Va.: Mount Vernon Ladies' Association of the Union, 1966), pp. 34–36; Celia Jackson Otto, "French Furniture for American Patriots," *Antiques* 79, no. 4 (April 1961): 370–71; Stephen Decatur, "George Washington and His Presidential Furniture," *American Collector* (February 1941): 8–10; Marie Kimball, "The Original Furnishings of the White House," *Antiques* 15, no. 1 (June–July 1929): 481–86; Esther Singleton, *The Furniture of Our Forefathers, with Critical Descriptions of Plates by Russell Sturgis*, 2 vols. (New York: Doubleday, Page and Co., 1906), 2: 515–16; Frank M. Etting, *An Historical Account of the Old State House of Pennsylvania, now Known as the Hall of Independence* (Boston: James R. Osgood and Co., 1876), pp. 180–81; Benson J. Lossing, *Mount Vernon and Its Associations: Descriptive, Historical and Pictorial* (1859; reprinted, Cincinnati: J.C. Yorston, 1883), pp. 228–29.

47. Hepplewhite, *The Cabinet-Maker and Upholsterer's Guide*, p. 24.

48. Cadou, *The George Washington Collection*, pp. 169–71, 182–83. The Washingtons commissioned these pieces, as well as a tambour writing table and bookcase (MVLA W-158) that Washington used in his study, and a bedstead (MVLA W-194) that the he and Martha used in their bedchamber. For a fuller discussion of the meaning of "plain, neat, and simplicity" in early national America, see Henderson, "Furnishing the Republican Court," ch. 5, especially pp. 333–36.

49. George Washington to Mary White Morris, Mount Vernon, May 1, 1797, PGW Digital. Washington went to such lengths in explaining the situation because he had intended to present Mary Morris with the large lustre with eight lights as a gift—but Lear had shipped it home to Mount Vernon instead of directly to her house in Philadelphia. John Adams to Abigail Adams, Philadelphia, January 28, 1798, AEA. In a letter to his secretary, Bartholomew Dandridge, Washington wrote that Tobias Lear informed him of the Adamses' decision; however, this letter has not been found so the actual date of communication is unknown. George Washington to Bartholomew Dandridge, Mount Vernon, April 3, 1797, PGW Digital.

50. Inventory and Appraisement of the estate of Gen.l George Washington Deceased, Fairfax County Will Book J, 1801–1806, fol. 326, Fairfax County Archives, Springfield, Va., available online at http://chnm.gmu.edu/probateinventory/index.php. "The Will of Martha Washington," March 4, 1802, reproduced in *Worthy Partner: The Papers of Martha Washington*, compiled by Joseph E. Fields with an introduction by Ellen McCallister Clark (Westport, Conn.: Greenwood Press, 1994), p. 407; and "Account of Sales of the Personal Estate of Martha Washington (not specifically devised) late of Mount Vernon deceased—as rendered to me by Thomas Peter the Executor," [July 20] 1802, reproduced in Fields, *Worthy Partner*, pp. 407, 411. Eliza Parke Custis Law purchased one chair for $20.00 in 1802; Martha Parke Custis Peter inherited the "writing table and the seat to it" in 1802, and the square stool also descended in the Peter family; and Eleanor Parke Custis Lewis inherited the "Great Chair" and purchased the green bottom chair and the white arm chair.

51. The many questions of authenticity that surround these armchairs is beyond the scope of this project, although the author is currently preparing a related article on this topic. Washington-owned objects assumed a status of mythical relic at the time of George's death in 1799 and were the subject of profound interest in the 1830s, 1850s (on the eve of the Civil War), 1870s (Centennial Celebration), and 1930s (Washington's 200th birthday celebration). For this cycle of interest (and the industry promoting fake Washington objects), see Edward G. Lengel, *Inventing George Washington: America's Founder, in Myth and Memory* (New York: Harper, 2011). The four pieces compared here are: the armchairs at Mount Vernon (MVLA W-30), the Museum of the American Revolution (MoAR 2003.00.l501), and the White House Historical Association Collection (WHHA 962.401.1); and the private sofa that has been passed down through multiple generations in a Maryland family. The similarities in appearance and construction between the arms and legs of WHHA 962.401.1 and the sofa indicate they could have been made in the same shop and once formed a set; MVLA W-30 and MoAR 2003.00.l501 also match. Provenance research into the pieces has yet to confirm a solid association with the Washingtons' presidential suite, and curators at the three museums cannot trace the ownership beyond ca. 1900. Moreover, the sofa that matches the armchair at the White House has an oral tradition of being owned by a single family since the nineteenth century. This family also owned a matching chair until the early twentieth century, when it was stolen from an upholsterer's shop (where it was undergoing repairs), bringing into question the fabrication of the Washington association after the theft.

52. Furniture upholsterer and historian Xavier Bonnet inspected MVLA W-30 and noted the construction technique of the single leg/arm support, plus the high number of flutes (12) on the leg, concluding that the chair was made after 1795 (Xavier Bonnet, report, October 15, 2012, Curatorial Files, George Washington's Mount Vernon, Mount Vernon, Va.).

53. As part of the recent refurnishing plan at Montpelier, Grant Quartermous led a team of conservators and historians conducting research into six chairs with a James and Dolley Madison provenance. The chairs in the study included one at Montpelier owned by the National Trust for Historic Preservation (NT1988.6); one in a private collection; two at the Chrysler Museum of Art's Moses Myers House (CMA 51.1.32, 51.1.33); and two (with Washington histories) at Mount Vernon (MVLA W-217/A, W-217/B). Quartermous worked on provenance, conservator Thomas A. Snyder focused on wood and style analysis, and conservator Susan L. Buck provided paint analysis. They were able to demonstrate that four of the chairs (NT1988.6, private collection, MVLA W-217/A, and W-217/B) had the same paint history, and two chairs (CMA 51.1.32 and 33) did not match; three of the chairs were made in France, and one was made in the United States. The similarities in the feet, plus the style and materials of the carved rosettes in the corner blocks, suggest that three chairs (NT1988.6, private collection, MVLA W-217/B) were made in the workshop of Jean-Baptiste Lelarge (MVLA W217/B has his maker's mark) and the remaining chair (MVLA W-217/A) was one of the copies Washington commissioned from Georges Bertault in Philadelphia. Although Quartermous was unable to find conclusive evidence that James and Dolley Madison attended the Washingtons' auction in

March 1797, he speculates that they (or an agent) did and purchased several of the chairs. The Madisons did not leave for Virginia until March 28, 1797, upon Madison's retirement, when the couple shipped home a considerable amount of household goods that could have included the chairs. Moreover, lateral Madison descendants who later owned these chairs, the earliest of whom likely purchased them from James Madison or Dolley Madison's estate sales (1836 and 1849), recorded the Washington association. The first such instance was when Mary Cutts (Dolley's niece) bequeathed MVLA W-217/A to W. W. Corcoran in 1852 and noted it had "belonged to Gen. Washington." A second reference was made by Jane Chapman in 1932 when she informed the Mount Vernon Ladies' Association that her parents taught her to treat the chair with care as "it was a relic of General Washington." In 2015 curators at Mount Vernon commissioned Susan L. Buck to conduct additional paint analysis on the Law *bergère* (MVLA W-877), and in 2018 they coordinated with Quartermous to conduct paint analysis on the round stool at Tudor Place (TP 4005.1). In her October 2018 report directly comparing the paint histories of MVLA W-217/A and W-217/B, W-877, and TP 4005.1, Buck confirmed that the paint layers for the chair and stool made in Philadelphia (MVLA W-217/A and TP 4005.1) start two generations later than the chairs made in France (MVLA W-217/B and W-877). Further, in the first three generations of paint, she identified three different colors—light grey, cream, and light grey—suggesting that the Moustier suite was painted one or two times prior to Washington's acquisition, and then a third time when Bertault was commissioned to make the additional six side chairs and two stools.

Quartermous uncovered the provenances of the six pieces from the green drawing room suite, and they are:

MVLA W-217/B: Made by Jean-Baptiste Lelarge, Paris, France. Cômte de Moustier; purchased by George Washington; possibly purchased by James Madison; purchased by Dr. and Mrs. Thomas Towles Slaughter; by descent to their daughter, Jane Chapman Slaughter; purchased by Mount Vernon Ladies' Association of the Union, 1932.

MVLA W-217/A: Made by Georges Bertault, Philadelphia, Pa. George Washington; possibly purchased by James Madison; by purchase or descent to Mary E. E. Cutts; by bequest to W. W. Corcoran; by bequest to Mount Vernon Ladies' Association of the Union, 1878.

NT1988.6: Made by Jean-Baptiste Lelarge, Paris, France. Cômte de Moustier; purchased by George Washington; possibly purchased by James Madison; possibly purchased by, or by descent through marriage to, John Hancock Lee; purchased by W. W. Scott; purchased by Thomas S. Winston; by descent to his daughter Alice W. Kean; purchased by National Trust for Historic Preservation, 1988.

Private Collection: Made by Jean-Baptiste Lelarge, Paris, France. Cômte de Moustier; purchased by George Washington; possibly purchased by James Madison; possibly purchased by Benjamin Thornton; by descent or purchase to his nieces, the Thornton sisters; purchased by Frank Littleton; purchased by Mrs. Eugenia Reed DeLashmutt; by descent to private owner.

MVLA W-877: Made by Jean-Baptiste Lelarge, Paris, France. Cômte de Moustier; purchased by George Washington; purchased by Eliza Parke Custis Law or Eleanor Parke Custis Lewis [?]; by descent to Eliza Law's granddaughter Eleanor Agnes Rogers Goldsborough; by gift to Mount Vernon Ladies' Association of the Union, 1882.

Tudor Place 4005.1: Made by Georges Bertault, Philadelphia, Pa. George Washington; possibly purchased, or by descent to, Martha Parke Custis Peter; by descent to Britannia Peter Kennon; by descent to B. Kennon Peter; to his brother Armistead Peter Jr.; by descent to Armistead Peter III; to the Tudor Place Foundation as part of the 1983 bequest of the property and its contents by Armistead Peter III.

Ron Blank conducted the earliest conservation survey of any of these pieces (Blank, "French Furniture in the American President's House" and "Did George Washington Sit Here?"). For the Montpelier studies, see Grant Quartermous, "Summary of French Chair Research" (report prepared for the Montpelier Foundation, Orange, Va., August 19, 2009); Susan L. Buck, "Cross-Section Paint Microscopy Report for James Madison's Montpelier. Six Madison Upholstered Side Chairs: National Trust for Historic Preservation #NT1988.6, Chrysler Museum of Art Chairs #51.1.32-33, Privately Owned Madison Chair, Mount Vernon Chairs #W-217/A and W-271/B" (report prepared for the Montpelier Foundation, Orange, Va., June 1, 2010); Grant Quartermous, "The Montpelier French Chair Research Project: Summary of Provenance and Historical Research" (report prepared for the Montpelier Foundation, Orange, Va.,

March 1, 2011); Thomas A. Snyder, "A Comparative Analysis of Six Louis XVI-Style Chairs for James Madison's Montpelier" (report prepared for the Montpelier Foundation, Orange, Va., January 29, 2012); Susan L. Buck, "French Armchair (*Bergère* W-877, Paint Analysis" (report prepared for George Washington's Mount Vernon, Mount Vernon, Va., October 15, 2015); Susan L. Buck, "Analysis of the Paints on the Tudor Place Stool 4005.01" (report prepared for George Washington's Mount Vernon, Mount Vernon, Va., February 10, 2018); Susan L. Buck, "Analysis of the Paints on the Tudor Place Stool 2005.1 Compared to the Mount Vernon French Chairs W-217/A, W-217/B, W-877" (report prepared for George Washington's Mount Vernon, Mount Vernon, Va., October 11, 2018). For references by Madison descendants that the chairs had a Washington association, see Will of Mary E. E. Cutts, August 1852, box 24, Wills, National Archives; and Jane Chapman Slaughter to Alice Lee Sheltie, Charlottesville, Va., October 5, 1931, Curatorial File W-217/B, George Washington's Mount Vernon, Mount Vernon, Va.

54. Furniture conservator Ron Blank's study of the stool represents the most in-depth research of Moustier's belongings. In searching for records of *L'Aigrette*, he learned that Moustier's personal papers are housed at the Centre des archives diplomatique de Nantes. In folios 135 and 138 are two letters indicating that the minister brought a significant amount of furniture with him to America, implicit in receipts he submitted for repairs he made following damage on the crossing. In the first letter Moustier writes: "Dans son passage de Brest à Newyork il a souffert une perte d'une partie de son mobilier d'environs dix mille francs qu'il a été obligé de remplacer" ("In his passage from Brest to New York he suffered a loss of some of his furniture estimated at ten thousand francs which he was forced to replace"). The second version is dated December 8, 1789: "Dans la traverse de Brest à Newyork il a souffert par l'effets des gros temps une perte d'une partie de son mobilier d'environs dix mille francs qu'il a été obligé de remplacer" (Dossier of the comte de Moustier, vol. 53, folio 135, 138 [folios 71 à 149, 1772–1792], coté 1 Mi 46 au CADN] Centre des archives diplomatique de Nantes, France, as cited in Blank, "French Furniture in the American President's House," p. 15). Moustier also referred to the damaged furniture in a February 13, 1788, letter to Thomas Jefferson: "To be fully compensated for what I have suffered and for the sacrifice I made of my interests, which were mostly harmed by the loss of a part of my furniture, I need only know that your compatriots noticed, not only the eagerness of the King's Minister, but also that of the Cte. of Moustier," PTJ Digital; as cited in Travis M. Bowman, "Federal Hall Chairs at John Jay Historic Site" (report prepared for New York State Office of Parks, Recreation and Historic Preservation, Waterford, N.Y., 2018, p. 115).

55. Moustier's secretary, Victor du Pont, kept a journal during the voyage. A complete transcription and translation may yield more information on the weather and its impact on the ship. Victor du Pont, "Journal de mon passage en Amerique sur la frigate du Roy L'Aigrette commandée pr Mr. de Beauslier," November 1, 1787–January 15, 1788, Papers of Victor du Pont, group 3, series B, box 19, W3-3535, Hagley Library and Museum, Wilmington, Del. For the exchange rate calculations, see Bowman, "Federal Hall Chairs," p. 116. Another frame of reference for this price can be found in a July 9, 1793, bill for a similar set of drawing room furniture that Bertault made for Andrew Craigie: Craigie paid £387.16.2 ($1,034.14) for 12 mahogany armchairs, 2 settees, and 4 curtains, which together required 82 yards of green and white silk damask; boards, boxes, and nails; 8 yards of coarse linen to back the window curtains; 56 yards fancy chintz for chair and sette slip covers; and shipping. See Kathleen Catalano and Richard C. Nylander, "New Attributions to Adam Hains, Philadelphia Furniture Maker," *Antiques* 117, no. 5 (May 1980): 1114.

56. *New York Journal*, March 26, 1789, p. 2; as cited in Bowman, "Federal Hall Chairs," p. 39. In his comprehensive study on the Federal Hall chairs, Bowman makes a strong argument that Georges Bertault furnished the chairs originally used in the Senate hall. Noting the craftsman's sophisticated use of neoclassical elements in the carving and their departure from details on New York chairs made before 1788–1789, Bowman posits that the chairs must have been made by a recently arrived, European-trained craftsman. Although Bowman and his colleague, furniture conservator David Bayne, have observed differences among the surviving Federal Hall chairs (not all exhibit the same two-part seat rail construction, so at least two craftsman's shops may have collaborated on the order), those objects share enough similarities in carving of the feet and reeded legs to harmonize with one another; and the same details are present on the side chair (MVLA W-217/A) and round stool attributed to Bertault. Whether Bertault was contracting with both French-trained and American-trained turners and cabinetmakers for the wood frames or not, it seems likely he instructed local woodworkers to provide frames that corresponded with the latest French styles.

57. There are multiple references to upholsterer Georges Bertault in Philadelphia, and many examples of his furniture are in museum collections. His working relationship with cabinet-maker Adam Hains is especially well documented. In recent years, several scholars have been attempting to verify Bertault's arrival in the United States as well as his training in Paris. Ron Blank has found naturalization papers for a Georges Bertault in Philadelphia in 1808; yet Bowman notes that the dates on that document could be interpreted to mean that that Bertault began his American residency in 1791 or, more likely, in 1801. The presence of a Georges Bertault in New York by the early 1790s is implied by two purchases George Washington made in January 1792. After Congress relocated the capital to Philadelphia, Washington paid a "Mr. Barteau" to buy buttons and gloves in New York for Martha Washington and have them sent to Philadelphia. The Jacques Georges Bertault identified by Xavier Bonnet seems to be the most promising candidate among the three "Georges Bertaults" that he has found in archival records. More research is needed to determine if the son was trained as an upholsterer and when he emigrated to the United States. Blank, "French Furniture in the American's President's House," pp. 34–39; Xavier Bonnet, "From Paris to Philadelphia, Georges Bertault (1733/?)" (short-term research fellowship proposal, Winterthur Museum, Winterthur, Del., 2012); personal correspondence with Xavier Bonnet, January 23, 2018; Bowman, "Federal Hall Chairs," pp. 41–42. For chairs attributed to Georges Bertault in the United States, see Lisa Minardi, "Adam Hains and the Philadelphia-Reading Connection," in *American Furniture*, edited by Luke Beckerdite (Lebanon, N.H.: University of New England Press for the Chipstone Foundation, 2014), pp. 143–201; Carlyle, *Cherished Possessions*, pp. 221–23; Jonathan L. Fairbanks, Introduction, in *Collecting American Decorative Arts and Sculpture, 1971–1991* (Boston: Museum of Fine Arts, 1991), p. 40; Ruth Davidson, "Museum Accessions," *Antiques* 103, no. 2 (February 1973): 250. Between 1791 and 1797 Washington made fifteen payments to Bertault for buttons and gloves, fixing furniture, feather beds, mattresses, making and putting down carpets, and the chairs and stools. Washington's receipts are in a number of repositories including: Winterthur Library, Joseph Downs Collection of Manuscripts and Printed Ephemera (No. 65 x 571 [November 19, 1791; July 2 and 9, 1792; January 24, 1793; and December 29, 1795]); Beinecke Library, Yale University ("Household accounts and monies received, 1789–1792," Gen. Mss. 201 [January 22 and 24, 1791; March 21, 1791; May 21, 1791; and July 9, 1792]); and published as "Washington's Household Account Book, 1793–1797," *Pennsylvania Magazine of History and Biography* 29–31 (1905–1907), 29: 392; 30: 165, 325; 31: 70, 348 (April 8, 1793; February 13, 1794; November 15, 1794; December 9, 1795; and March 16, 1797, respectively). A complete list of the expenditures and costs can be found in Blank, "French Furniture in the American's President's House," p. 93, appendix A: "Ledger Entries for Georges Bertault."

58. The Peter *berg*ère remains in a private collection and the author thanks Grant Quartermous for the opportunity to study it in person. The oral tradition of the chair is published in William Armstrong, "Some New Washington Relics," *Century Illustrated Monthly Magazine* (May 1890): 14–22, cited in Blank, "French Furniture in the American's President's House," p. 64. The author postulates that the "seat" to the desk in Martha's will is the Peter *bergère* and that it came with the square stool; there is otherwise no indication in the written record for how the stool also came into the possession of the Peter family; "The Will of Martha Washington," Fields, *Worthy Partner*, p. 407. Conservator Marc A. Williams has noted that the lady's writing desk had prominent, deep wear marks on both of its front legs that matched the curved profile of the square stool (MVLA W-731), and since the stool fit the location and wear on the desk, it is possible the stool was used for a lengthy period of time as a seat to the desk. Marc A. Williams, "Square Stool Object Report" (report prepared for George Washington's Mount Vernon, Mount Vernon, Va., March 25, 1992). Period examples of the *bergère* being used in private or more intimate settings may be found in the illustrated works of Jean Michel Moreau the Younger (French, Paris, 1741–1814). In the 1770s and 1780s Moreau published several prints that record fashionable dress and domestic interiors in the final years of the ancien régime. A *bergère* is visible in "Le Lever," "La petite Toilette," and "Le Matinèe," from *Monuments du costume physique et moral de la fin du dix-huitième siècle, ou Tableaux de la vie* (1789).

59. In previous studies of these Bertault-Hains sets, scholars have suggested that MVLA W-30 could have served as the model, and that Washington also commissioned several matching chairs in 1797 (two examples are in the White House collection, 975.1182.92). However, since MVLA W-30 dates more precisely to ca. 1795, this connection seems unlikely, and the evidence that the Washingtons purchased more chairs from Bertault upon their departure from Philadelphia does not accord with Washington's receipts for that period. For the literature on these various sets of chairs, see Catalano and Nylander, "New Attributions to Adam

Hains," pp. 1112–16; Monkman, *The White House*, p. 279; and Minardi, "Adam Hains and the Philadelphia-Reading Connection," fn. 11. Furniture scholar Richard C. Nylander also noted similarities between the legs of the square stool and the legs of the chairs Bertault and Hains made both for Andrew Craigie and for Theodore and Lydia Williams Lyman, further suggesting that Bertault produced the Peter *bergère* and square stool. Richard C. Nylander to Christine Meadows, Boston, March 3, 1781, Mount Vernon Curatorial Files, George Washington's Mount Vernon, Mount Vernon, Va.

60. Mercier wrote in the 1780s that there were so many specialized words to describe all of the new furniture forms in Paris that "our inventories would astonish a visitor from classic times returning to this world." This observation makes one question what monsieur Le Prince could have meant when he listed "12 armchairs" in the 1790 sales list. Historians have presumed this was a reference for open armchairs only (*cabriolet* or *fauteuil a la reine*), yet it seems possible the word "armchair" could have been used to indicate a mixed collection of different forms. Mercier, *Panorama of Paris*, p. 70.

Figure 1 John Banks, armchair, New York City, 1819. Mahogany with ash and white pine. H. 37¾", W. 21½", D. 27¾". (Courtesy, Bernard and S. Dean Levy, Inc.; photo, Richard Goodbody.) The letter designations provided for some of the seating illustrated here are derived from accesion numbers assigned by the New-York Historical Society. This armchair is "H".

Philip D. Zimmerman

A Beekman Legacy:
1819 French Tapestry
Chairs by John Banks
of New York

▼ THE HISTORICAL RECORD FOR early American furniture seldom releases its secrets about who made a particular piece of furniture, when and where it was made, for whom, or under what circumstances. Some objects survive with oral traditions of descent in particular families, but often those reconstructed histories are more aspirational than factual. Similarly, long-time attributions to makers may signal over-eagerness or other evidence of wishful thinking. Early written records of such object histories or provenances do much to eliminate speculation. Such is the case with two sets totaling sixteen armchairs and two sofas, all upholstered in rare French woven tapestry (figs. 1–3).

Furniture historian Esther Singleton first published this seating in *The Furniture of Our Forefathers* (1901), her serialized history of American furniture regions and styles, as belonging to the Beekmans, a leading family of New York and direct descendants of Wilhelmus Beekman (1623–1707), who immigrated to New York in 1647 with Peter Stuyvesant and others. Singleton included the chairs and sofas among pre-1776 "Dutch and English Periods," apparently influenced by caption author Russell Sturgis (1836–1909), an architect, art critic, and founder of the Metropolitan Museum of Art. He dated one sofa (and by implication the other sofa and all of the armchairs) circa 1760 (fig. 4). Sturgis's sense of furniture history may have been influenced by the prominence of James Beekman (1732–1807), a great-grandson of Wilhelmus but better known as the builder of Mount Pleasant, a grand country seat constructed in 1763–1764 and overlooking the East River near what is now First Avenue and 51st Street (fig. 5). The house was demolished in 1874. Sturgis, born in Maryland but educated in New York City where he subsequently practiced architecture, may have seen the house and furnishings, but regardless, Mount Pleasant was known through drawings, photographs, interior paneling, and the carved parlor chimney breast given to the New-York Historical Society in 1874. Sturgis went on to identify the extraordinary upholstery as "French tapestry, Gobelins or Beauvais, of the same or a somewhat later epoch."[1]

A remarkable family reminiscence recorded on December 30, 1876, was more accurate. In it, Mary Beekman de Peyster (1800–1885), a great niece of James Beekman, recalled:

> The gobelin tapestry chairs and sofas were bought by the same uncle James Beekman–from a French nobleman who had fled to the West India Island about the year 1818 or 1820 the chair and sofa frames were made here in New York.

Figure 2 John Banks, sofa, New York City, 1819.
Mahogany with cherry, ash, and white pine.
H. 38½", W. 72", D. 27". (Courtesy, Bernard and
S. Dean Levy, Inc.; photo, Richard Goodbody.)

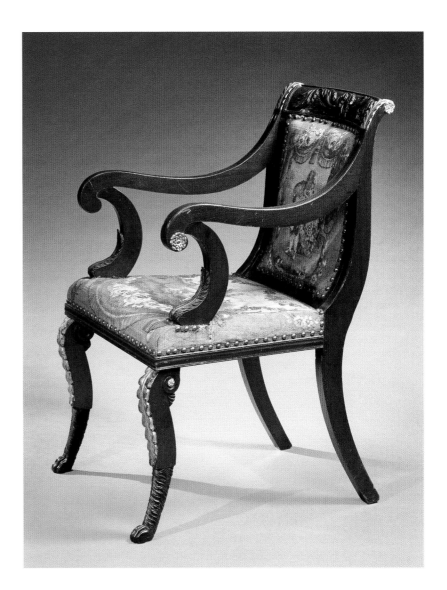

Figure 3 John Banks, armchair, New York City, 1819. Mahogany with cherry, ash, maple, and white pine. H. 37¾", W. 21½", D. 27¾". (Courtesy, Bernard and S. Dean Levy, Inc.; photo, Richard Goodbody.) This is armchair "K".

Figure 4 Frontispiece to Esther Singleton, *The Furniture of Our Forefathers,* pt. 4, (New York: Doubleday, Page, August 1901).

SOFA OF GOBELIN TAPESTRY
Owned by Gerald Beekman, Esq., New York. See page 289.

MOUNT PLEASANT

Country Seat of
James Beekman
East River about four and one quarter

Concerning the gobelin tapestry chairs and sofas, I was told by Catharine Moulton (Catharine Hill) – who lived for many years as housekeeper with my uncle James Beekman at the mount [i.e., Mount Pleasant] – from about 1817 till his death in 1837.) a few months before her death in 1875 that she remembered that these chairs and sofas were bought by my uncle – they were not inherited by him she said, but he bought the tapestry, and had the frames made in New York – She remembered that they were bought while she lived with him. This confirms Mrs. de Peyster's recollection and establishes the history of the gobelins – which have therefore been in our possession only about 55 years.

"Uncle James" was Beekman's son and namesake, James Jr. (1758–1837). This younger James was correctly identified as the original owner when the Beekman armchairs and sofas were exhibited at the New-York Historical Society throughout most of the twentieth century, but the furniture maker's identity proved elusive. A modest exhibition pamphlet published by the society in 1976 dated the seating circa 1820 and attributed it to the "workshop of Duncan Phyfe," a generalized form of identification that is sometimes understood to be code for confusion. Given the ambitiousness of the Beekman seating, its upholstery, and its esteemed provenance, furniture historians of the 1970s might have thought that the chairs and sofas *should* have been made by Duncan Phyfe, although this furniture does not sit comfortably among Phyfe's known work. In 2001 furniture historian Elizabeth Bidwell Bates laid uncertainty to rest by discovering several Beekman invoices and accounts that address different aspects of the seating, including its manufacture by New York furniture maker John Banks (ca. 1789–1826).[2]

The earliest manuscript is a bill of sale describing James Beekman's purchase of two "Set Tapastry" and a carpet from New York auctioneer Robert McMennomy (ca. 1769–1842) in May 1818 (fig. 6). As multiple newspaper notices beginning in 1801 attest, McMennomy regularly sold a variety of goods along the New York City waterfront. By 1805 he advertised selling "valuable property" specifically at "public vendue" (i.e., auction), and in 1817 he was listed among some thirty other New York City auctioneers as having paid duties on auction sales to the city in the previous year. Although newspapers often detailed auction offerings, no notice has yet been found that describes the precise circumstances of McMennomy's tapestry sale to Beekman. It is possible that the tapestry sets were sold to him privately rather than at public auction.[3]

In light of the Beekman bills of sale, Mary de Peyster's personal reminiscence assumes an interesting dimension. Historians of all kinds rightfully challenge the accuracy of such reminiscences—and historical memory in general. With the help of psychological studies, they point out regular reportings of factual misstatements, enhancements, and wish-fulfillments. From the perspective of furniture history, one need only consider the number of beds George Washington slept in or all of the furniture that supposedly came over on the Mayflower. But Mary de Peyster's recollections are substantiated by independent and reliable historical evidence. Her Uncle James inherited Mount Pleasant in 1817, as she said, the year in which his mother and surviving parent died. The seating in question was in fact bought by her uncle and not inherited, as Sturgis erroneously assumed. And, inasmuch as the "gobelins"—that is, the tapestry coverings—were bought at an auction or private sale, even the fleeing French nobleman story may contain an element of truth.

Figure 6 Robert McMennomy to James Beekman, invoice for tapestry sets, May 1818. (Courtesy, New-York Historical Society.)

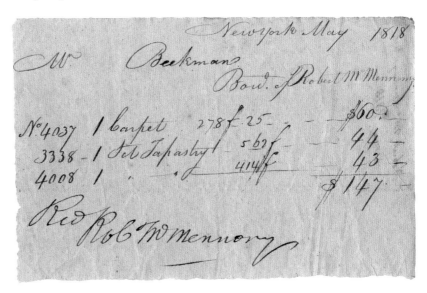

De Peyster did not mention that all of the Beekman seating comprised two separate sets of eight armchairs and one sofa each, although she surely must have noticed the differences. Casual inspection of the sixteen armchairs readily divides them into two groups of eight. Eight have upholstery covers with green backgrounds and eight have red. There is one green sofa and one red one. Details of construction and carving also divide the sixteen chairs into two groups of eight, but those groupings are not the same. Six of one construction type have green covers and the remaining two have red. The other eight chairs complement this six-and-two distribution of covers on frames. The two sofas exhibit less obvious carving and construction differences from one another. More detailed analysis below links construction of one sofa to one set of eight chairs and the other to the second set.

The McMennomy tapestry bill listing two sets leaves open to question what designated a set in the early nineteenth century. No single definition prevailed, but various contemporary listings often enumerated eight chairs and one sofa. For example, in 1811 the auction company C. and H. F. Barrell in Boston offered for sale "1 Sopha, and 8 Chairs, Gobelin Tapestry." Another set of eight chairs accompanied three sofas "of Goblin Tapestry in perfect order" in an 1801 offering by Arden and Close of New York City as part of "a variety of superb and costly household Furniture." Still other references remind the modern researcher that the number of chairs that constituted a set was not constant. Nonetheless, the evidence suggests that in the United States after 1800, sets of eight were both common and reasonable alternatives to sets of six, which seem to have prevailed (but with exceptions) in the eighteenth century.[4]

John Banks's two furniture bills, which support the concept of a set representing eight chairs and one sofa, require some explanation. The first one, dated June 26, 1819, specifies a "Square grecian Sopha" and eight matching chairs (fig. 7). Although the seating forms are straightforward, use of the term "Grecian" is not. This early reference is not the first in New York

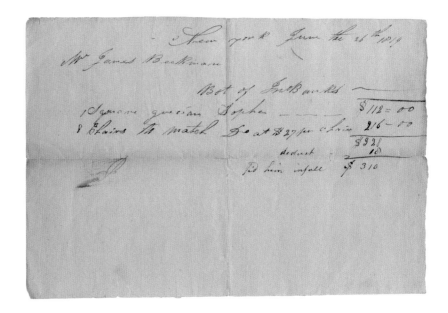

Figure 7 John Banks to James Beekman, invoice for a set of eight armchairs and one sofa, June 26, 1819. (Courtesy, New-York Historical Society.)

usage. Upholsterer William W. Galatian, for example, offered "a handsome Grecian Couch" among wallpapers, upholstery textiles, and other items in an 1814 advertisement. Several different tradesmen listed Grecian sofas and couches in 1817 advertisements. And the next year, the auction firm of Franklin and Minturn mentioned a "Grecian sofa and chairs to match" among "the furniture of a parlour and bed room" they offered for sale.[5]

What, precisely, did the term Grecian communicate to those living in the early nineteenth century? As is so often the case in furniture history, exact definitions are elusive. Typically, either the historical term survived or the piece of furniture in question did, but not the two linked together, leaving

Figure 8   Thomas Seymour, Grecian card table (one of a pair), Boston, 1816. Mahogany. H. 30⅛", W. 36¼", D. 18". (Courtesy, Adams National Historic Site; photo, David Bohl.)

scholarly application of one to the other open to various possibilities. The Beekman chairs and invoices are a rare exception. Another rare instance is Bostonian Peter Chardon Brooks's purchase of "a p[ai]r of Grecian card-tables" from Thomas Seymour in December 1816 (fig. 8). Comparison of the Beekman chairs to the Brooks card tables yields little to define what "Grecian" might have signaled. Other written references to Grecian, lacking direct ties to the individual pieces of furniture that could illuminate the term to modern viewers, contribute little. For example, the 1810 *New-York Revised Prices for Manufacturing Cabinet and Chair Work* lists a "Grecian Sofa" but offers no image or further description. The 1815 *Additional Prices* edition includes a telling phrase, namely "the foot to form a Lion's leg and paw at bottom." Such reference to an animal paw foot was probably a meaningful feature in American usage at the time. "Lion's paws" accompanies the term Grecian in an entry for stools in an 1808 London price book, but as in America, English usage was never precise. In other contexts, Grecian denoted certain "antique" features, such as in-curved front legs (popularly called saber legs today) and "Grecian cross" chair-backs or front stretchers shaped as two semicircles, one above the other and joined (lapped) where they touch. English designer Thomas Sheraton, writing in *The Cabinet Dictionary* of 1803, captured the vagueness associated with the term by explaining that it signified anything in the taste of the Greeks.[6]

To return to the Banks payment records, Beekman received a deduction of $18 from the total of $328 for the one set listed on the 1819 invoice. No explanation accompanies this deduction, but it probably rewarded prompt payment. A single Beekman receipt bearing three separate payments beginning with $100 on June 26, 1819 (the invoice date), shows that purchase of this first set was completed on August 3, 1819. Documentation for the second transaction is indirect. On November 15, 1819, some five months after billing for the first set, Banks acknowledged receipt of "fifty Dollars on account of a Sopha & eight mohagony Chairs that I am making for the said Beekman," clearly designating a second set (fig. 9). On December 13, Banks issued a bill of exchange in the amount of $111.75 that he owed to a third party, namely J. R. Hardenbergh, a gunpowder manufacturer. Those funds, due in sixty days, were to be charged to James Beekman's account,

Figure 9 John Banks to James Beekman, accounting for a set of eight armchairs and one sofa, November 15, 1819. (Courtesy, New-York Historical Society.)

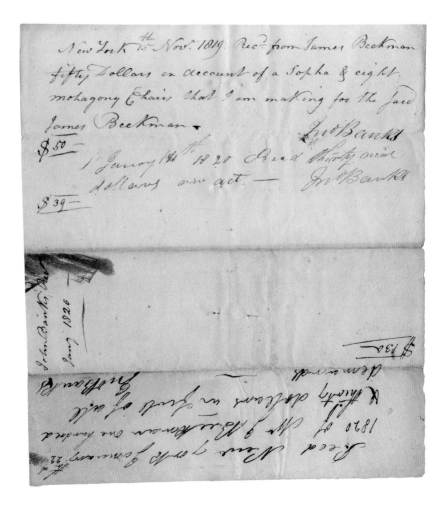

in essence representing a payment from Beekman to Banks. The following January, Banks received two payments of $39 and $130, bringing the grand total for the second set to $330.75, or slightly more than the cost of the first set. The last reference to Banks in the Beekman manuscripts is a receipt dated June 17, 1820, for $9.00 "in full of all Demands."[7]

Furniture maker John Banks is enigmatic. He is first recorded as a cabinetmaker in the 1818–1819 New York City directory, working at 66½ Beekman Street. Henry Banks, cabinetmaker, occupied 66 Beekman Street that year. Two years later, John and Henry were both listed at 60 Beekman Street. Henry died on December 31, 1821, "in the 62d year of his age. His friends and acquaintances are respectfully invited to attend his funeral tomorrow afternoon at 3 o'clock, from his late residence No. 60 Beekman street." Given Henry's age, occupation, and residence, he was likely John's father, or perhaps an uncle. Regrettably, no information about John's birth, parentage, or upbringing has come to light. The 1819 New York City Jury Census, which recorded adult males eligible for jury duty, identified their occupation and age. John's age was given as thirty in 1819, indicating a date of birth about 1789. Curiously, no New York City resident of that name is listed in the 1820 U.S. Census, although Henry's name is. "John Banks, cabinetmaker," disappears from repeated listings in New York City directories after a final address at 51 Beekman Street in the 1825–1826 edition. A court document dated February 2, 1827, directs that "Ann Banks the Mother of John Banks, late of the city of New York, Cabinet-maker, Deceased," be given power of attorney for John, who died without leaving a will. No probate records, notably an estate inventory (which furniture historians find immensely valuable to fill out details of a furniture maker's life), have yet been found. However, a death record conforming to the timing of the court decree states that John Banks, age thirty-three, born in Dublin, Ireland, died on December 24, 1826. It introduces a four-year discrepancy in John's age.[8]

If these records were all that survived about John Banks, furniture historians would bemoan the paucity of information, note the uncertainty of his birth year, and move on—but there is more to his story. The *New-York Evening Post*, the same newspaper that published Henry Banks's death notice in 1821, reported on August 18 of that year, "DIED Yesterday morning, in the 24th year of his age, Mr. John Banks, of a tedious illness, which he bore with a manly and christian fortitude, entire [sic] resigned to the will of his Maker." The newspaper notice does not identify this John Banks by any trade that might have distinguished him from others of that name in New York City, but it follows another item published on May 5, 1821:

> Elegant and Substantial Cabinet Furniture.
> On Monday at 11 o'clock, at No. 62 Beekman street, the entire stock of fashionable Cabinet Furniture, of Mr. John Banks, consisting of 8 sideboards, 3 handsome pillar and claw card tables, large and small sets of dining do. ["ditto," i.e., having pillar and claw bases] ladies work do. 2 bed chairs, bureaus, secretarys, mahogany high post bedsteads, maple field do. candle and wash stands, cradles, &c, &c.—will be sold without reserve for cash.
> Robert McMennomy, Auctioneer

Figure 10 John Banks, tall case clock, New York City, 1820–1826. Mahogany, light and dark wood inlays and stringing with tulip poplar. H. 96", W. 21½", D. 11¼". (Courtesy, Sotheby's.)

Taken together, these references provide strong evidence that the young John Banks (this one born in 1797 according to his stated age of twenty-four when he died), an active and accomplished furniture maker working at 62 Beekman Street (the same address as listed in the 1820–1821 New York City directory), terminated his business because of a serious illness, which subsequently caused his death. Yet Banks's name continued to be listed as a cabinetmaker on Beekman Street until his apparent death again in 1826. Resolving this dilemma with certainty requires further historical evidence, which is simply lacking. Early New York City records are notoriously less numerous than those for most other large American cities. Fires, British occupancy during the Revolutionary War, constant building and rebuilding in the rapidly growing city, and other forces all contributed to substantial gaps and losses. Until some confirming evidence comes to light, the court record of 1826 seems to be more plausible than the newspaper notice. Instead, that notice likely referred to another John Banks. New York City was home to several men of that name, including three listed in the 1830 U.S. Census. Newspapers noted the death of a Mr. John Banks, described only as "a native of England," on July 17, 1818; in April 1819, Mrs. Elizabeth Banks, wife of another John Banks (unidentified, but not the furniture maker), died; John Banks, shoemaker, appears in the 1822–1823 city directory; combmaker John Banks is listed the next year; and "John Banks, cartman," appears in the year following. Again, details are not rich enough to confirm how many different people these several listings represented.[9]

Four pieces of furniture bearing the printed label or stencil of John Banks are known. They include a profusely inlaid mahogany tall case clock, a gilt-stencil lyre-base work table of rosewood veneer and mahogany, a mahogany chamber table, and a pair of elliptic dining table ends known only by photographs (figs. 10–13). Banks's printed label and stencil each give his address as 60 Beekman Street, where he first appears (with his father Henry) in the 1821–1822 city directory and where he remained for the next four years (figs. 14–15). No further evidence allows this labeled furniture to be dated more specifically, except the work table. It has the name "LAFAYETTE" worked into decoration on the top in honor of the marquis de Lafayette's triumphal visit to America. That thirteen-month tour to all twenty-four states began in New York City with his celebratory landing at Castle Garden (now Castle Clinton in Battery Park), at the lower tip of Manhattan, on August 16, 1824. Otherwise, comparisons between and among these documented pieces of furniture contribute little to defining Banks's shop production beyond demonstrating a broad range of forms, decoration, and practices. More important, nothing suggests why the wealthy and influential James Beekman might have chosen the young Banks to make two sets of seating furniture intended to be upholstered in exotic French tapestry. The commission, however, may have inspired Banks's description of himself as "Cabinet Chair & Sofa Maker" on his stencil. The printed paper label, in contrast, advertises "John Banks / Cabinet Warehouse," with the address.[10]

Banks's "Cabinet Warehouse" at 60 Beekman Street was probably a first-floor room, visible from the street, where he stored and showed readymade

Figure 11 John Banks, work table, New York City, ca. 1824. Mahogany, rosewood, and walnut with tulip poplar and white pine. H. 31½", W. 24¾", D. 20¾". (Courtesy, Winterthur Museum; photo, Laszlo Bodo.)

Figure 12 John Banks , serving table, New York City, 1820–1826. Mahogany with tulip poplar and white pine. H. 33¼", W. 36¼", D. 18". (Courtesy, Locust Lawn.)

Figure 13 John Banks, dining table section (one of a pair), New York City, 1820–1826. Mahogany. H. 28¼", W. 46", D. 21". (Courtesy, Decorative Arts Photographic Collection, Winterthur Museum.)

Figure 14 Printed label of John Banks on the tall case clock illustrated in fig. 10.

furniture. Living quarters were upstairs. Before he and his father moved to that address from a few doors up the street, cabinetmaker John L. Everitt occupied that space. Beekman Street, which ran from south of New York City Hall (built 1802–1811) southeast to the East River, supported a small enclave of furniture makers living (and renting) in buildings numbered from 40 to 66, clustered near the middle of the street and mostly on one

Figure 15 Stenciled label of John Banks on the work table illustrated in fig. 11.

side. In 1819 James Poillon's "Cabinet Warehouse" was at number 40, fancy chair painter William Brown was at number 50, and cabinetmaker Andre Froment occupied number 66. The proximity of all these furniture makers introduces the possibility that they cooperated with one another on work from time to time, but the historical record is simply not rich enough to document or detail such circumstances. Personal relationships, rather than proximity, might also have driven cooperative ventures, which could easily have established connections to other furniture enclaves in the city. Duncan Phyfe was at 168–172 Fulton Street a few blocks away, and Michael Allison was at 46–48 Vesey Street, another block or so farther. Many other furniture makers were scattered elsewhere. New York City and the furniture trade it supported were rapidly growing in scale and complexity in the opening decades of the nineteenth century.

Construction and Decoration of the Armchairs

The Beekman armchairs and sofas represent ambitious design and stylishness on the one hand and telling documentation for American furniture history on the other. Examination and analysis of physical features yield significant evidence and generate engaging questions. For purposes of this study, construction features, rather than more readily apparent upholstery cover colors, will be used to identify the two sets of eight armchairs.

The sixteen armchairs readily divide into two sets of eight defined by the presence or absence of a medial brace running front-to-back underneath the upholstered seats. In one group of eight, a cherry brace is dovetailed into the front and rear rails, each of which is made of ash and covered by mahogany molding strips and veneer, respectively (fig. 16). Long and narrow front glue blocks made of cherry attach to the side rails, a configuration that helps resist front-to-rear wracking of the chair. The other group of eight has no medial brace; instead, large, square blocks made of ash stabilize the front corners of the seat frame (fig. 17). These no-medial chairs also have slightly

Figure 16 Underside of armchair "P" showing medial brace and corner blocks.

Figure 17 Underside of armchair "F" showing no medial brace and one remaining corner block.

thicker seat rails, and their seat frames taper in plan slightly more toward the back, bringing the rear legs closer together than those on the set with braces. The stay rails (the lowermost horizontal framing member of the back) curve to echo the shape of the crest rail, whereas the stay rails on the medial chairs are straight. The crest rails of the no-medial chairs are noticeably thinner in depth or thickness than those of the other group, a small detail that has further implications for the way the former were assembled (discussed below). Other, less visible construction details that separate the two groups are noted in Appendix A.[11]

The two sets of chairs have three different surface colors, in keeping with stylish principles of the day. The uncarved mahogany has a clear coating that saturates the deep reddish hue of the nearly grainless wood selected for these chairs. Certain carved passages—the deeply modeled foliage in the armchair crest rails, the cornucopia arm supports on the sofas, carved acanthus fronds on the fronts of the armchair arm supports, and all of the feet—have a dark green- and deep yellow-tinted coating that yields a "patinated bronze" (or *verte antique* as it is also known today) appearance, recalling classical antiquity. Finally, strategic highlights are gilded and punctuated with stamped brass ornaments nailed in place. Gilded details include the acanthus-carved tips of the rear stiles and upper leg sections on the armchairs and several

Figure 18 Leg detail of medial armchair "P".

Figure 19 Leg detail of no-medial armchair "F".

locations on the sofas. More subtle manipulations of the surface include recessed panels of bookmatched mahogany veneers that introduce distinct grain patterns on the sofas.[12]

Variations in surface treatment and carving between the two seating groups are minor but sufficient enough to indicate work by different craftsmen, whose identities remain unknown. On the chairs with medial braces, the tops of the arms have two broad flutes cut into them; on the no-medial chairs, the arms are molded to a serpentine profile. The gilded waterleaves that run down the tops of the front legs are different (figs. 18, 19). On the medial chairs, the leaves are naturalistically shaped and have undulating contours and pronounced ruffled edges; on the no-medial chairs the ruffling is less defined and the leaves have flatter surfaces. The leg fur and feet also differ from group to group. On the no-medial chairs, the fur has thick clumps and the paws are ovoid in shape; on the medial chairs, the fur is finer and more uniform and the feet are blockier. The foliate panels in the crest rails diverge in similar ways (figs. 20, 21). The no-medial leaves undulate more. In these iterations, the leaves look more natural than the flatter medial leaves. The grounds of the foliate panels in the no-medial crest rails have been smoothed to remove more toolmarks than in the medial counterparts (Appendix B provides a more complete listing of carving differences between the two groups).

Carving and construction features are consistent within each set; differences occur only between the sets. Although numerous, these differences

Figure 20 Crest rail of medial armchair "K".

Figure 21 Crest rail of no-medial armchair "A".

exist within a narrow spectrum of possibilities. That, combined with the absence of any formal design sources and the relative rarity in New York of the features decorating this seating, argues persuasively that the craftsmen working on the second set had to have seen the first set to understand what they were required to make. The differences represent alternative and concurrent solutions to small problems—for example, how to frame a seat or how to decorate the top of an arm. Given that the seat plan is a trapezoid, at what angle should the side rails meet the rear rail of the chair to achieve a gentle taper toward the back? Should the tops of the arms be molded using a molding plane with a cutting blade of a certain profile, or should a shallow fluting plane be used twice (once for each of the two flutes) to ornament that surface? Considered together, the several variations represent intriguingly different approaches to chair making, which furniture historians readily identify elsewhere as evidence of different artisans or shops. But the Beekman armchairs hold further surprises for historians.

The upholstered backs of both sets are made with an inner frame, similar to a slip seat frame, to which the woven tapestry cover is tacked on the front

Figure 22 Backs of medial and no-medial armchairs "I" (left) and "D" (right).

Figure 23 X-ray showing the back construction of no-medial armchair "A".

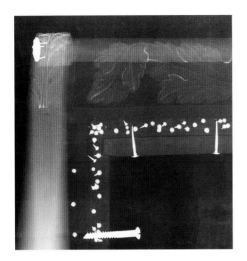

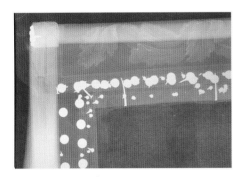

Figure 24 X-ray showing the back construction of medial armchair "P".

face. Nails driven through this inner frame hold it within the rectangular chair back formed by the crest rail, stay rail, and narrow framing members attached to the insides of the rear stiles. Cross banding covers these additional side members and the stay rail, thus forming the border around the tapestry panel except at the crest. Decorative tape or gimp covers the tack holes on the front, and cloth bordered in more tape covers the chair back (fig. 22). X-radiography reveals internal construction (figs. 23, 24). On the no-medial chairs, the inner frame incorporates a lapped joint and is held in place with wrought, rosehead nails. On the medial chairs, the frame is butt-jointed and secured with L-shaped cut nails. Differences also occur in the construction of the crest rails. The chairs with medial braces have substantial crest rails with mortise-and-tenon joints, whereas the no-medial chairs have thinner crests attached with three dowels. Dowels are wooden pins, each end of which inserts into a drilled hole. Round tenons, in contrast to dowels, are projections cut from a larger piece of wood, shaped round rather than in the more common rectangular shape. The advantage of dowels over tenons in this location is easy to understand. The thin crest rail curves across the front plane, creating a hollow back for the sitter; the crest also rolls backward (in what was often described as a Grecian fashion). A rectangular tenon cut from the ends of these crest rails had to fit into the rear stiles at the correct angle. That angle was enough to risk breakage due to sheering or splitting along the grain. The thicker crest rails of the medial group provide more wood mass behind and in support of their tenons.[13]

Conventional marketplace wisdom holds that dowels are evidence of late construction. They are popularly associated with mechanized furniture manufacturing in the late nineteenth century, when they all but replaced the more labor-intensive mortise-and-tenon joints. Indeed, use of dowels in certain aspects of construction is prima facie evidence of out-of-period workmanship. But the presence of dowels in the Beekman armchair construction inspires reassessment of their role and asks for more precision regarding when and under what circumstances they were introduced into American furniture.[14]

Dowels appear in the 1828 *Philadelphia Cabinet and Chair Makers' Union Book of Prices for Manufacturing Cabinet Ware*. That publication specifies "Doweling piece of stuff on top of back to form cape, from two to three feet long" (i.e., the shaped and finished wood cap above the upholstered back) in an entry for a "double scroll." In contrast, an entry for a plain sofa describes

Figure 25   Charles Honoré Lannuier (1779–1819), pier table, New York City, 1815–1819. Rosewood with white pine, tulip poplar, and ash. H. 37", W. 54", D. 22½". (Courtesy, Historic Deerfield, Inc.; photo, Amanda Merullo.)

stump feet that had "tenons prepared by the turner," indicating the need to turn the rounded tenons on a lathe to true their cylindrical shape. Clearly, both joining techniques were in use by 1828. Similar wording occurs in the 1834 *New-York Book of Prices for Manufacturing Cabinet and Chair Work*: the labor charge for "dowels in sofas" was valued at two cents each, whereas tenons were four cents, acknowledging the additional work necessary to make the latter. The fifteen-year hiatus from when the Beekman chairs were made reflects the absence of any known New York price books published in the interim. The 1817 *New-York Book of Prices for Manufacturing Cabinet and Chair Work* is not explicit: it describes "Dowelling tenons, each dowel" two pence, which may refer to rounding a tenon but likely denotes a true dowel. This particular interpretation of ambiguous wording stems from the common practice of copying ideas and wording from earlier price books, whether published in the United States or London. The 1802 *London Chair-Makers' and Carvers' Book of Prices for Workmanship* brings to light a revealing reference to dowels. The manufacture of chairs with "oval, round, or bell [shaped] seat," as described in the price book, specifies: "Dowels in the tenons, each" one-half pence. This construction detail did not refer to pinning tenons in place, despite the similarity of a pin to a dowel, because that common practice affected all chairs (and other furniture forms), whereas "dowels in the tenons" was only noted with rounded seats. The particular problem it addressed was the need to cut a tenon from the end of a curved piece of wood. The angle of the tenon veered away from the direction of the wood grain, thereby weakening the tenon, a circumstance similar to that encountered with the thin, curved crest rails on the no-medial group of Beekman chairs. Furniture makers typically call this circumstance "short grain." American chairs with bell-shaped seats were made in Philadelphia and New York, but only one set survives with historical documentation of when it was made: a set of ten side chairs and two armchairs made in 1807 by Duncan Phyfe for New Yorker William Bayard.[15]

The use of dowels in American furniture that can be dated firmly before 1820 is rare, although ongoing observations and research bring new instances to light. A pier table bearing the engraved label of Charles Honoré Lannuier (1779–1819), which dates it between 1815 and 1819, has two dowels securing each of the rear pilasters to the platform base (fig. 25). In work related to furniture making, a tavern sign for the Williams Inn of Centerbrook, Connecticut, bearing the date 1826 painted over 1803—its probable time of manufacture—is made from two boards that are glued together and have four original dowels reinforcing the joint (fig. 26). Undated pieces of New York furniture that may be dated in the late 1810s by style and construction include a scroll-back side chair made with a harp banister, which attaches to the underside of the crest rail with dowels.[16]

An x-ray of an arm support, repaired along a grain split at the juncture of the arm, shows a dowel through the middle of the tenon and continuing into the underside of the arm and the curved portion of the support beyond the break (fig. 27). The grain split occurred at the site of short grain, precisely the problem that the 1802 London price book reference to dowelling tenons

Figure 26   Tavern sign for the Williams Inn of Centerbrook, Connecticut, 1803. Pine and maple. 54¾" x 35⅛". (Courtesy, Connecticut Historical Society.)

sought to avoid. The strong, longitudinal grain of the dowel stabilized this inherent weakness and was an effective repair. X-ray of another arm support, which is unbroken, shows the presence of a much longer dowel that runs from the tenon through the cross- or short-grain section of the curved

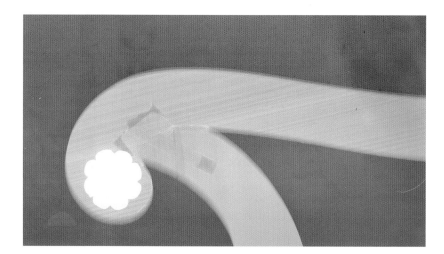

Figure 27 X-ray of a broken arm support showing an internal dowel on no-medial armchair "F".

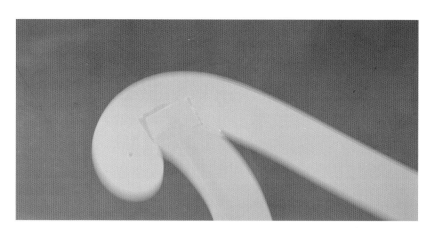

Figure 28 X-ray showing the long original dowel in an arm support on medial armchair "P".

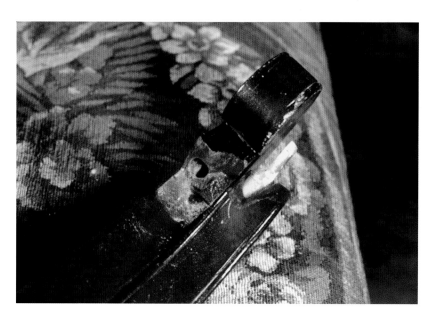

Figure 29 Detail showing a dowel with tenon notch. (Photo, Philip Zimmerman.)

arm support (fig. 28). Given the undisturbed appearance of the arm and arm support, this dowel is clearly preventative in function and could only have been installed at the time of manufacture, representing a variant of "dowels in the tenon." A loose arm support on another armchair shows insertion of a dowel, which at first glance appears to be an attempt to repair the break. But disassembly of this break reveals that this dowel has a shoulder cut out of it (fig. 29). Such a cut only makes sense if the dowel was originally inserted into the arm support before the arm tenon was completely shaped. It and the long, undisturbed dowel both come from the medial-group armchairs, whereas the shorter dowel—which appears to be a repair—is in a no-medial chair. Thus, both sets of armchairs have dowels in different places, in the crest rail on one and in the arm support on the other.

Construction and Decoration of the Sofas

The striking differences between the two groups of armchairs beg comparison with the two sofas (see Appendix C). As with the armchairs, the sofas are different from one another, but in less obvious ways. Each is built around a rectangular frame with four medial braces made of cherry and dovetailed into the front and rear rails. The sofa with green upholstery has cherry seat rails with long, narrow cherry glue blocks attached to the side rails in the front corners and large ash blocks in the rear corners. The medial braces have full dovetails cut into each end. The other sofa, with red upholstery, has ash seat rails with small rectangular blocks in front and small triangular ones in back. Medial braces are half-dovetailed. The lushly carved foliate brackets above the animal feet of the red sofa lie within the plane of the side seat rails, as does the richly carved cornucopia above the seat. In contrast, those elements on the green sofa are more massive and project a half inch beyond the side rails. This difference in scale applies generally to the construction of each and parallels the heavier scale of the medial group of armchairs compared to the no-medial group.

Both sofas stand on carved hairy paw feet (fig. 30). Unlike most other sofas of this style, the feet face forward rather than to the sides. This ninety-degree change in orientation derives from the unusual cornucopia arm supports. Their curve is visible from the sides, like that of the feet. When viewed from the front, the cornucopias appear more or less straight. Were the feet to point to the sides, they would look detached and awkward. Each foot has the customary winged bracket above, although a composition of deeply carved scrolls and acanthus fronds replaces the usual feathers encountered on other sofas. The thickness of wood required to create these robust feet and motifs was achieved by laminating thinner boards. The laminations can be difficult to discern by eye, especially when surfaces are painted or gilded and foot bottoms are scarred by long use. The legs of the green sofa appear to be laminated from two pieces of wood, whereas those of the red sofa appear to be made of three or four pieces. Again, the number of laminations reflects the scale of the components, which are larger in the medial chairs.[17]

The modeling of the feet and fur does not readily associate the feet on each sofa with the feet on either group of armchairs. Better physical evidence

Figure 30 Detail of the red sofa showing a leg and arm support.

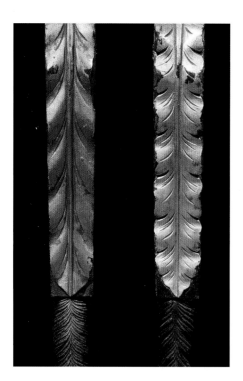

Figure 31 Comparative detail showing the leaf-carving on the front legs of no-medial armchair "F" (left) and medial armchair "P" (right).

lies in the acanthus leaves immediately above the feet and in the stylized floral squares or rosettes at the base of the arm supports. The leaves on the green sofa are more serrated than those on the red sofa. Similar variations in detailing can be seen on the leaves of the armchairs, which have ruffled edges on the medial group and smooth edges on the no-medial group (fig. 31). The tops of the arms provide the most definitive links between the sofas and armchairs. On the red sofa and no-medial armchairs, the surface is molded; on the green sofa and medial chairs, the surface is fluted (figs. 32, 33). Thus, physical evidence of the two sofas ties each firmly to a particular set of eight armchairs.

The lushly carved arm supports use an iconic cornucopia motif in an unusual and notable way (fig. 34). The tops of the spiral horns of plenty join the undersides of acanthus-decorated arm volutes. Each cornucopia rests on the back of a sea monster, whose oversized head and even larger gaping mouth and teeth face backwards (fig. 35). The tail of this scaly sea monster sticks out of the center of the rosette in front and below the cornucopia as

Figure 32 Comparative detail showing the arms of a medial (left) armchair and a no-medial (right) armchair.

Figure 33 Comparative detail showing the arms of the green (left) and red (right) sofas.

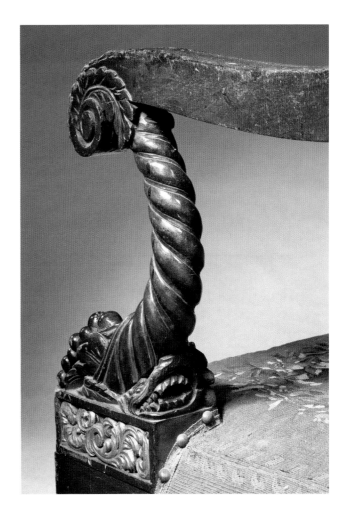

Figure 34   Detail of the arm support of the red sofa.

Figure 35   Detail showing the back of the arm support of the red sofa.

Figure 36   Detail showing the sea monster tail inside the rosette of the arm support base of the red sofa.

Figure 37 Detail showing the arm support of the green sofa.

it coils around itself (fig. 36). One can only imagine what comments these little details might have inspired during polite conversation at a Beekman social gathering in the 1820s.

Although exhibiting similarities in subject and arrangement, the arm supports of the sofas differ in several respects (figs. 34, 37). On the green sofa, the cornucopias are laminated, and on the red sofa, they are not. Carving differences are also evident in: the edge treatment of the cornucopia openings; the modeling and composition of the fruit; the direction and detailing of the spiral sections; and execution of the leaves on the arm terminal bases. Despite these differences, the sofas have shared idiosyncrasies establishing that one must have been copied directly from the other. The green sofa frame is about 2½ inches shallower front-to-back than the red one, although the length is approximately the same at 72½ inches. Finally, vertical in-fills flanking the sides of the tapestry back panel on the green sofa are almost two inches wider than those on the red sofa, indicating that the red back panel was four inches longer than the green, although the seat panels appear approximately equal in length.

Upholstery Evidence and Techniques

When James Beekman purchased the tapestry upholstery, the origin of the textile was not identified. However, contemporary newspaper references to similar textile offerings regularly called them "Gobelin," referring to the Parisian manufactory, first established in the sixteenth century by the Gobelins family and then acquired in 1662 by Jean-Baptiste Colbert (1619–1683) on behalf of Louis XIV. The factory enjoyed royal patronage for several generations thereafter. Russell Sturgis, in his 1901 captions, introduced the possibility of Beauvais origin, another French manufacturer named for its locale, a city some fifty miles north of Paris. Similar tapestry covers were also manufactured in the factories of Aubusson, France, over two hundred miles to the south of Paris. Identifying the origins of early nineteenth-century and later tapestry upholstery can be problematic. These uncertainties stem in part from inconsistencies, disruptions, and reorganizations throughout the French tapestry industry in the years following commencement of the French Revolution in 1789. Royal patronage ended, and quality became uneven and generally declined. Nonetheless, tapestry producers needed new markets, and some French tapestries found their way to America. The earliest reference found to date is an advertisement for "A very orname[n]tal sett of tapestry covering for a room, consisting of 2 arm, 6 common chairs and sopha, beautifully worked in rural emblems" that was to be auctioned in Philadelphia on May 6, 1793, barely four months after the execution of Louis XVI. Tapestry upholstery was occasionally sold in the years immediately following. Tapestries were sold in Boston and New York as well, such as Aubusson "sopha and chair Bottoms and Backs, in a great variety of sets" to be auctioned in Boston on November 17, 1796. By the turn of the century, the most frequent references came from New York, such as an advertisement in 1801 for "4 handsome pcs [pieces] of tapestry of Gobelin manufacture, . . . these articles would command a very high price in Russia." Some tapestry sets were sold with larger pieces that may have hung on walls. The "eight chairs and three sofas of Goblin Tapestry" discussed above had "five pair curtains to suit, with elegant trimmings," which might also have been tapestries but could have been color-coordinated silks made en suite. Gouverneur Morris (1752–1816), who lived in France from 1789 to 1794, described the tapestry hanging in the drawing room of his house, Morrisania, as a picture of "Telemachus rescued from the charms of Circe by the friendly aid of old Mentor." In all of the advertisements, whether printed in New York, Philadelphia, or Boston, "Gobelin" likely referred generically to French-made tapestries rather than to the specific products of that factory, although in some cases it accurately identified the source of the tapestries in question. The names Aubusson and Beauvais were rarely mentioned; however, at least one set of Beauvais tapestry was used in America. A set of twelve armchairs and one sofa made in Philadelphia for Eliza (1793–1860) and Edward Shippen Burd (1779–1848), probably about the time of their marriage in 1810, survived into the early twentieth century with Beauvais covers. Despite the esteem with which tapestries were marketed in America in the late eighteenth and early nineteenth centuries, examples other than those on the Beekman sofas and armchairs—and the tabouret discussed in Appendix D—that survive on American-made frames are virtually unknown.[18]

The upholstery on the Beekman chairs encompasses the woven wool tapestry covers, decorative tapes or trim, and the foundation or under upholstery. The tapestry chair covers depict thirty-two different scenes—one for the back and one for the seat of each of the sixteen armchairs. The sofa covers add four more scenes to the total. Back panels show people; the seats show animals, in keeping with the convention that people did not sit

Figure 38 Green tapestry back and seat from medial armchair "K".

Figure 39 Red tapestry back of armchair "O" with a composition similar to that of armchair "L", illustrated in fig. 40.

on people (fig. 38). The backs exhibit young women or men in tranquil settings, usually engaged in peaceful garden- or farm-related tasks such as feeding domesticated animals, tending plants, gathering fruits and vegetables, or fishing. The broad sofa panels narrate courting scenes. The scenes featuring animals on the seats range from peaceful and bucolic compositions to more violent encounters between the hunter and the hunted. The red tapestry set has oval floral borders, whereas the green set has elaborate drapery, tassels, and floral festoons. Each of these decorative strategies occurs in other late eighteenth- and early nineteenth-century French tapestry covers.

Figure 40 Green tapestry back of armchair "L" with a composition similar to that of armchair "O" illustrated in fig. 39.

Similarly, the specific panel designs, reproduced from cartoons, turn up elsewhere. Within the Beekman seating, the sofa backs illustrate duplication of the image: they depict the same composition of two people dancing in the center, a cluster of three in conversation on the left, and a piper on the right. These two tapestry panels differ in foliated background details, and one is against green and the other red, each accompanied by the appropriate drapery and floral devices. This repetition of design must have been happenstance; no armchair scenes repeat, although two backs—one red and one green—are similar (figs. 39, 40): they each show a boy or young man hold-

ing an oval portrait-like device, possibly a shield. This particular design may
have been adapted from another design of a young actress holding a mask,
an image woven by the Gobelins Manufactory in 1725, and taken in turn
from a painting or print source. Specific sources have not yet been identified
for the images on the Beekman covers. Esther Singleton identified them as
representing Aesop's fables. Indeed, some may have been inspired in general by that fountain of imagery, but the animals appear to be representa-
tions without Aesop's characteristic narrative cues. All of the back designs
are tranquil and appear devoid of moral or ethical themes.[19]

The designs on the tapestry covers do not fit the armchair seat frames
precisely. The curved drapery motif across the bottom of the green seat
covers and the outermost stylized vine border on the red chairs intersect
the straight seat rail moldings in front (figs. 39, 40). The relatively thin
upholstery stuffing and correspondingly thin seats accentuate this visual
awkwardness. Most French chairs, in contrast, have thicker upholstered seat
foundations, creating a higher vertical dimension in front. Many French
chairs—but not all—have bowed seat rails in front, which conform better to
the green and red designs. Yet like the Beekman chairs, tapestry covers used

Figure 41   Detail of the green sofa showing the
wide veneer border between the upholstered
panel and the rear stile.

in some other French seating sometimes do not coordinate exactly with the shape of the chair frames either. The decision to make the Beekman chairs with straight rails may also have taken into consideration the sofas, whose overall rectilinear design favored a straight front.[20]

Fitting the back panels was simpler and yielded better aesthetic results. The width of the mahogany crossbanding around the upholstered panel and the width of a horizontal insert across the bottom allowed adjustment within the frame of the back. No discernable adjustment was necessary from chair to chair, even from one set to the other, because the tapestry back covers are all approximately the same dimensions. The sofa covers, however, are of notably different dimensions. Although each sofa frame is about seventy-two inches wide, the red tapestry sofa back cover is about four inches longer from side to side than is the green back. The difference is visible where mahogany veneers have been glued to the frames just inside the rear stiles and arms (figs. 41, 42). Those on the green sofa are two inches wider, thereby compensating for the shorter dimension. More ambitious design adjustments compensate for the narrower depth of the green seat cover. The overall frame of the green sofa is about 2½ inches shallower than

Figure 42 Detail of the red sofa showing the narrow veneer border between the upholstered panel and the rear stile.

that of the red sofa. Even with that adjustment, the seat cover had a narrow strip of green wool sewn along the back border to extend its depth and provide a tacking edge. The wool strip was covered with a strip of wood, now missing. The raw bottom edge of the tapestry back cover is visible in figure 37. The original strip was probably made of mahogany, cut to a simple cove molding, and veneered with mahogany crossbanding similar to that on the armchairs. Each sofa, whose construction and carved detail tie it to either the medial or no-medial set of armchairs, bears the matching tapestry covers—namely green on the medial set and red on the no-medial set.[21]

The unusual problem of fitting pictorial tapestry covers onto New York chair and sofa frames brings into consideration a pair of sofas originally owned by

Figure 43   Sofa, New York City, 1805–1810. Mahogany and light and dark wood inlays and stringing with beech, ash, and other unidentified woods. H. 39", W. 73½", D. 26". (Courtesy, New-York Historical Society; photo, Glenn Castellano.)

Figure 44 Sofa, New York City, 1805–1810. Mahogany and light and dark wood inlays and stringing with ash, oak, cherry, tulip poplar, and white pine. H. 40", W. 73½", D. 25½". (Courtesy, New-York Historical Society; photo, Glenn Castellano.)

Robert L. (1775–1843) and Margaret Maria (1783–1818) Livingston (figs. 43, 44). The sofa frames, made in New York, retain their original French tapestry covers, outer side and back panels (colored red on one sofa and a now-faded blue on the other), and complete foundation upholstery. The Livingstons likely acquired the tapestry covers when they lived in France from 1801 to 1805, assisting Margaret's father, Robert R. Livingston (1746–1813), whom Thomas Jefferson had appointed to serve as the United States minister to France. The Livingston sofa frames were probably made soon after the couple returned to New York. Following Robert's death in 1843, the sofas passed through generations of Livingston ownership. Much of that time, from about 1865 until 1950, they were in storage at the Manhattan Storage and Warehouse

Figure 45 Detail showing patched-in tapestry inside the arm of the sofa illustrated in fig. 43.

Company—a remarkable circumstance that preserved these important artifacts of furniture history. The sofas are in extraordinarily good condition, with no patches and no extra nail holes indicating any alteration of the upholstery. Examination of the wool tapestry not exposed to light shows that much of the blue now visible was originally green, the yellow colorant in the dyes having faded. The sets of backs and seat covers for each sofa are similar in design, suggesting manufacture in the same time and place, but no two covers appear to be specifically paired. The pictorial image of one back looks fuller and richer than the other, and the draped and floral borders differ in details. More important in terms of aesthetics, the inside arm panels differ substantially from the backs and seats (fig. 45). In fact, they look patched-in from unrelated sources, although the integrity of the upholstery application confirms their originality to these frames. Their differences, as well as the less obvious differences among the large back and seat panels, suggest that matched sets were not available to the Livingstons for purchase. Instead, they had to be content with more limited selections of these rare covers.[22]

Unlike the Livingston sofas, the Beekman sofas and armchairs were used throughout the nineteenth century and into the opening years of the twentieth. Accordingly, they exhibit evidence of upholstery repairs and refreshenings. Three generations of decorative trim outline the tapestry panels on the chairs, and two generations survive on the sofas. Correspondingly colored tapes made of woven wool, and others of silk, each appear on the green and red armchair sets. Brass tacks spaced about an inch apart accompany the silk tapes (fig. 46). In addition, some red-set chairs display a third, brighter, woven tape colored a deep red that is modern, possibly applied when the chairs were in the custody of the New-York Historical Society,

Figure 46 Detail showing tapes at the arm supports of a chair from each group (armchairs "D" [left] and "L" [right]).

Figure 47 Detail of armchair "A" showing deep red, modern tapes.

although no records document their application (fig. 47). Each of the sofas has silk and brass tack treatments on the backs and brass tacks with a different woven tape on the seats. Making sense of this assortment of materials requires sorting through all of the upholstery evidence on the various chairs and sofas to determine sequences of restoration through several generations of ownership. However, examination still does not resolve all of the questions, including basic sequences.

Twelve of the sixteen armchairs have original upholstery foundations for the seats. Although not exposed to view, the back foundations are also likely intact, because backs receive significantly less wear and tear than seats do. A few of the Beekman chairs appear to have had stuffing (cotton batting) added from the outside back so as to push the front surface of the upholstered back forward (i.e., towards the sitter), making it fuller. The original seat material, which is readily visible from underneath, was applied in two different ways. The seats of chairs with medial braces have three strips of webbing two inches wide running front to back and two running side to side. On the no-medial chairs, the webbing arrangement is reversed (figs. 16, 17). The foundation upholstery of the backs is covered by the tapestry panels in front and by solid green or red cloth panels (coordinated with the

Figure 48 Detail showing the foundation upholstery of medial armchair "P".

Figure 49 Detail showing the arm support mortise and upholstery blocks of medial armchair "J". (Photo, Philip Zimmerman.)

Figure 50   Detail showing the arm support mortise and grass seat roll on no-medial armchair "D".

tapestry background color) in the back. On one chair in the medial group, the back panel is open enough to reveal one vertical and two horizontal strips of webbing (fig. 48). A broken and reglued arm support on another chair in that group reveals the use of wood blocks to define the corners of the seat upholstery (fig. 49). Thin grass rolls atop the front rail and along the side rails square out the seat. On the no-medial chairs, a more substantial grass roll without wood blocks in the corners shapes the front edge all the way across the seat (fig. 50). The sides have no grass roll and taper from the middle of the seat to the edges. Without the large wood blocks to provide shape, the seat corners look and feel softer. Figures 49 and 50 also show differences in how the tapestry seat covers were cut to fit around the rectangular base of the respective arm supports (see also fig. 46). In the medial or green set, the upholsterer cut in from the side edge of the seat cover aligned with the back edge of the arm support, whereas in the no-medial or red set, his cut intersected the middle of what became the rectangular arm-support opening. In each instance, diagonal cuts within the rectangle allowed the upholsterer to fold or cut away the triangular tabs to open the rectangle and minimize fraying of the woven tapestries. Decorative tapes bordered the rectangle and covered the cut on the side edge of the seat. On both sets of chairs, the upholstered backs were padded without rolls or other shaping devices. Other differences exist between the two sets regarding specific types and weaves of upholstery webbing and cloth used to contain the stuffing.[23]

The differing techniques (and materials, to a lesser degree) used on each set of seating indicate that at least two upholsterers were responsible for that work. An invoice to James Beekman from William Denny documents his upholstery of one set, (fig. 51), but no invoice for the other has come to light. Denny wrote his invoice on June 26, 1819, the same day as Banks's first furniture bill, indicating coordination between these two craftsmen.

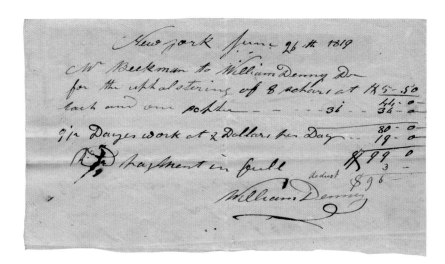

Figure 51 William Denny to James Beekman, invoice dated June 26, 1819. (Courtesy, New-York Historical Society.)

Like Banks, Denny is somewhat enigmatic. He is listed as an upholsterer at 64 Nassau Street in the 1819–1820 New York City directory. That directory also lists a William Denny with no accompanying trade designation at 44 Nassau Street, and a third William Denny, referred to as a blockmaker, at 40 Washington Street. Blockmaker Denny had been listed each year since 1815 at various addresses, but no other William Denny appears in those earlier directories. More interesting, Denny's name disappears from the directories entirely after the 1819–1820 edition. The disappearance of one William Denny from the written record was noted in the *New-York Gazette* on October 23, 1819: "DIED. Suddenly, on Saturday evening last, Mr. WILLIAM DENNY, of the firm of John Fine & Co. aged 31 years." Denny might have suffered a fatal accident or possibly succumbed to yellow fever, which plagued the city until 1823.[24]

But what about the two other William Dennys, especially the one listed as an upholsterer? The 1819 New York City Jury Census provides some insight. Organized by street, this census lists Thomas L. Jennings, a forty-year-old tailor, at the 64 Nassau address, and Thomas D. Penny, a tavern keeper (identified as "porterhouse" in the census, reflecting the term's use in early New York for establishments that served porter), age thirty-eight, at 44 Nassau Street. The only William Denny mentioned is the blockmaker, listed at the Washington Street address. Given all of this evidence, it seems unlikely that three William Dennys resided in New York City for a brief moment, yet were not recognized in the 1819 Jury Census. Instead, all three city directory listings probably refer to the same person, who began dividing his time as he pursued a new trade: he could be found at the Washington Street blockmaker establishment, where he had worked for several years; he probably resided at 44 Nassau Street; and he may have begun his new upholstery trade on a tailor's premises. Denny's sudden death late in 1819 may explain why the U.S. Census lists a William Denny in 1820, assuming census takers began their work before year-end. Regardless, no one by that name appears in the 1830 U.S. Census of New York City.

With Denny gone, the second set, which Banks began making in the autumn of 1819, had to be upholstered by someone else. No evidence suggests who that person might have been, but many upholsters were active in New York City during the opening decades of the nineteenth century. Moreover, James Beekman had dealings with several upholsterers around the time he commissioned the seating. For example, he paid upholsterer John Voorhis $20.00 for sixty-four yards of fringe on October 5, 1818, an amount equal to the trim requirements of a single set. Each armchair required about six yards, for a total of forty-eight; one sofa took about fifteen yards, leaving a mere yard left over from the order. Beekman bought yard goods and "Borders" from another upholsterer, Peter D. Turcot, on July 18, 1819, but neither the price nor the yardage suggests any association with the tapestry seating. And Lawrence Ackerman charged him £5.14.00 on July 12, 1821, for "repairing sofa." Since John Banks had just made Beekman two new ones, which presumably did not yet need repair, Ackerman's bill must have referred to some other piece of furniture.[25]

Although variations in construction and upholstery techniques place the seating made by Banks into two clearly discernable groups, inconsistencies occur with regard to the tapestry covers: two chairs from the medial group have red covers and two chairs from the no-medial group have green covers. Denny's and Banks's bills for the earlier set indicate that it was completed by June 1819, more than six months before the second set. Given all of the similarities in upholstery and woodworking that exist within each set, imagining a mixing of the red and green tapestry sets from the outset seems untenable. Consequently, some covers from both sets must have been removed from the frames at a later date and reinstalled on different frames, and in some instances, installed on frames from the other (i.e., "wrong") set.

Payments to craftsmen in the mid-nineteenth century, although cryptic, suggest that such a switch likely occurred. In 1844 James William Beekman (1815–1877), who had inherited Mount Pleasant and other estate assets from his childless uncle James Jr., paid H. Haddaway (possibly Henry Hathaway of uncertain birth and death dates) for "rubing & varnishing" and occasionally oiling, polishing, and repairing a lot of furniture. In addition to one entry for twenty-two chairs, the bill lists the two tapestry sets, continued on the back as "2 sofas" and "16 chairs." Haddaway's work is not detailed but can be inferred by the associated charges, which are the same as the rubbing and varnishing costs on the front side. Three years later New York upholsterers Joseph Dixon and Henry Stoney of 555 Broadway billed James William for "repairing Tapestry chairs, $30.00." Several other entries in Beekman's cash book reference "repairing chairs," "arm chair, &c," "cleaning furniture," and "repairing furniture" over several years in the 1850s, although none specifically mentions the tapestry-covered furniture or gives further details. Various payments for house carpentry, wall papering, and new pieces of furniture signaled a lot of activity, all of which seems appropriate and customary, reinforcing ongoing use of and interest in the armchairs and sofas throughout changing domestic circumstances. About 1897, when Cornelia Augusta Beekman (1849–1917) had her full-length portrait executed in pastel (fig. 52), she appreciated these nearly eighty-year-old chairs enough that she posed with one, which can be recognized specifically

as the chair illustrated in figure 53. Regrettably, these references are too vague to determine more precisely what repairs to the sets were made and when.[26]

Physical evidence is more revealing. One of the two red-upholstered armchairs from the medial group has its red wool back panel cut away to the brass-tacked borders, exposing an old repair across the top rail of the back framing (see fig. 48). The slightly arched piece of wood immediately below the mahogany crest rail was wrapped in a strip of linen impregnated with glue. The only apparent function of the linen covering was to repair or stabilize damage. This mending technique, commonly used in the furniture making and upholstery trades, cannot be dated, but it demonstrates that some of the Beekman seating needed repair. Similarly, a row of unoccupied holes underneath the bottom edge of the outside-back panel is from an earlier campaign to secure a textile, perhaps this same fabric if the back panel had been switched at an earlier time.[27]

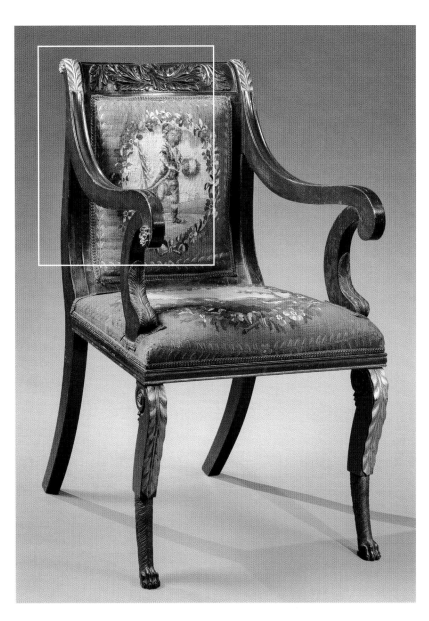

Figure 53 Armchair "F", with highlighted detail showing the area depicted in the portrait illustrated in fig. 52.

The remains of the present back panel are held in place by silk tape and brass tacks. Much of the silk on the Beekman furniture has deteriorated over time, and sorting through the physical evidence of the various tapes does not yield conclusive results. Accurate dating of upholstery trim typically requires accompanying bills of sale or other manuscript evidence of manufacture or purchase. If original, trims can also be dated by bills, documents, or other evidence related to the seating on which they are installed. In the case of the Beekman seating, there is little basis for concluding whether the silk or the wool tapes present are earlier, and reasonable scenarios can be posited in support of either sequence. One could assign the earlier date to the silk tape because it is the finer material and more in keeping with the ambitious qualitys of Beekman's tapestry seating. Original attachment of the silk tape may have consisted of few place-holding tacks and glue, neither of which would have left an imprint on the tapestry or chair frame definitive in establishing that it was the first trim used. The brass tacks have iron shanks, and some of their heads appear to have a gold or other metallic coating. These tacks may have been added later in the nineteenth century, both as a decorative treatment and as a way of reinforcing attachment of the fragile silk trim.

Of the three types of trim on the Beekman seating, silk tape is by far the most widely present, and on the sofas silk is the only decorative trim. The sofas also have a second, partially woven silk tape, representing a fourth trim. Used around the seat covers but not the back covers, it is the later of the two silk tapes. Both sofas have replaced foundation upholstery in the seats, which required removal of the original tapes and the tapestry seat covers when that work was done. As with the armchairs, the sofa backs are less disturbed. Although the outside back panels have been removed

Figure 54 View of the red sofa showing the open back.

and additional webbing has been installed over the original webbing and stuffing, the tapestry back covers seem not to have been removed (fig. 54). The new seat foundations were made with different materials and techniques. The new webbing, which matches that added to the backs, is wider and made of jute rather than linen (and possibly hemp), and it was installed with no gaps between the straps. The work was probably done in the late nineteenth or early twentieth century. Four of the no-medial armchairs have new foundations made of similar materials applied in a similar fashion. The repair of original foundation upholstery on seating from that group does not indicate that the materials and workmanship were inferior to that of the set with medial braces. Rather, the braces deflected the sitter's weight off the webbing and helped preserve the foundation upholstery. The four armchairs with newer foundations have deep red tapes, which represent the third and most recent generation found on that seating form (see fig. 47). Somewhat jagged renailing of the seat covers at the upholsterer's scissors-cut below the arm support also indicates reapplication of the seat covers following installation of the new foundations on these four chairs.

Examination of two armchairs with original foundation upholstery and wool trim yielded evidence that their tapestry covers had never been removed. Sections of upholstery were carefully detached from the back frame of one chair and the seat of the other. Separation of the back panel revealed a clear and solitary line of ten tacks spaced roughly an inch apart (fig. 55). In contrast, lifting a section of upholstery just below the crest rail of an armchair with new trim revealed multiple rows of tack holes, indicating that this back cover was either removed from the frame and reapplied or was from another chair in the set (fig. 56). There was no evidence of additional

Figure 55   Detail of the exposed back upholstery and tacks of armchair "F" with original trim (fig. 53). The loosened tacks were kept in place.

Figure 56   Detail of the exposed upholstery and multiple tack holes in the back of armchair "A" with replaced trim.

holes on the tapestry covers of the chairs with original trim, indicating that they were never on any other example. Two unoccupied nail sites were observed in the seat frame of yet another chair. The purpose of those sites remains unknown, but two holes is far too few to suggest the presence of an earlier upholstery cover. The extra holes may have been introduced by the upholsterer when he positioned and temporarily tacked the seat cover in place before attaching it permanently. Alternatively, the holes may have come from sprigs holding silk trim, now replaced for some unknown reason.

Finish evidence from the green sofa establishes the originality of these tapestry covers much more conclusively. That sofa has a shorter back panel than the red one, requiring the use of wide strips of mahogany veneer to cover the side edges of the inner frame that supports the tapestry panel between the mahogany rear stiles (see figs. 41, 42). Microscopy establishes that the finish layers on the veneer strips match those on other primary-wood components of the frame, indicating that they are original to the sofa frame. Had the green sofa been upholstered previously with any other back panel, it is highly likely that the dimensions of that textile would have covered the side edges, thus eliminating the need for this awkward solution. The veneer strips represent original modifications, as do the adjustments along the back edge of the seat covering—namely, the added strip of green textile and the now-missing mahogany coved molding.[28]

Establishing the originality of the tapestry covers to the seating frames is more than an exercise in connoisseurship. It directly challenges another physical finding—a yellow textile fragment trapped under a nail head on the frame of one of the armchairs. While this might suggest that the tapestry upholstery was preceded by an earlier covering, the evidence presented above precludes that conclusion.[29]

Understanding the Beekman Seating

The Beekman seating is innovative, extraordinarily well documented, and was owned by a leading New York City family—an unusual and potent combination for early American furniture history. Yet detailed study and focus on this furniture occurs only now, rather than decades earlier. A likely cause for this delay stems at least in part from some of the unfamiliar features integral to the two suites, coupled with the lack of manuscript documentation of manufacture that only recently has come to light. Although all aspects of the chair and sofa designs drew from an ornamental vocabulary in place in New York City by the late 1810s, the particular combinations and expressions in the Beekman seating differ from other New York work (as well as from that of other American urban centers), and the tapestry upholstery is unconventional. The rich historical documentation that now accompanies this furniture reveals craftsmen and circumstances that add a degree of mystery to the narrative. Collectively, this furniture raises engaging questions for which there are not ready answers. Nevertheless, the contribution of the Beekman seating to a more comprehensive understanding of early American furniture history is substantial.

Differences between the two seating groups are significant. In short, had manuscript evidence not survived for both sets, they likely would not have been assigned to the same maker. This circumstance alone makes the Beekman seating notable. The two sets are a reminder that accurate furniture history cannot be written without adequate manuscript references and support. These sets also document the occasional departure from consistency that occurred within or between historically related suites.

Notions of consistency deserve more attention. Setting aside construction and upholstery details that may be noticeable only to a small group of furniture historians, collectors, and connoisseurs, the differences in carving, curve of the chair backs, and other particulars may be seen clearly by more casual observers of the two Beekman sets. These differences exceed modern ideas about what degrees of consistency are generally "acceptable" in handwork. Did not James Beekman and his family notice, or care? Since one set copied the other, why were the workers in question not motivated to replicate the first set more accurately? From the perspective of furniture history, the differences between the two sets generate concerns. Specifically, they undermine generally accepted notions of consistency that characterize or define individual pre-industrial furniture shops in America. In turn, those identified shops form the building blocks of further maker identifications of anonymous furniture. What happens when furniture historians try to generalize about John Banks's work from this well-documented—yet inconsistent—furniture or use it to help interpret related furniture?

Some comfort may follow from recalling other anecdotes in American furniture history that, quite frankly, are equally disquieting. Specifically, there are a few, perhaps even several, well-documented instances in which furniture pairs (represented here by the two Beekman sets) are significantly different from each other. Other Beekman-owned furniture, for example, includes a "pair" of Chippendale-style cabriole-leg card tables that resemble each other only generally. Differences include front skirt veneers, carving details, shaping along the bottom edges of the rear fixed and swing rails, and construction details. Long considered a pair because they survived together with the same provenance, these two card tables may have been purchased at different times. To this point, furniture historian Lauren Bresnan found manuscript evidence for only one table—purchased in 1768 by James Beekman, builder of Mount Pleasant, from New York furniture maker William Proctor. A pair of turret-corner Philadelphia Chippendale card tables appear very similar but have significant construction differences. In 1770 Philadelphia cabinetmaker Thomas Affleck billed John Cadwalader for another pair of card tables that exhibit a similar range of differences. This pair was unambiguously listed as "2 Commode [i.e., serpentine] Card Tables @ £5" apiece. Their differences contrast with another pair of Cadwalader card tables, not listed in that or any other extant bill, composed of two truly identical tables, thus clearly demonstrating the degree to which craftsmen could match pieces of furniture if they intended. In the Affleck-Cadwalader easy chair, made at the same time, noticeable variations in carving exist between one side seat rail and the other. The set of chairs made for Samuel or Daniel Crommelin Verplanck of New York divides into two groups based on differences in the splat patterns and in decorative carving details. Last, the Livingston pair of New York sofas with original tapestry covers exhibit significant differences in the frames, upholstery materials and construction, and tapestry covers. Although both are believed to have been made in New York at the same time, they are structurally dissimilar from one another. In addition, inlay decoration in the crests and arms looks different. Aside from subtle differences in the pictorial qualities of the tapestry covers and disparities—but unnoticeable to the casual viewer—in the size and placement of upholstery webbing that supports the seats, the original outer side and back panels are strikingly different. One sofa uses a red harrateen or moreen, whereas those of the other combine blue velvet out sides, applied with the nap on the inside (see figs. 43, 44), with the same red outside back as the first sofa. The color selections of the out sides create inexplicable differences in the appearance of this pair.[30]

Explaining the differences between the two groups of Beekman seating is as difficult as understanding other unmatched pairs that occur in American furniture history. Some scholars propose that mismatches stemmed from adverse circumstances related to filling large furniture orders promptly, leading shop owners to subcontract into the broader furniture-making community and to lower their expectations and standards accordingly, since these irregular work relationships led to disparities in the finished products. That may be so, but it does not explain why a customer accepted such differences. Any discontentment would likely undermine future commissions, both from customers and their social connections to other potential customers. In short, it seems to be an unnecessary risk. Alternatively, those peccadillos may not have been meaningful to owners and consequently were simply not noticed. In contrast, the modern material world of highly regulated production, in which product differences simply do not exist, may indelibly have shaped and biased modern interpretations accordingly. In the case of the Beekman seating, acceptance of the differently colored and designed tapestry sets appears to represent expediency: two or more identical sets of eight, single larger sets, or other alternatives were simply not available when Beekman wished to acquire. Similarly, the lack of direct pairing of the Livingston sofa covers indicates that even in Paris tapestries must have been insufficient in the early nineteenth century. But the parallel differences between the two Beekman sets of frames (and the Livingston sofa frames) argues against expediency, since both Beekman sets used the same readily available materials and were made mere months apart by the same maker. Teasing out reasons from available evidence to address these differences remains a challenge.

Another elusive question addresses why Beekman chose Banks to do the work. James Beekman was sixty years old when he purchased the tapestry covers in 1818. According to historian Elizabeth Bates, he had just completed a new and expensive octagonal room added onto Mount Pleasant, which was the likely destination for the new seating. The architectural work began soon after his mother, Jane Keteltas Beekman, died and he assumed full control of the house. Clearly, this building addition, the exotic tapestry covers, as well as an expensive "carpet" listed on the same invoice at $60, versus $44 and $43 for each of the two seating sets, signaled Beekman's pursuit of the opulence and status appropriate to his position in society. But why Banks? If Beekman sought to convey worldliness and refinement through his new seating furniture, why not use the services of such proven and prestigious craftsmen as Lannuier or Phyfe, to say nothing of their many notable and established competitors? Young John Banks was just on the verge of adulthood when he received this commission. His father, Henry, a year or two younger than Beekman, seems a more likely candidate for the work. Nonetheless, John Banks acquitted himself well. Perhaps he had signaled his capabilities in some way that history simply does not reveal.[31]

To get each set of eight armchairs and one sofa made, Banks engaged four different types of craftsmen. Furniture makers made the wooden frames. Carvers carved the feet and ornamentation. Gilders and finish specialists applied the gilded, bronzed, and varnished surfaces. Upholsterers built up the foundations and tacked on the tapestries and tapes. In each instance, the resulting physical features of one set differed from those of the other, indicating that the team assembled to make one set was not the same as the one for the other. Even the frames must have been made by different furniture makers, despite Banks's being one himself. Aside from William Denny, the historical record does not reveal the names of any of the other craftsmen besides Banks. It is tempting to think that Banks drew his teams from geographically proximate sources. His immediate neighbors on Beekman Street included cabinetmakers; a chairmaker named William Brown Jr. (1785–1819), who apprenticed to Duncan Phyfe in 1802 but is listed in directories as a maker of inexpensive, painted fancy chairs from 1811 to 1819; a carver; and a finisher or "varnisher." As attractive as this picture of proximity and cooperation may be, specific historical evidence argues otherwise. William Denny worked some four blocks away, as far or farther than other furniture-making enclaves, confirming that proximity was not the reason Banks hired him. Similarly, James Beekman's dealings with other upholsterers between 1818 and 1821 (cited above) led him to different neighborhoods in the city. What is striking about these documented relationships with craftsmen is the seeming absence of allegiance to specific individuals.[32]

Given the differences between the two Beekman sets, dramatically underscored by the red and green sets of tapestry covers, the question arises as to which set came first (figs. 57, 58). Far from prompting an idle historical exercise, this question brings into sharp focus a wide assortment of beliefs, assumptions, and theories that drive American furniture identification in general. No compelling answer emerges. In fact, almost every observation that might argue one set is the earlier has neutralizing counter-evidence in the other set.

The green and red tapestry covers display designs that suggest different style periods. The green covers have scenes below tasseled festoons and flowers of varied sizes, evoking classic eighteenth-century design. In contrast, the red set has more constrained oval pictorial medallions with floral borders in the center of each rectangular panel; delicate rows of single leaves

Figure 57   Medial armchair "G" with green upholstery.

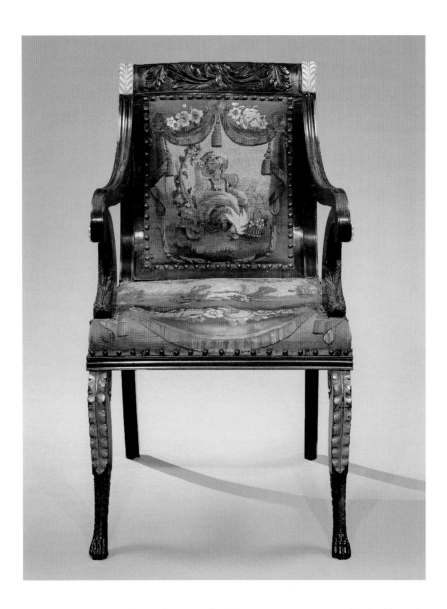

define the outer borders. The overall effects appear more neoclassical in scale and arrangement. Regardless of the styles suggested by the decoration, each tapestry set was likely new when acquired in 1818, a timeframe that underscores the persistent stylishness of these decorative schemes. Throughout the long history of tapestry weaving in France, designs were copied and re-copied, revived and reproduced.

A case can be made that the chairs with medial braces are earlier based on construction. The practice of making chairs and other seating forms with front-to-rear bracing was well established in New York long before Beekman commissioned his chairs and sofas. It is conceivable that Banks started out using braces but abandoned them to save labor and material costs. Decorative arts scholars have shown that seminal objects were ocassionally over-engineered. However, the larger seat rails of the no-medial chairs make those objects structurally equivalent, or at least nearly so.

At first glance, nail types might help establish a chronology. Use of rose-headed wrought iron nails in the no-medial chair set, and cut nails in the

Figure 58   No-medial armchair "A" with red upholstery.

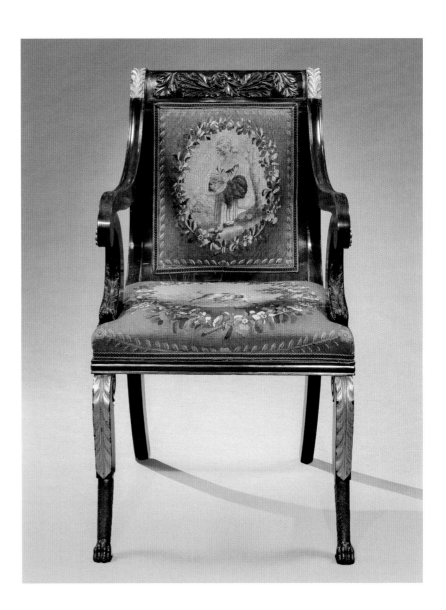

other, is clearly visible in x-rays (see figs. 23, 24). Wrought nails were used throughout the seventeenth and eighteenth centuries. Machine-made cut nails, which were more efficient to make and produced a more effective fastener, came later, broadly entering the marketplace in the late eighteenth century. However, wrought nails continued in regular use through the 1820s, creating an overlap that subverts the value of this piece of evidence in arguing for the earlier chair set. Indeed, the presence of each type of nail in these two sets, made in the largest urban environment and market in America, underscores the ongoing availability and acceptability of each to craftsmen.

The presence of dowels as original construction in each set also eliminates that feature as a determinant of which set came first. However, where and how the dowels were used suggests another strategy. Use of the long reinforcing dowels in the curved arm supports of the medial group was undoubtedly a response to short-grain splitting in other, similar circumstances. Short-grain splitting did not occur immediately, nor did it happen all of the time. Experienced furniture makers knew the risks of such construction and, like the compilers of the 1802 London price book who inserted an extra charge for dowelling tenons, they learned how to compensate. But why weren't reinforcing dowels used in the arms of the no-medial group? Did John Banks decide to forego them, or did someone working for him on this commission make that decision without Banks's knowledge?

The dowels used in the no-medial group performed a different function. They attached a thin crest rail that curved in two directions to the abutting rear stiles without a tenon. This dowel use underscores the more daring qualities of the thinner crest. Who was responsible for this design change? Did John Banks make this decision? Broad-based surveys of documented work from individual shops have established that some furniture makers produced highly consistent results, whereas others exhibited considerable—sometimes great—variation in construction and workmanship. Furniture historians have often explained these circumstances by postulating large and changing work forces within the shop in question, but that does not explain consistent qualities of the work from other large and complex shops. Perhaps that depended more upon the personality of the shop master. One shop master may have been interested in getting the job done, whereas the other was more interested in getting the job done his way. In sum, although there are many striking differences between the two sets of chairs—differences that appear to embody great potential for informative analysis—the differences are evenly distributed between the sets on the one hand and have concurrent use on the other. Identifying one set as earlier than the other is impossible without benefit of further evidence.[33]

All details and historical nuances aside, the Beekman seating anchors style and construction practices in New York with substantial physical and written evidence. Because New York was the leading city in the nation, its products and procedures surely influenced early American furniture history in general. The Beekman seating also explores new territory in the use of French woven tapestry covers—elite textiles for the bourgeoisie. The armchairs and sofas test the limits of connoisseurship and the ability to "read" non-verbal documents, namely the furniture itself.

ACKNOWLEDGMENTS For assistance with this article, the author thanks Mark Anderson, Elizabeth Bidwell Bates, Travis Bowman, Nancy Britton, Stuart Feld, Hugh P. Glover, Gretchen Guidess, Amy Henderson, Margaret K. Hofer, Yadin Larochette, Ridgely Kelly, Peter Kenney, Marjin Manuels, Robert Mussey, Susan Newton, Michael S. Podmaniczky, William Rutledge, Melanie Smith, Kenneth F. Snodgrass, Amanda Thompson, Gino Vidal. Throughout this long and complex writing project, Frank Levy and the Levy Gallery have provided invaluable assistance.

1. Esther Singleton, *The Furniture of Our Forefathers*, pt. 4 (New York: Doubleday, Page, August 1901), pp. vii, x, 289–90. This serial publication was subsequently reissued as a monograph in several subsequent editions. Illustrated and discussed in Luke Beckerdite and Margaret K. Hofer, "Stephen Dwight Reconsidered," in *American Furniture*, edited by Luke Beckerdite (Hanover, N.H.: University Press of New England for the Chipstone Foundation, 2016), pp. 154–55. Singleton, *Furniture of Our Forefathers*, pt. 4, p. vii, "List of Illustrations" captions.

2. "Family recollections dictated by Mary Beekman de Peyster, widow of William Axtell de Peyster [1793–1856] and daughter of John Beekman [1768–1843]," museum accession notebook X.200+, accession sheet X.470a-p, New-York Historical Society. *The New York Cabinetmaker & His Use of Space*, loan exh. cat., New-York Historical Society, January 6 to May 31, 1976, organized by Mary Black with assistance of Berry B. Tracy and other Metropolitan Museum of Art curators (New York: New-York Historical Society, 1976). Banks's birth and death dates are not clear. The New York City Jury Census of 1819 gives his age as 30 years. The time of his death is discussed below.

3. *Morning Chronicle* (New York), March 5, 1805, p. 3; *Columbian* (New York), February 21, 1817, p. 2.

4. *Repertory* (Boston), July 12, 1811, p. 3. *New-York Gazette and General Advertiser*, April 27, 1801, p. 3. A perusal of Geoffrey Beard, *Upholsterers and Interior Furnishings in England, 1530–1840* (New Haven: Yale University Press, 1997), shows that sets of eight chairs, often accompanying a sofa, became increasingly common through the second half of the eighteenth century in furniture ordered for grand English country houses (see pp. 201, 234, 236, 250).

5. *New-York Gazette and General Advertiser*, May 7, 1814, p. 4. *New-York Daily Advertiser*, March 5, 1818, p. 3.

6. Robert D. Mussey Jr., *The Furniture Masterworks of John & Thomas Seymour* (Salem, Mass.: Peabody Essex Museum, 2003), cat. no. 113. *The New-York Revised Prices for Manufacturing Cabinet and Chair Work* (New York: Southwick and Pelsue, 1810), p. 57. *Additional Prices Agreed Upon by the New-York Society of Journeymen Cabinet Makers* (July 1815): 5. *Supplement to the London Chair-Makers' and Carvers' Book of Prices* (London: printed by T. Sorrell, 1808), pp. 22–24, 62–63. "Grecian Front Legs" are noted in the 1802 *London Chair-Makers and Carvers' Book of Prices for Workmanship* (London: printed by T. Sorrell, 1802), pp. 24–26, with references to number illustrations in figs. 4–5 showing what today are popularly called saber legs. Thomas Sheraton, *The Cabinet Dictionary*, 2 vols. (1803; reprint, New York: Praeger Publishers, 1970), 1: 182; 2: 245–47. Thomas Hope in his *Household Furniture and Interior Decoration* (1807) and George Smith in his *Collection of Designs for Household Furniture and Interior Decoration* (1808) occasionally used the term as a modifier but gave it no specific definition.

7. Beekman Family Papers, box 37, file "1819," New-York Historical Society. For discussion of these three-party bills of exchange, see W. T. Baxter, *The House of Hancock: Business in Boston, 1724–1775* (New York: Russell and Russell, 1965), pp. 29–32. These financial instruments helped balance accounts in lieu of specie, which was chronically in short supply.

8. All city directories referenced were published by David Longworth until 1817 and by Thomas Longworth thereafter, typically with the title *Longworth's American Almanac, New-York Register, and City Directory*. John Banks occupied 62 Beekman St. in 1819–1820, 60 Beekman St. from 1822 to 1825, and 51 Beekman St. in 1825–1826. *New-York Evening Post*, December 31, 1821, p. 2. New York City Department of Records, Municipal Archives. Censuses were taken in 1816, 1819, and 1821 only. They are organized by street address. "Letters of Administration (New York County, New York), 1743–1866," vol. 21, 1825–1826, item 224, New York, Wills and Probate Records, 1659–1999," for John Banks, Ancestrylibrary.com, https://www.ancestrylibrary.com/interactive/8800/005523639_00591?pic=5999219. That John's mother, rather than his father, was given power of attorney reinforces the likelihood that his father, namely Henry, was no longer living. "New York City Municipal Deaths, 1795-1949" FamilySearch.org database. The death record states that Banks died of consumption. New York Municipal Archives, New York; FHL microfilm 447,545.

9. *New-York Evening Post*, August 18, 1821; *New-York Spectator*, August 21, 1821. *New-York Evening Post*, May 5, 1821. *New-York Columbian*, July 18, 1818, p. 2; *Mercantile Advertiser* (New York), April 9, 1819, p. 2. In 1806 newspapers reported the trial and execution of John Banks of Nieuwpoort, Belgium, who murdered his wife, Margaret, in March 1805. *Morning Chronicle* (New York), June 5, 1806, p. 2.

10. Tall clock: Sotheby's, *American Paintings, Furniture, Folk Art and Silver*, New York, September 27–28, 2011, lot 90; dining table: Sotheby Parke Bernet, *Americana*, New York, October 23–24, 1981, lot 456. Patriotic sentiments stirred by Lafayette's visit occasioned mass-

production of several domestic objects, such as English transfer-printed ceramics and American-made molded glass flasks and salts.

11. William Rutledge, "Measures of the Beekman Armchairs" (unpublished research paper, author's possession, January 2001). All wood identification is by eye. The front legs of both sets are 21 inches apart, but the back legs of the no-medial set measure 18 inches apart whereas the medial set back legs measure 18⅜ inches apart.

12. Finish characterization for each of the two sets is beyond the scope of this study. Marijn Manuels (Metropolitan Museum of Art) has examined the finishes on some of the Beekman seating. For history and analysis of patinated bronze, see Robert D. Mussey Jr., "Verte Antique Decoration on American Furniture: History, Materials, Techniques, Technical Investigations," in *Painted Wood: History and Conservation*, edited by Valerie Dorge and F. Carey Howlett (Los Angeles: Getty Conservation Institute, 1998), pp. 242–54.

13. Square tenons cut from curved furniture parts are diagrammed in pl. 7 of the 1817 *New-York Book of Prices for Manufacturing Cabinet and Chair Work*, reproduced as fig. 45 in Peter M. Kenny, Frances F. Bretter, and Ulrich Leben, *Honoré Lannuier: Cabinetmaker from Paris* (New York: Metropolitan Museum of Art, 1998).

14. Philip D. Zimmerman, "The Art and Science of Furniture Connoisseurship," *Antiques* 152, no. 1 (July 1997): 97. Lucy Wood illustrates an x-ray of an Italian armchair, ca. 1806, that uses dowels to hold a carved griffin's head arm support in place (*The Upholstered Furniture in the Lady Lever Art Gallery*, 2 vols. [New Haven: Yale University Press with National Museums Liverpool, 2008], 2: cat. no. 67, fig. xxiii 67j). Wood notes dowels in several English-made chairs, but she does not always distinguish carefully between round tenons and true dowels.

15. *Philadelphia Cabinet and Chair Makers' Union Book of Prices for Manufacturing Cabinet Ware* (Philadelphia: printed for the Cabinet and Chair Makers by W. Stavely, 1828), pp. 36–37. *The New-York Book of Prices for Manufacturing Cabinet and Chair Work* (New York: Harper Brothers, 1834), p. 185. *The New-York Book of Prices for Manufacturing Cabinet and Chair Work* (New York: J. Seymour, 1817), p. 143. Charles F. Montgomery, *American Furniture: The Federal Period* (New York: Viking Press, 1966), pp. 19, 23–25. Among other price books, he discusses *The Cabinet-Makers' Philadelphia and London Book of Prices* (1796), an agreement on prices that directly converted London circumstances to Philadelphia. *The London Chair-Makers' and Carvers' Book of Prices*, p. 17. Another construction complication with curved seat frames was that they were typically made of two or more separate pieces of wood glued or "laminated" together with the grain direction of each laminate at an angle to the adjoining wood. This construction prevented warping and splitting of the rails. Montgomery, *American Furniture*, cat. nos. 66–67. For examples of other New York and Philadelphia round- or bell-seat chairs, see cat. nos. 68, 71, 94, and 95.

16. Kenny et al., *Honoré Lannuier*, no. 99. Thanks to Hugh Glover, conservator of furniture and wooden objects, Williamstown Art Conservation Center, for this observation. The 1803 date appears underneath an 1826 repainting campaign. Tavern licenses confirm that the tavern was first established in 1803 and changed hands some twenty years later. *Lions & Eagles & Bulls: Early American Tavern and Inn Signs from the Connecticut Historical Society*, edited by Susan P. Schoelwer (Hartford, Conn.: Connecticut Historical Society in association with Princeton University Press, 2000), cat. no. 36. The sign made ca. 1825–1835 for the Collins Hotel, Straitsville, Connecticut (a section of Naugatuck), also uses four dowels (ibid., cat. no. 42). Montgomery, *American Furniture*, cat. no. 74. Thanks to Michael S. Podmaniczky for this observation.

17. For a well-documented 1816 sofa with winged paw feet by Duncan Phyfe, see Jeanne Vibert Sloane, "A Duncan Phyfe Bill and the Furniture It Documents," *Antiques* 131, no. 5 (May 1987): pls. 1, 2, fig. 3.

18. Edith A. Standen to Philip D. Zimmerman, letter, February 28, 1997, author's possession, February 28, 1997; Philip D. Zimmerman, "The Livingston Family's Best New York Federal Furniture," *Antiques* 151, no. 5 (May 1997): 721. *Dunlap's American Daily Advertiser* (Philadelphia), May 15, 1793, p. 1. *Columbian Centinel* (Boston), November 9, 1796, p. 3. Thanks to Robert Mussey for providing this reference. H[arman] G. Rutgers and Co. (active 1796–1808) of New York City, advertisement, *New York Daily Advertiser*, June 17, 1801, p. 3. Arden and Close advertised an auction of "eight chairs and three sofas of Goblin [sic] Tapestry, in perfect order" in the *New York Daily Advertiser*, April 27, 1801, p. 3. Monson and James Hayt offered "several elegant sets of tapestry for covering chairs, sofas, &c." in the *New York Daily Advertiser*, July 28, 1801, p. 3. *New-York Gazette and General Advertiser*, April 27, 1801, p. 3. Diary entry of

May 24, 1803, *The Diary and Letters of Gouverneur Morris*, edited by Anne Carey Morris, vol. 2 (New York: Charles Scribners Sons, 1888), p. 438. Morris served as minister plenipotentiary from 1792–1794. David Hanks, "Armchair," in *Philadelphia: Three Centuries of American Art: Bicentennial Exhibition, April 11-October 10, 1976* (Philadelphia: Philadelphia Museum of Art, 1976), cat. no. 170. Original tapestry covers remain on a set of eight American armchairs and one sofa owned by the New York State Office of Parks, Recreation and Historic Preservation (acc. nos. JJ-1987.23–.31). The seating, made of rosewood and rosewood veneer on ash and likely made in New York City in the 1830s or 1840s, seems to have descended in the John Jay family, although its provenance needs confirmation.

19. For example, compare the red sofa to Sotheby's, *Important French and Continental Furniture and Tapestries,* London, June 14, 1991, lot 191. See Edith Appleton Standen, *European Post-Medieval Tapestries and Related Hangings in the Metropolitan Museum of Art*, 2 vols. (New York: Metropolitan Museum of Art, 1985), 1: 376–377 and cat. no. 54; 2: 595, fig. 86h.

20. For a sofa with a rectangular seat that has an oval back, which cuts through the rectangular tapestry border, see Christie's advertisement for the Fermor-Hesketh Collection, *Antiques* 133, no. 6 (June 1988): 1277.

21. Similar treatment is visible on the John Jay sofa.

22. Zimmerman, "The Livingston Family's Best," pp. 716–21.

23. These straps may incorporate hemp as well as linen. This and other technical analyses of the Beekman upholstery materials, including dyes, are beyond the scope of this study. Nancy Britton, textile conservator at the Metropolitan Museum of Art, has analyzed materials for some of the Beekman seating. The presence of wood blocks can be determined by pressing the upholstery at that corner location.

24. *New-York Gazette*, October 26, 1819, p. 2. Notice of the dissolution of the partnership between Denny and Fine appeared in the *Mercantile Advertiser* (New York), November 10, 1819, p. 3.

25. Beekman Family Papers, box 37 "Beekman Family Estates, Accounts, and Correspondence," files "1818" and "1819."

26. Ibid., box 7(A) "Household Recipts," folder 13, 1843–1844, invoice dated September 14, 1844. Ibid., bound volume 36 "James W. Beekman Cash Book, 1843–1858," p. 152, November 6, 1847. Ibid., p. 288, Joseph Dixon, May 30, 1851; p. 354, F. A. Vrede, February 5, 1853; p. 372, F. A. Vrede, October 30, 1853; p. 416, James E. Connor, March 3, 1857.

27. There is a slim chance that this thin, linen-wrapped piece of wood represents original construction and upholstery, but no evidence of such a practice is known. Another medial-set armchair "J" also has glue-impregnated linen on this chair part. Other Beekman armchairs were not examined for this detail because existing upholstery hides this construction location from view.

28. Susan Buck, "Cross-Section Microscopy Report: Beekman Sofa Finish Analysis" (report written for Bernard and S. Dean Levy, Inc., October 9, 2018).

29. Nancy Britton, textile conservator, Metropolitan Museum of Art, to the author, various personal communications, 2005–2006.

30. One is published in Morrison H. Heckscher, "The New York Serpentine Card Table," *Antiques* 103, no. 5 (May 1973): 981, pl. 3. Heckscher notes that one table bears chalk initials "IWB" on the underside of the top, probably for James William Beekman (1815–1877), the same person who inherited the John Banks seating from his uncle, James Beekman Jr. For comparative photographs of the two tables, see Sotheby's, *Important Americana*, New York, January 21–22, 2000, lot 718. On January 15, 1768, Beekman purchased "a card table, a china ditto and four windsor chairs" for £11.4.0. Lauren L. Bresnan, "The Beekmans of New York: Material Possession and Social Progression" (master's thesis, University of Delaware, 1996), p. 54. Gregory J. Landrey, "Two Gaming Tables: A Comparison," *Antiques & Fine Art* 8, no. 6 (summer/autumn 2008): 172–79. Nicholas B. Wainwright, *Colonial Grandeur in Philadelphia: The House and Furniture of General John Cadwalader* (Philadelphia: Historical Society of Pennsylvania, 1964), pp. 44, 118–21; Mark Anderson, Gregory Landrey, and Philip D. Zimmerman, *Cadwalader Study* (Winterthur, Del.: Henry Francis du Pont Winterthur Museum, 1995), pp. 3–17, 21–23, 32–33. Morrison H. Heckscher, *American Furniture in the Metropolitan Museum of Art. 2: Late Colonial Period: The Queen Anne and Chippendale Styles* (New York: Random House for the Metropolitan Museum of Art, 1985), no. 34. Zimmerman, "The Livingston Family's Best," pp. 716–21.

31. Historical evidence confirming where the Banks seating was used has not come to light. Aside from the obvious inferences provided by sixteen new armchairs and a new octagonal

room, the only explicit mention of this seating used in that room occurs in Fenwick Beekman's introduction to Philip L. White, *The Beekmans of New York in Politics and Commerce, 1647–1877* (New York: New-York Historical Society, 1956), pp. xviii–xix. Fenwick Beekman was born in 1882, eight years after Mount Pleasant had been demolished. In 1840 Mount Pleasant was relocated a block south to avoid demolition for the eastward continuation of 51st Street. An article in the *New York Times*, October 12, 1872, details the house interior but makes no mention of an octagonal room. The 1840 foundation did not preserve or recreate the ground floor. Possibly, the octagonal room was not reconstructed in the new location.

32. Peter M. Kenny et al., *Duncan Phyfe: Master Cabinetmaker in New York* (New York: Metropolitan Museum of Art, 2011), p. 46.

33. For additional comment, see Philip D. Zimmerman, "Method in Early American Furniture Identification," in Thomas P. Kugelman and Alice K. Kugelman with Robert Lionetti, *Connecticut Valley Furniture: Eliphalet Chapin and His Contemporaries, 1750–1800* (Hartford: Connecticut Historical Society Museum, 2005), pp. 480–81, 484.

Appendix A

Medial Group

- A medial seat brace made of tulip poplar is half-dovetailed (i.e., one side of the brace is a dovetail, whereas the other side is straight) at each end into the front and rear seat rails.
- The rear seat rail attaches to the rear stiles with double tenons; the side rails attach to each front and rear stile with one tenon (positioned near the outside of the rail); the front rail attaches to the stiles with double tenons.
- Long, narrow tulip poplar glue blocks are attached to the side rails and abut the front seat rail.
- The seat rails, made of ash, are less than 1-1/2 inches thick and are thinner than those on the no-medial group. The seat rails have slight chamfers at the inside rear corner where they meet the rear stiles.
- The rear seat rail is longer (measured from chair side to chair side) than that on the no-medial group. The longer rail creates a squarer seat frame in plan.
- The rear stay rail of the back (the lowermost structural element) is straight.
- The crest rail is thicker than that on the no-medial group. It attaches to the stiles with tenons.
- The tops of the arms have two broad flutes terminating in half-round niches.
- A scratch-bead defining the edge of the arm runs the length of the flutes and continues around the scrolled handhold.
- Blocks of wood above the seat rails and hidden by the tapestry upholstery define the height and shape of the seat upholstery in the front corners.
- The top crosspiece of the interior framing members of the chair back (visible in X rays) buts against the vertical side pieces.
- The interior frame of the chair back attaches to the mahogany crest rail with L shaped cut nails.

No-medial Group

- The seat framing has no medial brace.
- The rear seat rail attaches to the rear stiles with double tenons; the side rails attach to each front and rear stile with one tenon (positioned near the center of the rail); the front rail attaches to the stiles with a single tenon.
- Large square glue blocks made of ash and chamfered on the inside corners are attached to the front corners of the seat frame.
- The seat rails are about 1-5/8 inches thick—more substantial than those in the medial group. These thicker seat rails are noticeably wider than the rear legs and exhibit no chamfering, as on the medial group.
- The rear seat rail is shorter than that on the medial group, creating a greater taper of the side seat rails in plan toward the rear.
- The rear stay rail of the back is curved (concave when viewed from the front of the chair).
- The crest rail is thinner than that on the medial group. It attaches to the stiles with three dowels.

- The tops of the arms are molded to a serpentine profile. The termination of this molding continues farther down the top of the arm into the handhold than does the fluted decoration in the medial group.
- A scratch-bead on the arms stops before the handhold.
- Edge rolls made of grass create the square loft of the seat upholstery.
- The top crosspiece of the interior framing members of the chair back (visible in X rays) fits into a notch cut into the vertical side pieces.
- The interior crosspiece of the chair back attaches to the mahogany crest rail with rose-headed nails.

Appendix B

ARMCHAIR CARVING DIFFERENCES

Medial Group

- The foliate carving within the crest rail panel appears flatter and exhibits surface texture; the ground is not as smooth as on the no-medial crests.
- Volutes atop each front leg coil around farther than those on the no-medial group. The carved bracket beneath each volute has one fewer chisel-cuts than that on the no-medial group.
- The water leaves on the legs undulate to a greater degree, and the leaf ends are shaped.
- The center spine down the legs has a shallow hollow in the upper section.
- The fur carved into the feet has larger strands of fur, which clump into coarser and more irregular groupings.
- Massing of the toes of the animal paw feet is more ovoid, and toes are longer and more rat-like.

No-medial Group

- The foliate carving within the crest rail panel appears more three-dimensionally modeled and has smooth surfaces throughout.
- Volutes atop each front leg do not coil around as much as those in the medial group. The carved bracket beneath the volute has more chisel cuts than in the medial group.
- The water leaves on the legs do not undulate as much, nor are the leaf ends scalloped; the triangular tip at the bottom has noticeably less inset cutting and edge detail.
- The center spine has a narrow, but deeper hollow down the center in the upper section.
- The leg fur lies in finer and more regular strands.
- The toe knuckles of the animal paw feet stand higher and squarer, more like lion's paws, and they have prominent and sharply defined claws.

Appendix C

Green sofa (associated with the medial group)

- The seat rails are made of cherry, as are the large, rectangular glue blocks in front. The large square glue blocks in the rear are made of ash.
- The four tulip poplar medial braces attach to the front and rear seat rails with full dovetails.
- The foliate carved side panels below the cornucopia arm supports project about one-half-inch beyond the plane of the side seat rails.
- Fruit inside the cornucopia spills outside the plane of the side seat rail.
- The arm support has a ruffled collar around the cornucopia opening, the volute-carved handhold has more spirals, and the carved leaf out of the spiral angles back rather than down. The cornucopia is laminated.
- The arms are fluted along the top surface.
- The front-facing surface of the rear stiles is flat with beads cut into each outside edge.
- The stylized rosettes below the arm supports have imbrecated leaves (i.e., a row of leaves with another overlapping row in front). The leaves have notched edges and are set against a stippled background.
- The recessed panels in the front seat rail have square edges without beading.

Red sofa (associated with the no-medial group)

- The seat rails are made of ash, as are the small rectangular glue blocks in front and small triangular blocks in the rear.
- The four tulip poplar medial braces attach to the front and rear seat rails with half dovetails.
- The foliate carved side panels below the cornucopia arm supports lie within the plane of the side seat rails.
- Fruit inside the cornucopia remains within the plane of the side seat rail.
- The arm support has an inclined, narrow collar around the cornucopia opening, the volute-carved handhold has a single spiral, and the carved leaf out of the spiral angles down rather than back. The cornucopia is not laminated.
- The arms are molded along the top surface.
- The front-facing surface of the rear stiles is molded in a serpentine shape with beads cut into each outside edge.
- The stylized rosettes below the arm supports have overlapping—but not imbricated—leaves. The leaves do not have notched edges, and they are set against a plain background.
- The recessed panels in the front seat rail have beaded edges around the inside.

The mahogany curule-base tabouret or stool was probably owned by James Beekman, Jr., the original owner of the tapestry armchairs and sofas, or by his nephew, James William Beekman, who inherited the bulk of James, Jr.'s, estate upon his death in 1837 (fig. A). Among Beekman family papers, H. Haddaway's September 14, 1844, bill for finish work on Mount Pleasant furniture then owned by James W. substantiates Beekman family ownership of two tabourets. Below the tapestry entries, described as "2 sofas" and "16 chairs" and a reference to "1 sideboard," is a charge for the same kind of finish work on "2 tabourets." Author Esther Singleton mentioned two tabourets among the tapestry sofas and armchairs in *The Furniture of Our Forefathers*, published in 1901. She published images of one sofa and two armchairs but did not illustrate a tabouret. Her description, "the sofas and tabourets show hunting and pastoral scenes," carelessly misidentified the top of the tabouret, assuming it is the one she referenced (fig. B). No record of a second tabouret exists at the New-York Historical Society.[1]

Physical evidence does not resolve the matter. The rare tapestry upholstery is very similar to the red set, which argues for a common manufacturing origin. Specifically, the floral vines that encircle the side panels and describe a rectangle on the top resemble the oval picture borders on the backs and seats of the set. However, its design does not tie it directly to the armchair and sofa set. The rose sprig featured in the center has no counterpart, and the tabouret tapestry lacks the simple stylized vine at the outer edges of the seat and back covers. Similarly, the original under upholstery of the tabouret is more similar to that of the red set than the green, but it does not seem to match. Design of the tabouret frame also separates it from the Beekman chair and sofa sets. No correspondence exists between the curule base, the turned stretcher, or the frame moldings and any features of the chair and sofa sets.

Historical circumstances argue that the tabouret was made later than the two chair-and-sofa sets. By convention, American curule furniture is dated as early as 1810, presumably based on designs printed in plate 3 of the 1808 *Supplement to the London Chair-Makers' and Carvers' Book of Prices* or design books of Thomas Hope and George Smith. The earliest evidence in America, however, does not occur until Duncan Phyfe presumably sketched a side chair with a curule (called a Grecian cross) front and chairback on a piece of paper that accompanied a January 4, 1816, bill to Charles N. Bancker of Philadelphia. Historical manuscripts document Phyfe-made curule stools from about 1837 to 1841, thus nearly reaching the 1844 Haddaway date. The tabouret is not mentioned in the several documents related to James, Jr.'s, tapestry, armchair and sofa frames, and upholstery purchases that range from 1818 to 1820, shortly after he inherited Mount Pleasant in 1817. Suggesting a date for the tabouret afterwards fits his documented circumstances, and it corresponds better stylistically, given the presence of the turned feet, bold ogee molding around the rails, and the complex turned medial stretcher.[2]

Figure B Detail of the top panel of the tabouret illustrated in fig. A.

Figure C Original foundation upholstery of the tabouret illustrated
in fig. A.

1. New-York Historical Society, Beekman Family Papers, Box 7(A) "Household Receipts,"
Folder 13, 1843-1844. Esther Singleton, *The Furniture of Our Forefathers*, Part IV (New York:
Doubleday, Page, August, 1901), pp. 289-290.

2. Thomas Hope, *Household Furniture and Interior Decoration* (1807; reprint ed., New York:
Dover Publications, 1971), pls. VI, VII, XII, XX, XXIX; George Smith, *A Collection of Designs
for Household Furniture and Interior Decoration* (1808; reprint ed., New York: Praeger, 1970),
pl. 53. Charles F. Montgomery, *American Furniture: The Federal Period* (New York: Viking
Press, 1966), cat. no. 72a. Peter M. Kenny, Michael K. Brown, Frances F. Bretter and Matthew A. Thurlow, *Duncan Phyfe: Master Cabinetmaker in New York* (New York: Metropolitan
Museum of Art, 2011), pp. 234-35, Appendix 2, nos. 2.5, 2.19.

Figure 1   Edward M. Rosenfeld, "Southwest
View of Old Swedes Church," Wilmington,
Delaware, April 20, 1934. (Historic American
Building Survey, Library of Congress.) The
church was built between 1698 and 1699.

Philip D. Zimmerman

Early Eighteenth-Century Swedish-American Furniture from Wilmington, Delaware

▼ A DOVETAILED CHEST prominently displayed today in the nave of Old Swedes Church (figs. 1, 2) prompts several questions that ultimately inform broader issues relevant to the history of early furniture made in Delaware and Pennsylvania. A paper label, framed and attached to the lid, quotes a 1713 church record mentioning "the chest given by Christian Joransson." By implication, the viewer is meant to assume that Joransson made this chest. But did he? No early American furniture made by Swedish settlers has yet been identified with reasonable certainty, and the Delaware Valley Swedish community in general remains poorly portrayed. This chest and two other early eighteenth-century pieces of furniture, all owned by the same church, warrant further investigation.

In 1638 part of a larger Swedish migration to the Delaware River Valley disembarked at Fort Christina (now Wilmington). They and others who arrived in successive years established farms in the area where the Christina and Brandywine Rivers empty into the Delaware. The settlers formed a Lutheran church in 1640, led by the Reverend Reorus Torkillus (1608–1643). Fifteen years later, armed Dutch forces under Peter Stuyvesant (1610–1672) took control of the fledgling colony of New Sweden, but with neither an influx of their own countrymen nor a minister of their own, the Dutch who remained worshiped in the Swedish church. That church, named Holy Trinity but commonly called Trinity Parish, sustained Swedish vitality

Figure 2   Chest, probably made by Christian Joransson (1664–1716), Wilmington, Delaware, 1700–1713. Walnut and tulip poplar. H. 24½", W. 48", D. 20¾". (Courtesy, Trinity Episcopal Church; photo, Gavin Ashworth.)

through much of the eighteenth century despite changes and gaps in pastoral leadership. In the seventeenth century, Trinity Parish enjoyed a modest presence in the young colony until the arrival of the Reverend Erik Björk (1668–1740) in 1697. Björk was one of three pastors dispatched by Swedish King Charles XI (1655–1697) to bolster struggling congregations of the Swedish Church in the Delaware Valley. Within a year, the energetic and capable Björk had unified the divided church community on both sides of the Christina River and persuaded its parishioners to build a substantial stone church building, which stands today as Old Swedes.[1]

The Chest

On June 24, 1701, Björk wrote: "Talked of a Church chest in which the income of the Church should be put, and I relieved from the reckoning which is now burdensome to me." This entry in the Old Trinity Church records reveals that Björk persuaded lay leadership, called wardens or vestry, to assume responsibility for overseeing church finances. Pew rents and periodic collections at church services contributed toward paying the ministers' salaries and other costs. Careful management entailed regular account reconciliations. Given the absence of banks or other repositories, specie and other items of value had to be stored safely—hence the call for a church chest. At a general meeting of the congregation exactly twelve years later, Björk recorded:

> "resolved that the church money shall be deposited in the chest given to the church by Christian Joransson for that purpose, which should always stand in the church, the Churchwardens keeping the key of the same, so that whenever any of the members of the congregation want to make change in payment, it can be made to them by the Churchwardens in the church, and thus all mistakes and misunderstandings be obviated."

Christian Joransson (also called Christiern and Urinson) appears elsewhere in the church records as well. He pledged £1.10 in 1697 in support of the new church and appears in the accounting of those who contributed time, having worked 33 and 1/2 days on the roof and other carpentry tasks. He is named as the carpenter on the priest's house built in 1701. At a special meeting called in August, a year after the record of his gift of the church chest, Joransson was elected one of two "church watches," whose duties were to "keep good order and propriety both within and without the church during God's service" in an effort to stem the lack of "improvement" that the pastors observed among the congregation. Joransson died in 1716 at age fifty-two.[2]

The large chest on four ball feet still stands in Old Swedes Church. Its design, materials, and construction support its identification as Joransson's church chest. The front, sides, and lid are each made of two boards. Dovetails secure the front and side boards, but the rear—a solid piece of tulip poplar in excess of one inch thick—fits into a rabbet cut into the back edge of the chest sides and is nailed in place. Likewise, two tulip poplar bottom boards are nailed to the bottom edges. Four ball feet, the left front of which appears to be original, have round tenons that engage holes bored in the

Figure 3   Detail showing an original ball foot on the chest illustrated in fig. 2. (Photo, Gavin Ashworth.)

Figure 4   Interior view of the chest illustrated in fig. 2. (Photo, Gavin Ashworth.)

bottom (fig. 3). The top has cleats that are secured with clinched wrought nails and long wrought-iron hinges attaching it to the chest (fig. 4). Inside, the tulip poplar till on the left side has runners for a drawer below, now missing, as is the lid. None of these features contributes much to dating or regionalizing the chest beyond the very general. However, its extraordinary iron security couples with its provenance to fit neatly into the church record.

Twelve nailed and clinched wrought-iron brackets reinforce the structure of this chest. Although some bottom boards have detached from the nails holding them, the structural integrity of the chest remains intact. Two box locks set into the front are further indications of this object's function as a strong box (fig. 5). The locks are different—one measures 6" x 4½" and the other 5" x 3½"—but their escutcheons are identical and each keyhole is 15"

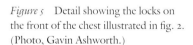
Figure 5   Detail showing the locks on the front of the chest illustrated in fig. 2. (Photo, Gavin Ashworth.)

in from the corner. This suggests that the locks were installed at the same time. The lock catches on the underside of the lid are old replacements over holes for the originals. There is no evidence of any type of locking device in the center, where a single lock would normally have been placed. The wrought-iron lifting handles at each end of the chest are sturdy and original.

Medieval Britain and Continental Europe (including Sweden) have strong traditions of iron-reinforced chests, typically with two or more locks, used to store cash and valuables securely. That tradition guided seventeenth-century church practices in which the multiple locks typically required two or more people in positions of authority to access the contents, thus ensuring another level of security. Chests of this type are exceedingly rare in America, perhaps due in part to the general lack of specie, which compelled church leaders to depend on written records to a greater extent. Unlike cash and valuable metals, written records were not readily negotiable, hence not a target of theft. Some iron-reinforced chests of European origin protected the possessions of immigrants during ocean crossings. These objects, commonly referred to as "sea chests," typically lacked feet. Assuming the Trinity Parish records correctly identify this chest as Joransson's gift, the question arises how and where he got the design, since he was American-born and probably had little exposure to this particular form. The Rev. Björk may have verbalized specifications when he "talked of a Church chest." Based on his stated relief from money oversight responsibilities, each of the two wardens of the church likely had a key.[3]

After Björk returned to Sweden with his family on June 29, 1714, Andreas Hesselius (1677–1733), an assisting pastor and brother of painter Gustavus Hesselius (1682–1755), assumed a leading role. Although not specifically named in the church records, Andreas was surely among "the pastors" who found church discipline wanting. Evidently, responsibility for the church chest had also lapsed. An accounting from July 9, 1715, reported a loss of seven shillings that should have been in the chest. More troubling,

> "the chest had been for the whole year without a lock, and the church on various occasions had stood open . . . . And to prevent any further loss . . . , the church wardens were ordered to procure a lock for the chest, they to remain hereafter responsible for all loss which may happen on account of the chest standing open in case they do not procure a lock."

A February 26, 1716, account entry records the purchase of "1 Key to chest for the money in the Church." At issue regarding identification of the iron-reinforced chest is the number of locks. Did two locks and two keys not provide adequate redundancy and security to prevent such a theft, especially given the short amount of time that had passed since Joransson's original gift of that object? A three-shilling charge on January 22, 1727, for "Repairing the church key," although it indicates that the wardens attended to their responsibilities, does not resolve these ambiguities, since the key in question might have locked the chest or the church door.[4]

A history of New Sweden published in 1759 resolves most uncertainty. The author, Swedish-born Israel Acrelius (1714–1800), who had assumed leadership of Trinity Church in 1749, published his account in Stockholm after his return to Sweden in 1756. Describing Hesselius's tenure, he stated, "a church-chest was provided, in which the moneys of the church were placed, and two keys were kept—one by each Church-Warden." Church records reveal that during Acrelius's pastorate, he had the church chest carried to his (i.e., "the priest's") house to "stand on the lower floor, for fear of fire." After the chest was moved, as reported some nine months later, warden Henry Colesberg received "the key." The records make no mention of a second key that should have been held by the second warden. Thereafter, an inventory was made "of all papers contained in the chest" so that "nobody could say that anything had been lost after the chest came into the priest house." That inventory, which survives among Trinity Church records, lists some thirty land deeds, articles of and releases from agreements, and other valuable papers, but no cash.[5]

The Armchair
In contrast to the chest, the "wainscot" armchair illustrated in figure 6 is not mentioned in the records of Trinity Church. Domiciled at Trinity Episcopal Church, the 1890 Gothic Revival building and primary house of worship of the congregation today, the chair's long history of ownership by the church has been confirmed by senior members of the congregation. The armchair resembles many Delaware Valley examples from the first half of

Figure 6   Armchair with later hinged shelf, probably Wilmington, Delaware, 1710–1730. Walnut. H. 47", W. 27¾", D. 29". (Courtesy, Trinity Episcopal Church; photo, Gavin Ashworth.)

Figure 7 Detail of the writing arm support and underside of the arm of the armchair illustrated in fig. 6 showing evidence of grooves cut for a panel.

the eighteenth century. Points of similarity include the crest with ogee shaping, prominent finials, and a fielded-panel back with quarter-round moldings that enrich the edges of the framing members. However, notable differences abound. Unlike any other wainscot armchair from that time and place, this one displays no turning. Moreover, the front stiles, seat rails, and stretchers are massive, measuring 2" x 3¼" in cross-section. The especially wide rail separating the two back panels has a bold, bolection molding—a feature occasionally found on the stiles of schranks. Another detail that distinguishes this chair is the shaping of the arms, which curve along a horizontal plane rather than vertically.

The hinged writing flap attached to the left side of the armchair is a later addition. The upright portion of the flap support (the wing that swiveled underneath the flap is now gone) sockets through a clear residue line, indicating a previous and different arrangement (fig. 7). Filled channels along

Figure 8 Armchair, southeastern Pennsylvania, 1715–1735. Walnut with tulip poplar. H. 48½", W. 23½", D. 18". (Courtesy, Philadelphia Museum of Art.)

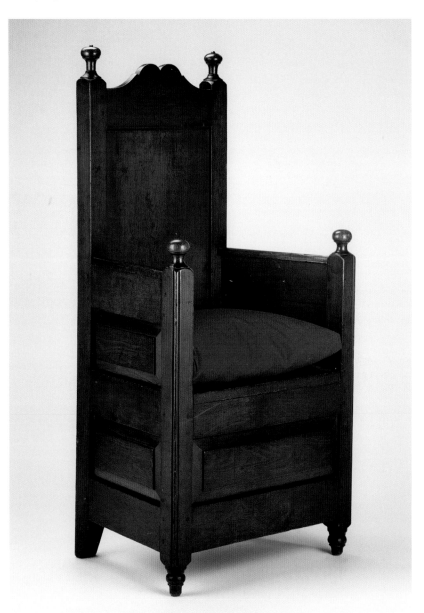

the tops, bottoms, and sides of the side seat rails, stretchers, and arms confirm the one-time presence of panels, which likely were removed when the flap was installed. Other enclosed wainscot armchairs, such as the one illustrated in figure 8, accommodated chamber pots, but the Trinity Church example never did, since the original two-board seat remains firmly attached to the seat rails (fig. 9). The seat overhang in front ends in shallow ogee corners that meet the front face of the stiles (fig. 10). When first installed, the seat boards were cut back at the sides to meet the now-absent panels. Wood pegs holding the seat in place do not enter the middle of the side rails, as in the front, but towards the inside edge to make room for the channel securing the base of the panel (fig. 11). The missing panels were probably fielded, similar to those in the chair back but without the surrounding quar-

Figure 9 Detail of the underside of the seat of the armchair illustrated in fig. 6, showing the original seat boards, a later board reinforcement, and evidence of drawer runners on the legs. (Photo, Gavin Ashworth.)

Figure 10 Detail showing the seat overhang and arm support of the armchair illustrated in fig. 6. (Photo, Gavin Ashworth.)

Figure 11 Detail showing the cut seat and filled channel for a panel on the armchair illustrated in fig. 6. (Photo, Gavin Ashworth.)

ter-round molding. Precedents exist for such paneling below the arms to face inward or outward, but the panels below the seat rails must have faced outward, as must have those at seat level. Patches on the inside corners of all four legs just below the seat rails, visible in figure 9, indicate the one-time presence of front-to-back runners that supported a side-hung drawer, which filled in the open space in front.

Figure 12 Side chair, probably Wilmington, Delaware, 1730–1750. Sassafras. H. 40½", W. 18¼", D. 20". (Courtesy, Winterthur Museum; photo, Lazlo Bodo.)

A prominent and distinguishing feature of this armchair is the upper arched panel of the back. It readily brings to mind several arched-panel spice box doors, but this treatment is different. Unlike the doors, in which the arch fits within a rectangle capped by the strong horizontal cornice molding of the box, the arch in the chair back follows and reinforces the arched outline of the center of the crest rail. Furniture historian Benno Forman, attempting to recognize the work of elusive Swedish furniture makers in the Delaware Valley, considered the arched crest rails he found in a few turned side chairs a possible Swedish feature. He was also aware of a sassafras side chair, acquired by Winterthur in 1991, associated with the Reverend John Eneberg (born 1689), pastor of Trinity Church from 1733 to 1742. It has a similar crest outline featuring prominent cusps at each side (fig. 12).[6]

A key to understanding this armchair more fully lies in considering another from the Limburg region of the Netherlands (fig. 13). This chair

Figure 13 Armchair, Limburg region of the Netherlands, 1764. (Courtesy, Rijksmuseum.)

bears the date 1764 on the crest rail along with "IHS" below a cross, suggesting church ownership and use. It shares several features that are otherwise not part of the Delaware Valley design vocabulary. The arms curve horizontally. The finials shaped from the tops of the rear stiles are not of the usual rounded form. The front stiles are massive like those on the Trinity Church chair and have similar trimming and ogee transitions above the seat. Lastly, the Dutch chair has panels under the arms as well as a front panel below the seat.[7]

The role of the Dutch in Delaware Valley furniture making is poorly defined at best. The Dutch conquest of New Sweden in 1655 did not foretell active and broad settlement. Rather, the Swedes remained culturally dominant until after 1682, when the English started to populate William Penn's grant quickly and thoroughly. The Reverend Andreas Rudman (1668–1708), pastor of Gloria Dei, the Swedish church in Philadelphia, wrote in 1700: "If anyone were to see Philadelphia who had not been there [before], he would be astonished beyond measure that it was founded less than twenty years ago." By the end of 1773, when Trinity Parish records begin to be written in English, acculturation of the Swedes into Anglican life was complete. Following the Revolutionary War and separation of the colonies from England, the Swedish Church recalled their pastors in America. Consequently, Trinity Parish joined the nascent Protestant Episcopal Diocese in Delaware, which adapted Church of England doctrine, and the vestry wrote a new charter in 1791. In contrast, the Dutch had little visible impact throughout this period, especially compared to their presence in New York and areas of New Jersey. In Delaware, their identity blurred as they became members of the Swedish Church—which was closest in language and custom—as the seventeenth century drew to a close.[8]

Distinctions between Dutch and Scandinavian furniture are similarly unclear. In rural furniture, often termed "rustic" by European furniture historians, the differences are ever more nebulous. Comprehensive surveys of Swedish furniture from different regions by Sigurd Erixon in 1925 and Sigurd Wallin in 1931 create useful profiles of the types of furniture made there. In addition to documenting Forman's observation of arched crest rails (although finding them in Swedish work does not eliminate their presence elsewhere), these multi-volume studies show similar Swedish finials and the arched panel below an arched crest as in the armchair. Because influences are mixed on both sides of the Atlantic, these favorable comparisons do not identify the American-made armchair firmly as Swedish in origin, but they convincingly establish that a Swede might have made it. Without this evidence, the 1764 Dutch chair would argue for Dutch manufacture assuming, despite its late date, that this chair represents a broader, yeomanry furniture form. No definitive answer is possible. Instead, it makes more sense to identify the ethnic source of the armchair in degrees of probability or likelihood. Accordingly, given its particular history of ownership within a Swedish community, it seems more likely to be of Swedish origin than Dutch, if such a distinction must be made. The chair could also represent the work of a Dutch craftsman who had joined the Swedish Church and community.[9]

The maker of the Trinity Church armchair was skilled. In addition to the design refinements around the seat, joinery of the back reveals detailed planning and effective execution. The quarter-round molding that borders each of the back panels was cut into the respective rails and stiles, meeting in miters at the corners. To continue the sight line from the edge of the molding upward into the seam between the stile and crest, the maker cut a rabbet into the stile to the same depth as the molding. Evidence of this work is only visible from the back looking down from the finial (fig. 14). The crest rail of the chair is made of a 9½"-wide plank, scalloped at the top and undercut with an arch at the bottom. Two tenons, rather than a single very long one,

Figure 14 Detail of the rabbeted joint securing a stile and the crest rail of the armchair illustrated in fig. 6. (Photo, Gavin Ashworth.)

Figure 15 Corner cupboard, probably Wilmington, Delaware, 1710–1740. Walnut with tulip poplar. H. 67½", W. 28½", D. 21". (Private collection; photo, Gavin Ashworth.)

likely attach it to the stiles. Four wooden pegs on one side and three on the other secure the joints. A similar redundancy of pegs in an arched rail occurs on a small corner cupboard with ball feet (fig. 15). Regrettably, the corner cupboard lacks an early history. Given all of the particulars of the Trinity Church chair, it and the corner cupboard were likely made by a joiner or a house carpenter who specialized in finer interior work.[10]

Dating the chair is more problematic. Forman maintained that wainscot chairs were made in the Delaware Valley from the time of Penn's settlement until the middle of the eighteenth century. Stylistic shifts were few, and those that occurred are often problematic as tools for dating. Considering the impact of ethnic origins or the woodworking capabilities of individual makers only complicates the picture. Assuming that this armchair was originally made for Holy Trinity Church, it almost certainly dates after completion of the priest's house in 1701—an important project that required a variety of woodworking resources—and fabrication of the chest, which might have been accomplished a few years before its documented presence in the church in 1713. A date range of 1715–1735 seems plausible for the chair. Swedish design features, like those associated with the chair, probably waned as British styles became increasingly dominant in the early decades of the eighteenth century. The absence of turned components on the chair may also speak to that object's date. Presumably the number of turners and other specialists in the woodworking trades increased during this period. In the absence of more precise dating tools, the corner cupboard assumes a more significant role in assessing the age of the chair. If the woodworking practices displayed in the arched rails of the chair crest and cupboard door are contemporaneous, then the presence of ball feet on the latter may offer clues to the age of both pieces. Although the feet on the cupboard and the Joransson chest are not identical, he remains a possible maker, despite his death in 1716. However, considerably more research is required to identify the capabilities of woodworkers in the lower Delaware River Valley before Joransson or any individual can be promoted without specific written references.[11]

The Desk

The slant-lid desk illustrated in figure 16 is roughly contemporaneous with the joined chair and the cupboard, but its place of manufacture is more difficult to determine. Although few contemporaneous Delaware examples are known, the desk's ownership by Trinity Church and the woods used in its construction—walnut primary with tulip poplar secondary (a common combination in the Middle Atlantic region)—suggest that it was made locally.

In the center of the fitted interior is a small drawer constructed with wedged dovetailed joints, a feature Benno Forman considered indicative of Germanic influence. The hinged lid is made of two boards. To counteract warping and to hold the boards together, the maker used two thick battens. The battens slide in dovetail-shaped channels cut into the underside and across the grain of the wood. This technique brings to mind similarly installed battens on the seat bottoms of Germanic board chairs, as well as the wooden cleats typically found on Germanic table tops.[12]

Although Germanic immigrants began arriving in the Delaware Valley during the 1680s, they came in significantly greater numbers beginning in the 1730s. The desk illustrated in figure 16 appears to predate that second wave of immigration. The inverted baluster shape and lower collarinos of the legs are rooted in seventeenth-century design. If the desk were made after 1730, legs with upright balusters or cabriole shaping would be more the norm. A Swedish table likely dating from the 1690s to the 1730s has leg turnings that are bolder than those on the desk but feature many of the same elements arranged in the same order: an inverted baluster with scored shoulders, a nearby ring or collar, and collarinos. In fact, this particular

Figure 16 Reading desk, probably Wilmington, Delaware, 1710–1740. Walnut with tulip poplar and hard or yellow pine. H. 36", W. 35¼", D. 26". (Courtesy, Trinity Episcopal Church; photo, Gavin Ashworth.) The second (middle) book stop on the desk lid and the two molding strips on the center top, all made of a resinous pine, are not original. Use of wire nails to secure them suggests they were added after about 1875. Other features of note include the iron lid hinges, which are especially well made, raising the question of whether they were made in the Delaware Valley or imported from Europe. The desk maker recessed slightly the underside edges of the lid along the front and sides. Presumably, this refinement was to smooth the surface that contacts the frame and perhaps to reduce the visible thickness of the lid. He also oriented the grain of the pigeonhole sides horizontally, so that end-grain shows. This departure from the norm may signal his lack of familiarity with construction details of this furniture form. Similarly, he reinforced the fitted interior by driving a peg through the exterior side of the case into the end of the low shelf that runs side-to-side.

elemental sequence appears to be common on Swedish tables if published examples are an indication of prevalence.

Forman acknowledged the widespread use of dovetailed battens on Italian board chairs; however, seating of the same basic type was made in much the same manner throughout Europe. Specific to this desk and its possible Swedish derivation, board chairs were common in Sweden. Most Swedish board chairs have stick-like legs that are socketed directly into the thick seat, but some have the legs socketed into dovetailed battens. On Swedish tables, dovetailed battens are commonly found on the undersides of tops; however, photographic evidence rarely if ever confirms the use of pins to secure the battens to the frame as on most Pennsylvania-German tables (fig. 17).[13]

Figure 17 Swedish table illustrated in Sigurd Erixon, *Möbler och heminredning i svenska bygder* (Stockholm: Nordiska museets förlag, 1925).

Similarly, the use of wedged dovetails may not be as indicative of Germanic work as Forman suggested. Conservator Christopher Storb has noted the use of wedged dovetails on three early chests of drawers signed by or otherwise documented to William Beakes III (1691–1761) of Bucks County, Pennsylvania, and later New Jersey, and on a Philadelphia scrutoir made in the 1710s. Because the origin and distribution of structural details like dovetailed battens and wedged dovetails are ambiguous, the Trinity Parish desk cannot be described definitely as Germanic. Indeed, slant-lid desks of this type were not a common Germanic furniture form. With its ethnic design origins open, a pre-1730 date for the desk is more plausible.[14]

As with the chest and the wainscot armchair, the desk has long been associated with Old Swedes Church. It is not specifically mentioned in the church records, but various entries support its use there. Following Swedish custom, the church provided schoolmasters who taught children to read and instructed them on the basics of Christianity. The Bible was the primary vehicle for literacy, and readings from that book were an integral part of church services. Parishioners were encouraged to bring their personal Bibles and psalm books, but such publications were scarce. In 1707 Holy Trinity received its share of "4 new church Bibles, Royal folio" and "40 Bibles octavo printed in Amsterdam" and sent by Swedish King Charles XII (1682–1718) in support of the several Swedish congregations in America. An entry in the records of Holy Trinity later that year mentions a reading from "the newly received big Bible." Folio books were typically as large as 18" x 12," thus requiring relatively large receptacles like boxes or desks to store, display, and use them.[15]

Several scholars have commented on the display of Bibles in Netherlandish contexts. In her book *Dutch New York* (1909), Esther Singleton wrote: "in many houses the great Bible . . . rested on a reading-desk . . . from which the head of the family read morning and evening." More recently, furniture scholar Peter Kenny observed: "Dutch Bibles were kept out for reference and display sometimes on a Bible desk or *bybellessenar*, a kind of desk on

Figure 18 Detail showing the backboard and dovetailed recess of the reading desk illustrated in fig. 16. (Photo, Gavin Ashworth.)

frame." Similar furniture forms were also common in Sweden. Most examples surveyed had flat tops, but those with slant-lids incorporated a book stop along the bottom edge that facilitated reading. The lids on these desks were hinged at the top, allowing convenient access to the interior but not enabling the lid to open outward to become a level writing surface. Reading, rather than writing, was the primary function.

The desk's long association with Old Swedes Church suggests that it may have been commissioned for use there rather than donated by a parishioner at some later date. If this is the case, the desk did not stand in front of the chancel on the side opposite the pulpit, a location traditionally occupied by lecterns, which were usually eagle-shaped and made of brass. The back of the desk is made of tulip poplar, indicating that it was not intended to be seen. The top has an old rabbet on the back edge and a dovetail-shaped recess cut into the center top edge that may relate to an early adaptation, such as the mounting of a bookshelf atop the desk (fig. 18).

Postscript

Trinity Parish's ownership of these three pieces of furniture establishes a provenance essential to their identification and interpretation. Although the chest is the only piece mentioned in church records, the other objects fit comfortably into the history of Old Swedes. The context is rich enough to suggest answers to another question: why did the church retain ownership of this furniture throughout the centuries? A combination of active interest and benign neglect preserved these objects. Neglect, probably the single greatest force in object preservation, occurred as a by-product of chronic funding shortages in the church, which undermined fashion-related obsolescence. Brief intervals of substantial expenditures for new buildings and related necessities provided appropriate shelter for this furniture. In the early nineteenth century, the parish acknowledged the growing inconvenience of Old Swedes Church as the population center drifted away from it. Accordingly, in 1830 the parish began worshipping in Trinity Chapel, at 5th and King Streets, just over a half-mile distant. Details of this building are remarkably absent from the historical record, but not so for Old Swedes Church. Within six years after the move, a group of parish women began efforts to repair and care for the old building, led by a sizable bequest of a Swedish descendant. This initiative helped preserve the 1699 pulpit and sounding board, made by John Harrison, "joiner and carpenter" of Philadelphia. When Old Swedes formally re-opened for services in 1842, it assumed an honored place in the life of the parish, which has actively supported its preservation ever since. In this changed climate, the old furniture had a specific and cherished place.[17]

In the late nineteenth or early twentieth century, Trinity Parish received donations of antique furniture, including a sixteenth-century, linen-fold chest and a press cupboard, each probably Northern European, and an early eighteenth-century oak one-drawer table with baluster-turned legs, also probably English or possibly Northern European. Although the historical record regarding the Delaware-made objects discussed here is vague, it is unlikely that those objects were gifts of parishioners. Aside from a general preference for English over American furniture during the late nineteenth and early twentieth century, Wilmington-area residents exhibited little interest in old furniture of any kind. The first piece of local furniture to enter the collections of the Historical Society of Delaware did not occur until 1929.[18]

Of the other antique furniture owned by Trinity Parish, the one-drawer table is the most intriguing (fig. 19). Church records disclose that in the early decades of the eighteenth century, when this table was made, the pastor and his assistants complained about the lack of furniture in the priest's house, which was completed in 1701. In 1714,

> "the pastor proposed to the congregation the purchase of two tables from the Provost Björk, to remain in the parsonage as an inventarium [i.e., church-owned inventory item] so that the present ministers as well as their successors may not have to go into the house without any table which they would deem very hard."

Figure 19 Table, probably England, 1710–1730. Oak. H. 27½", W. 29½", D. 16¾". (Courtesy, Trinity Episcopal Church; photo, Gavin Ashworth.)

A 1725 account records "a black walnut table" valued at twelve shillings "given as an inventarium to the Parsonage." Although the table in question is oak, and therefore likely not of local manufacture, it might have been acquired to serve needs not satisfied by the one walnut table.[19]

Assuming that the identification and interpretation of the chest, wainscot chair, desk, and cupboard are correct, those objects are the earliest furniture made in Delaware, a designation formerly assigned to a 1741 tall clock with a movement by William Furniss (working 1739–1749). Other early Delaware or southeastern Pennsylvania furniture, such as the turned chairs Forman identified as probably Swedish-American, may survive unrecognized. In time and with more research, a larger body of furniture may aggregate into a tangible narrative of furniture made by Swedish craftsmen in this long-settled but inadequately understood place. Like much early furniture made in Philadelphia and surrounding communities, these objects express influences from diverse European sources, reflecting the multitude of immigrant homelands. Subsequent interactions among colonists diluted distinctions. This diversity, however, did not yield a homogenous blend. Clearer characterizations await more research into the work of non-English and non-German furniture makers from the region.[20]

In addition to refining the history of Delaware furniture, initial findings about these three pieces of furniture improve our understanding of early Delaware Valley furniture, notably that made in Philadelphia. One key observation is the use of tulip poplar boards. Those on the chest and desk are thick and wide, not at all comparable to the kinds of tulip poplar boards commonly used for drawers, case backboards, and other applications in Philadelphia furniture of the second half of the eighteenth century. Early Philadelphia furniture seems not to have incorporated such large stock, nor does that furniture employ much, if any, tulip poplar during the early decades.[21]

A final observation with broad application concerns the findings presented here and the evidence on which they are based. Church provenance introduces rich documentation that, when compared with that for privately owned furniture, may seem very persuasive, leading furniture historians to accept without question those identifications and interpretations. But this—and much other furniture history—is provisional; it stands as the best narrative only until the next body of historic evidence surfaces. To ignore potential contradictions and consequences merely undermines the next generation of furniture scholarship.

ACKNOWLEDGMENTS   For assistance with this article, the author is indebted to Adam Bowett, Trevor Brandt, Max Dooley, the Reverend Patricia Downing, Rebecca Duffy, Angela Hewett, Margaret Johnson, Aniela Meinhald, Ed Richi, Christopher Storb, Sue Vernon, Rebecca L. Wilson, and Jon Zajackowski.

1. Peter Stebbins Craig, *The 1693 Census of the Swedes on the Delaware: Family Histories of the Swedish Lutheran Church Members Residing in Pennsylvania, Delaware, West New Jersey & Cecil County, Md., 1638–1693*, Studies in Swedish American Genealogy 3 (Winter Park, Fla.: SAG Publications, 1993), pp. 3–5, 8. Finland was under Swedish rule in the seventeenth century, although Finns spoke a different language. No attempt is made here to distinguish Swedes from Finns. The Reverend Anders Rudman served the church at Wicaco, now Gloria Dei in Philadelphia; the Reverend Jonas Aureen eventually assumed leadership of the church at Raccoon, New Jersey, now Swedesboro.

2. *The Records of Holy Trinity (Old Swedes) Church, Wilmington, Del., from 1697 to 1773*, translated by Horace Burr (Wilmington, Del.: Historical Society of Delaware, 1890), pp. 85, 182 [entry dated June 24, 1713], 194–95; Peter Stebbins Craig, "Samuel Petersson of Christina

and His Descendants," *Swedish Colonial News* 3:6 (Spring 2007): 11. Craig reports incorrectly that Joransson was elected a church warden. See also Jackie Killian, "Historic Furnishings Report: Trinity Episcopal Parish, Old Swedes' Church & Holy Trinity Church, Wilmington Delaware" (unpublished report, Trinity Parish archives, on deposit at the Old Swedes Historic Site, Wilmington, Delaware, Wilmington, Del., December 15, 2014).

3. Furniture historian Adam Bowett observes that the two-lock Joransson chest conflicts with the English tradition of three locks on such chest, thus reaffirming its attribution to a non-English maker. Wendy A. Cooper and Lisa Minardi, *Paint, Pattern, and People: Furniture of Southeastern Pennsylvania, 1725–1850* (Philadelphia: University of Pennsylvania Press for the Winterthur Museum, 2011), pp. 28–29; Jack L. Lindsey, *Worldly Goods: The Arts of Early Pennsylvania, 1680–1758* (Philadelphia: Philadelphia Museum of Art, 1999), p. 4, fig. 4.

4. "The Church Book, a Record of Trinity Church commonly called Old Swedes Church, Wilmington, Delaware. Translated from the original Swedish Record by John Gustaf Lindgren and transcribed by Henry H, J. Naff. 1857," pp. 62, 200, Old Swedes Church archives, on deposit at the Old Swedes Historic Site, Wilmington, Delaware; Burr, *Records of Holy Trinity*, p. 207.

5. Israel Acrelius, *A History of New Sweden, or, The Settlements on the River Delaware*, translated by William M. Reynolds (Philadelphia: Historical Society of Pennsylvania, 1874), p. 275; Burr, *The Records of Holy Trinity*, September 17, 1752, and June 12, 1753, pp. 446-48; "Accounts and Bonds Book," item 68, Trinity Episcopal Church Records, Delaware Historical Society, Wilmington, Del.

6. Lee Ellen Griffith, *The Pennsylvania Spice Box: Paneled Doors and Secret Drawers* (West Chester, Pa.: Chester County Historical Society, 1986), nos. 2, 9, 11, 13, 16, 18–21, 27, 31, 34, 43, 50–52; Benno M. Forman, *American Seating Furniture, 1630–1730: An Interpretive Catalogue* (New York: W. W. Norton, 1988), pp. 141–42, 175. See also cat. nos. 72–74, 82.

7. Forman, *American Seating*, p. 135, fig. 60.

8. Ruth L. Springer and Louise Wallman, "Two Swedish Pastors Describe Philadelphia, 1700 and 1702," *Pennsylvania Magazine of History and Biography* 84, no. 2 (April 1960): 207; Charles A. Silliman, *The Episcopal Church in Delaware, 1785–1954* (Wilmington, Del.: Diocese of Delaware, 1982), p. 12; Samuel Fitch Hotchkin, *Early Clergy of Pennsylvania and Delaware* (Philadelphia: P. W. Ziegler and Co., 1890), p. 38.

9. Sigurd Erixon, *Möbler och heminredning i svenska bygder*, 2 vols. (Stockholm: Nordiska museets förlag, 1925–1926), figs. 212, 634–37; Sigurd Wallin, *Möbler från svenska herremanshem*, 3 vols. (Stockholm: Nordiska museets förlag, 1931), figs. 276–77. The figures cited from the Erixon book are from vols. 1 and 2. The figures cited from the Wallin book are from vol. 1

10. Lindsey, *Worldly Goods*, no. 45, illus. p. 101, fig. 157.

11. Forman, *American Seating*, pp. 139–41.

12. Benno M. Forman, "German Influences in Pennsylvania Furniture," in *Arts of the Pennsylvania Germans*, edited by Scott T. Swank (New York: W. W. Norton for Henry Francis du Pont Winterthur Museum, 1983), pp. 111–12, 123.

13. Erixon, *Möbler och heminredning*, figs. 438–39, 449–50, 835.

14. Jacquelann Grace Killian, "United by Water: Cabinetmaking Traditions in the Delaware River Valley, 1670–1740" (master's thesis, University of Delaware, 2015), pp. 145–165. The scrutoir, now in the Dietrich American Foundation collection, is illustrated in pl. 1 in William Macpherson Hornor Jr., *Blue Book, Philadelphia Furniture: William Penn to George Washington* (Philadelphia: Privately printed, 1935).

15. Conrad Peterson, "The Beginning of Swedish-American Education [Prior to 1860]," *Yearbook of the Swedish Historical Society of America* 8 (St. Paul, Minn: Swedish Historical Society of America, 1923), pp. 29–30, 34–35; Burr, *Records of Holy Trinity*, pp. 118, 127.

16. Esther Singleton, *Dutch New York* (New York: Dodd, Mead and Co., 1909), p. 180; see also pp. 120, 166; Peter Kenny, "Ark of the Covenant: The Remarkable Inlaid Cedar Scrutoir from the Brinckerhoff Family of Newtown, Long Island," in *American Furniture*, edited by Luke Beckerdite (Hanover, N.H.: University Press of New England for the Chipstone Foundation, 2014), p. 24; Erixon, *Möbler och heminredning*, figs. 557, 1004–1007, 1009.

17. John W. McCullough, *Sacred Reminiscences: A Sermon Delivered August 21, 1842, in the Old Swedes' Church, Wilmington, Del.* (Wilmington, Del.: Old Swedes' Church, 1842), http://anglicanhistory.org/usa/misc/mccullough_sacred1842.html, accessed December 6, 2018; Gregory R. Johnson, *Holy Trinity (Old Swedes) Church: An Abridged History* (Wilmington, Del.: Trinity Parish, n.d.), pp. 5–6; Burr, *Records of Holy Trinity*, p. 35 [entry dated December 23, 1698].

18. Charles T. Lyle, "Foreward," in Deborah D. Waters, *Delaware Collections in the Museum of the Historical Society of Delaware* (Wilmington, Del.: Historical Society of Delaware, 1984), p. 8.

19. Burr, *Records of Holy Trinity*, p. 192 [entry dated June 24, 1714]; Naff, "The Church Book," p. 181, church expenses for the year 1725.

20. Philip D. Zimmerman, *Delaware Clocks* (Dover, Del.: Biggs Museum, 2006), pp. 8–9.

21. Thanks to Christopher Storb for this observation.

Book Reviews

Joshua A. Klein. *Hands Employed Aright: The Furniture Making of Jonathan Fisher (1768–1847)*. Fort Mitchell, Ky.: Lost Art Press, 2018. xii + 270 pp.; numerous color illus., bibliography. $57.00.

Now is a remarkable time to be studying American furniture. Technology plays an important role. The internet has provided collectors, researchers, and dealers with greater access to research materials. Advancements in photographic equipment have facilitated new ways of seeing objects. The ease with which images are taken and shared has led to their wide dissemination to researchers and the general public. A new generation of scholars and enthusiasts has also brought new perspectives to the field. After first working with early American furniture in my previous position at the Museum of the City of New York at the start of this decade, I was drawn to its complexity, the interdisciplinary nature of researching it, and the opportunities for original research. To paraphrase Patricia E. Kane of the Yale University Art Gallery, the field is young.

The past decade has produced several important studies of cabinetmaking, some based on the new discovery of primary source materials, others on known material due for re-evaluation. It is in the latter category that Joshua Klein's *Hands Employed Aright: The Furniture Making of Jonathan Fisher (1768–1847)* falls. Fisher was many things: preacher, educator, painter, engraver, newspaper reporter, author, and cabinetmaker; but he was also a disciplined documentarian of his own thoughts, surroundings, and daily activities. Fisher, born in New Braintree, Massachusetts, was a Harvard-educated minister who settled in Blue Hill, Maine, in 1796. The remarkable survival of his home, journals, drawings, furniture, and woodworking tools has left a rich trove of materials from which to study his life, his woodworking shop and tools, and the furniture he produced.[1]

An inherent challenge in the study of early American furniture is one shared among most art historians and scholars of material culture. Most of us simply do not practice the craft(s) we study. How many Michelangelo scholars can pounce a fresco design, or Bernini students can chisel marble? In his introduction, Klein describes his advantage in studying furniture: he is a proficient cabinetmaker. His woodworking experience allows him insights into Fisher's work as a cabinetmaker and carpenter that those without such skills could only hope to enjoy. A reader with or without cabinetmaking experience will benefit from the object descriptions in the catalogue section of the book, where Klein provides clear, detailed descriptions of each object's construction, including evidence of tool marks, documentation of inscriptions, orientation of wood grain, and notes on condition. The technical detail provided in these entries is excellent.

From my perspective—that of a museum curator without artistic training, let alone skill—this is a reminder of the necessity to study objects, particularly early American furniture, through interdisciplinary collaboration. Without conservators, materials scientists, dealers, auction house experts, collectors, and a host of other professionals, the study of objects suffers.

This experience deficit cuts both ways, and those trained in historic trades do not necessarily learn the skills of the art historian or historian. Unsexy as they might be, proper use and formatting of footnotes and bibliographies, and documentation of primary and secondary sources, are features of publications that can make them essential reference materials. Without making these sources of published information understandable to the reader, the resultant publication in many ways becomes unusable. This is the fundamental flaw of *Hands Employed Aright*. Examining similar studies of individual cabinetmakers whose records survive, such as Kemble Widmer and Joyce King's excellent *In Plain Sight*, would have provided Klein with inspiration on how to document and organize references to primary source materials. The partnerships that Widmer and King, and the authors of other recent publications, had with institutions is noteworthy. Klein too would have benefitted from partnering with an institution, historian, or curator. Working alongside a furniture scholar or museum professional could have obviated obvious errors in the text. Two, for example, appear on page 21. Klein states that the journal entries are significant because they document routine quotidian activities (which is common in day books and journals from this period), and he asserts that Fisher's body of objects and writings has been "unstudied." In fact, Klein's own footnotes and bibliography include ten publications that have Fisher's name in their titles. Many of these articles and books are not devoted to Fisher's cabinetmaking and woodworking, but he has most certainly been the subject of several focused studies over many decades.[2]

The readership of Klein's semi-annual *Mortise & Tenon Magazine*, which debuted in 2016, seems to be the intended audience for *Hands Employed Aright*. The magazine's target readership constitutes makers of period furniture who use pre-industrial hand tools. This group will find much to appreciate in and learn from *Hands Employed Aright*. In a chapter preceding the catalogue section of the book, Klein documents, in detail, Fisher's workshop and tools, organized by category.

Numerous detailed images, as well as period and contemporary photographs, beautifully animate and illustrate Klein's text. Fisher's extant furniture is sumptuously documented, and the descriptions of Fisher's furniture are one of the book's strengths. They include precise measurements, insightful commentary on construction characteristics, references to and sometimes excerpts from Fisher's writings on individual pieces, and documentation of inscriptions. Klein also copied a card table attributed to Fisher and a box he is known to have made, and he describes the manufacturing processes involved in each. All readers will find the wonderful photographs and illustrations throughout the book both helpful and handsome. Maps, interiors, paintings, photographs, details of tools, drawings, writings, and furniture made by Fisher richly complement both the text and the catalogue of tools and furniture.

The largest section of the book is the catalogue of furniture and tools. It helpfully includes accession numbers where applicable (the Jonathan Fisher Memorial presumably does not use them, as they are not included for objects from its collection). This section includes a wonderful selection of images of individual objects. A chest of drawers, for example, is depicted from the front, from the side with the drawers slightly open (revealing the drawer front construction), from the back, and from the underside, and includes skirt, foot, and interior drawer details. Catalogues of furniture rarely include such extensive photography. Fisher's furniture is practical, handsome, and, on occasion, even whimsical. The child's desk (cat. no. 10, pp. 150–51) features an apron and hinged crest at the top of the writing surface with tightly scalloped edges. With its concealed drawer under the ample desk compartment, the overall effect is an appealing, functional example of a normally unremarkable utilitarian form. Some of Fisher's furniture suggest inspiration from coastal points south of his home in Maine, in Massachusetts and Connecticut. A chest of drawers (cat. no. 4, pp. 138–39), a card table (cat. no. 12, pp. 154–55), a ribbon-back side chair (cat. no. 17, pp. 163–64), and a square tilt-top stand (cat. no. 25, pp. 176–77) are sophisticated and stylish. But most of the objects in the catalogue section of the book—numerous boxes, a dough tray, cabinets, and cupboards—are plain, straightforward objects built for daily use.

The furniture section could have benefitted from the author's collaborating with a wood anatomist in identifying woods microscopically or by eye. Precise wood identification is a challenge to anyone interested in early American furniture, and perhaps the use of general terms such as "pine" and "maple" are a way to address this challenge. But there are at least four species of pine and three species of maple native to Maine, assuming that Fisher exclusively used local woods for his furniture.[3]

Many questions remain about Fisher, his writings, and his belongings. When did he start keeping his journals? Klein alludes to this question, describing the period from 1790 to 1835 as when Fisher documented his daily activities (p. 20), and making other references to a forty-year range in his writings. What materials exist, and what time periods do they cover? How are the journals organized: in many volumes, or as loose sheets of paper? Are they day books, account books, diaries? Where in these materials do the numerous quotations that Klein has scattered throughout the text appear? Did Klein master the shorthand used in Fisher's original writings? Did he make any attempt to translate sections of the text himself, or did he rely solely on an existing transcription (by an uncredited person or persons, referenced in the introduction)? Even the most careful and skilled translations contain errors, some of which can impact the interpretation of the text.

One element that would merit publication is a finding aid or index to precisely what is in the collection of the Jonathan Fisher Homestead. Future studies that include these kinds of references and more careful documentation would make for a more complete study. What could have been a robust appendix is lacking. A glossary would have helped readers unfamiliar with cabinetmaking terminology, and the bibliography and index are thin. Klein's book can be seen as a critical step in the study of Fisher, but the significant volume of material he left out is ripe for further study. Being that the field is young, cataloguing is dynamic, and the kind of close study of a single cabinetmaker is laborious work, Klein has provided a critical chapter in revisiting a noteworthy maker of early American furniture.

Christine Ritok
Historic Deerfield

1. Peter Kenny, Michael Brown, et al., *Duncan Phyfe: Master Cabinetmaker in New York* (New Haven and London: Yale University Press, 2011); Kemble Widmer, Joyce King, et al., *In Plain Sight: Discovering the Furniture of Nathaniel Gould* (Salem, Mass.: Peabody Essex Museum in association with D Giles Ltd., London, 2014); Christie Jackson, Brock Jobe, and Clark Pearce, *Crafting Excellence: The Furniture of Nathan Lumbard and His Circle* (New Haven and London: Yale University Press, 2018); and Jay Robert Stiefel, *The Cabinetmaker's Account: John Head's Record of Craft & Commerce in Colonial Philadelphia, 1718–1753* (Philadelphia: American Philosophical Society Press, 2019).

2. Jane Bianco, *A Wondrous Journey: Jonathan Fisher & the Making of Scripture Animals* (Rockland, Me.: Farnsworth Art Museum, 2013); Rufus George Frederick Candage, *Memoir of Rev. Jonathan Fisher of Blue Hill, Maine* (Bangor, Me.: Benjamin A. Burr, 1889); Mary Ellen Chase, *Jonathan Fisher, Maine Parson 1768–1847* (New York: MacMillan Co., 1948); William Hinckley, "The Fisher House," *American Patriot*, August 28, 1975; Kevin D. Murphy, *Jonathan Fisher of Blue Hill, Maine: Commerce, Culture, and Community on the Eastern Frontier* (Amherst: University of Massachusetts Press, 2010); Albert L. Partridge, "Jonathan Fisher's Clock," *Antiques* 64, no. 2 (August 1953): 122–23; Raoul N. Smith, *The Language of Jonathan Fisher (1768–1847)* (Tuscaloosa: University of Alabama Press, 1985); Raoul N. Smith, *The Life of Jonathan Fisher (1768–1847)*, vol. 1: *From His Birth Through the Year 1798* (Acton, Mass.: R.N. Smith, 2006); John R. Wiggins, "'Parson Fisher's Funny Pronunciations' Show Up Alive and Kicking in Blue Hill," *Ellsworth American*, August 25, 1984; and Alice Winchester, *Versatile Yankee: The Art of Jonathan Fisher, 1768–1847* (Princeton, N.J.: Pyne Press, 1973).

3. Jack pine (*Pinus banksiana*), red pine (*Pinus resinosa*), pitch pine (*Pinus rigida*), Eastern white pine (*Pinus strobus*), red maple (*Acer rubrum*), sugar maple (*Acer saccharum*), and silver maple (*Acer saccharinum*). See Elbert L. Little Jr. *Atlas of United States Trees*, vol. 1: *Conifers and Important Hardwoods* (Washington, D.C.: United States Government Printing Office, 1971).

Conner-Rosenkranz LLC, with a foreword by Joel Rosenkranz and an introduction by R. Ruthie Dibble and Avis Berman. *The Art of Display: The American Pedestal, 1830–1910*. New York: Conner-Rosenkranz, 2018. 57 pp.; color and bw illus. $30.00 pb.

Works on individual furniture forms, with the exception of chairs and clocks, are not especially common. There are many exceptions, of course—books on federal-period card tables and Pennsylvania German chests come to mind, as does the Yale series of collection catalogues based on types of objects—but many forms still await their monograph. This slim volume on nineteenth-century American pedestals is thus a welcome addition to the literature. Short, well-written, and superbly illustrated, this digestible publication allows us to see the evolution of a single form in the changing context of its time. Moreover, the authors examine the social history as well as the artistic nature of the form.

As is the case with picture frames, pedestals are created in the service of others—in this instance, usually sculpture, but also vases, flower arrangements, and other things that need to be raised in height and highlighted in order to focus attention on them and thus to be seen to their best advantage. By their very nature they are thus part of an ensemble. Nineteenth-century American sculptors understood the importance of this (literally) supporting role. Hiram Powers, for example, had his famous *Greek Slave* mounted on a revolving pedestal, so that she could be seen in the round from all angles. Similarly, Thomas Crawford specified the materials, dimensions, construction, and finish for the pedestal for his massive *Orpheus and Cerberus* of 1843.

Despite its importance, the pedestal is often overlooked. The succinct essay here by R. Ruthie Dibble and Avis Berman addresses that gap by examining the "shift in the function, design, and aesthetics of the pedestal" (p. 5) from the neoclassical period through the end of the century and the advent of the arts and crafts movement, charting the evolution of the form as it was expressed in most of the major revival styles of the nineteenth century.

Dibble and Berman begin their survey with the early, neoclassical phase of the pedestal's history, during which it served largely a secondary role in the support of white marble sculpture. This slow beginning, from roughly 1820 to the 1850s, featured pedestals of marble, often in the form of columns or plinths that served the purpose without drawing much attention to themselves.[1]

Things began to change in the third quarter of the century, as an emerging art market and a focus on domesticity saw the introduction of more works of art into household interiors. During this time, a shift in the importance of the pedestal occurred: as the authors put it, "the object *for* display became an object *of* display" (p. 14) in and of itself. Wooden examples were produced by many of the major furniture firms in all of the au courant revival styles, and several examples by Pottier and Stymus, Kilian Brothers, and Edward Mahar of Boston demonstrate this point.

The next phase of the form's trajectory occurred in the last quarter of the century. The Centennial celebrations in 1876 marked the beginning of what is called here the "golden age" of the "ubiquitous" pedestal. Superb examples in the modern Gothic and aesthetic movement modes by Kimbel and Cabus, Herter Brothers, and others represent the apex of what the authors see as the highest aesthetic achievement of the form. They also call attention (pp. 36–38) to a hybrid form of pedestal that provided room for display on its top, as was traditional, but also allowed for the storage and display of additional objects on its lower level, on a shelf or in a small cupboard.

As the century came to a close, the heyday of the pedestal ended during a period that saw the "pedestal effaced." Rodin and other sculptors are cited as the principal agents of this decline. Rodin "challenged the norms governing traditional pedestals" and "after jettisoning heads, arms, hands, and legs" in his work, "Rodin eliminated the pedestal" (p. 46). No longer seen as indispensable, the pedestal "was discarded for the very elements that had once made it so desirable: elevation, veneration, and artfulness" (p. 46).

Richly illustrated with period prints, photographs showing pedestals in use, and pages from trade catalogues, as well as with images of many surviving examples in public and private collections, *The Art of Display* is a valuable addition, in microcosm, to our understanding of nineteenth-century material life.

Gerald W. R. Ward
Museum of Fine Arts, Boston

1. Pedestals in the classic mode can be very important, nonetheless. The plain rectangular marble pedestal for the sculpture now known as the Venus de Milo was discarded by conservators and curators in the Louvre in the 1820s because they thought it was not original, when in fact it was inscribed with the name and location of the sculptor, Alexandros of Antioch. See Gregory Curtis, *Disarmed: The Story of Venus de Milo* (New York: Alfred A. Knopf, 2003), pp. 74–77.

Jay Robert Stiefel. *The Cabinetmaker's Account: John Head's Record of Craft and Commerce in Colonial Philadelphia, 1718–1753*. Philadelphia: American Philosophical Society Press, 2019. xxi + 298 pp.; numerous color and bw illus., appendix, bibliography, index. $85.00.

The discovery of any eighteenth-century cabinetmaker's account book or ledger is a rare and momentous occasion in the decorative arts community, but particularly for students and researchers of early American furniture. This book ascends to the top level of publications in this area. Its importance is described best by noted English researcher Adam Bowett in the foreword: "The John Head account book is the earliest and most complete record of a cabinetmaker's work to have survived either in North America or in Great Britain" (p. xvii).

The publication of the Head account book would not have achieved its full impact without two critical elements: the commitment by the American Philosophical Society to publishing as complete a record as possible of every element of the book's journal entries as researched by Jay Robert Stiefel, and the comprehensive knowledge of Philadelphia's colonial history that the author was able to apply in researching and writing the book.

Head's accounts are part of the large Vaux Family Papers collection of documents donated to the society in 1992. They contain seven generations of manuscripts recording a Quaker family's relations with Philadelphia's elite merchant class. The collection, which contains documents dating prior to the Revolution, took some time to be fully catalogued due to its extensive size and time constraints. During an initial research trip to examine the Vaux files, Stiefel discovered the John Head account book in May 1999.

Not only did Jay Stiefel discover Head's ledgers, but he is uniquely qualified to research and interpret their contents. A lawyer by profession and lifelong resident of Philadelphia, he has been an avid collector and researcher of the city's history and decorative arts for the past thirty years. As a result, his contacts in the Philadelphia area are extensive, enabling him access to both private and public collections and manuscripts. His legal training, enabling him to pay close attention to the minutest detail, has resulted in extensive documentation of all aspects of Head's life between 1718 and 1753, creating a book that sheds new light on colonial life during the first half of the eighteenth century. Although furniture is a major component, this is not just a book about furniture making in Philadelphia. Stiefel takes Head's transactions and examines them in light of the reason for the entry, its implication for both Head and the other party to the transaction, its date, and its cost. But that is only the beginning of his work. He then examines every conceivable path of research that the transaction may disclose. It is difficult to imagine a book more carefully annotated. In addition to the normal reference sources from manuscripts and books, the footnotes document every conversation of importance with colleagues and professional historical staff members. The latter is extremely important for follow-up research in the wide range of subjects covered. The American Philosophical Society is to be commended for encouraging the inclusion of this level of reference sources.

A major objective of furniture research as a result of the discovery of cabinetmakers accounts is to tie surviving objects to specific entries in the account book. When one example is confirmed as being made by the craftsman, it inevitably leads to the confirmation of other objects of the same form being manufactured in the shop. Furniture manufactured in Philadelphia during the early to mid-eighteenth century is generally acknowledged to be unequaled in artistic design among connoisseurs and is eagerly sought in the marketplace. Three well-known conservators—Alan Miller, Alan Anderson, and Chris Storb—have collectively seen or worked on the majority of Philadelphia pieces in public and private collections or available to the market. They have made significant contributions to the book in discussing construction aspects of many of the entries. To date, more than sixty objects have been attributed to the John Head shop as a result of their work and Stiefel's research.

The first chapter, "The Discovery of the John Head Account Book," discusses the research project Stiefel initially had volunteered for—documenting a dressing table with a Benjamin Franklin provenance and a desk with an unbroken line of descent from John Head Jr. Both objects were in possession of the Vaux family. The chapter also documents the progression of publications connected to the discovery as more information was released.

The second chapter, "An Elusive 'Joyner,'" is an illustration of the persistence and attention to detail that characterizes the project. During the first quarter of the eighteenth century, Philadelphia, as well as many other American coastal cities, experienced a large influx of immigrant craftsmen from Europe, most fleeing oppressive conditions or searching for a more secure life. Surviving records from this time are scarce if they ever existed. Although John Head had been identified as a "Joyner" in his will and is one of a hundred woodworkers listed in Horner's *Blue Book,* there was little knowledge outside the Vaux family of his trade as a cabinetmaker—and certainly no recognition of the length of his practice in Philadelphia nor the prominence of his furniture. He was not listed among the Freeman's rolls in Philadelphia, nor does he appear as an appraiser of any woodworker's probate inventory. Since Head's original will and probate inventory have been lost, it is likely that he would have remained in obscurity without the discovery of his ledger. The second portion of this chapter discusses, in exquisite detail, Head's life in England and those of his ancestors prior to his immigration in 1717.

The following chapter outlines why this account book is so important. A number of other cabinetmakers' ledgers have been discovered over the years, most from the latter half of the eighteenth or early nineteenth century. Surviving business records from Head's era are not only scarce but fragmentary, most covering only a few years of a working career. In contrast, Head's accounts document his entire time in Philadelphia and cover a span of thirty-five years. Of equal importance to this documented longevity is his client base and the quality of furniture he produced: the pinnacle of the late baroque style in Philadelphia.

Other southeastern Pennsylvania furniture makers and their surviving records, primarily probate inventories, are discussed in detail, but Steifel's research fills in key pertinent information not available in inventories. Names, dates of purchase, object descriptions, and how and when payments were received are usually recorded. But the continuity of Head's entries also provides the opportunity for tracking trends in pricing, the decline or introduction of specific forms of furniture, and the interrelationship over time of the entire city's artisan community. There follows an extensive discussion of why so little surviving Philadelphia furniture from the early eighteenth century can be attributed to specific makers. Although the above factors are of interest to scholars, the most important result arising from any account book's discovery is the connection made between an entry and a surviving piece of furniture. To know when a piece was made, to whom it was sold, how much it cost, and to be able to study the object in detail in comparison to other objects of like design are the ultimate objectives of any researcher. If Head had only possessed an average skill at his craft, primarily selling output to Philadelphia's middle-class community, his ledger would have been important from a historical standpoint but would probably have resulted in a low number of surviving pieces. But he was not of average skill, which was recognized by the importance of his clientele, who demanded and received superior craftsmanship. His customers ranked among the highest level of Philadelphia society. Heirlooms, highly venerated by descendants, account for the survival, as mentioned, of at least sixty objects attributed to the Head shop. The confluence of all these factors defines this book's importance.

The fourth chapter discusses business practices of Head's shop that could apply to any other mercantile establishment during his era. The barter economy, economic circumstances in Philadelphia at time of his immigration and subsequent career, and a detailed explanation of currency in use are covered. Head was a stickler for detail in making entries. That allows Stiefel to explore the story behind transactions and bring to life everyday occurrences.

Chapter 5, devoted to the account book as artifact, is a useful primer for any researcher studying an early eighteenth-century document. If a tradesperson had little or no education, he or she often spelled phonetically, mirroring how the person spoke. Deciphering paragraphs becomes even more challenging if the phonetic spelling has been influenced by the dialect of the writer, as was the case with Head. Fortunately, the author explains both the problem and his approach to fully understanding the transaction. He points out that it takes time and patience, sometimes requiring visiting indecipherable entries numerous times in order to maximize an accurate interpretation. One complicating factor in the account book is the use of Julian dates in listing a transaction; later entries use Georgian dates. The author introduces the topic and interprets consistent dates throughout the book.

The depth of Stiefel's research is best illustrated in chapter 6, "Business Conducted at the Shop." The author traces the evolution of Head the cabinetmaker toward becoming a merchant and subsequently a wealthy property holder. That transition is covered in detail and includes an extended discussion of his offspring's occupations and their interconnectivity. Many cabinetmakers during this period aspired to develop a mercantile source of income. Making furniture was a hard, physical occupation that only became more difficult with age. More importantly, it was a profession dependent on the economic cycle. An alternative source of income to furniture production was not only desirable but a necessity during long periods of economic decline. One of Head's assumed apprentices, Thomas Maule, is also identified. This chapter illustrates the logical assumptions that can be drawn from the minute details of an account book entry.

The discussion of John Head's transition from an immigrant woodworker to a wealthy landowner continues in this section. Topics covered include the extent of his real estate holdings, rents paid and received, construction of his houses, and continued property development. As other people and trades are introduced in journal entries, their background and relationship to Head are considered. The discussion is extended by drawing conclusions from entries related to furnishing his home, food and drink consumed (chapter 10), dress and personal adornment (chapter 11), and livestock and transport (chapter 12).

An entire chapter is devoted to noted Philadelphia pewterer Simon Edgell. The account book documents business conducted between Head and Edgell from 1719 to 1732 and discloses the types of pewter forms Edgell manufactured as well as some aspects of Edgell's personal life. Of particular interest to specialists are the prices charged for specific forms, as no price list from the period exists. It is indicative of Head's early reputation in Philadelphia that some of his most expensive furniture was sold to Philadelphia's most prominent pewterer.

Having covered many aspects of thirty-two years of colonial life in Philadelphia, the reader is introduced to John Head's furniture, commencing with a discussion of "Shop Materials, Components, and Equipment," followed in the succeeding chapter by a discussion of other woodworking activities. Like many cabinetmakers of his time, Head evidently did not build chairs in the shop but depended on the specialized skill of chair making and turning. Due to the early period covered in these accounts, several unknown chair makers have come to light. Six chair makers are mentioned, with Head acting as a middleman in many transactions. Since no price book exists for these utilitarian objects, Head's accounts are particularly valuable to researchers in indicating a standard price for a set of six slat-back chairs.

As previously mentioned, for furniture specialists the ultimate objective of any discovery of a cabinetmaker's accounts is to connect a specific entry with an existing object. Chapter 16 starts this process. Three surviving case pieces of furniture sold to Caspar Wistar—a high chest and dressing table (1726), and a tall-case clock with works by William Stretch (1730)—are documented in Head's accounts and form the basis of attribution for many other pieces of furniture. No stone is left unturned in listing the full line of descent for each piece. Fortunately, all three are of superior design and condition and were sold to one of Philadelphia's wealthiest citizens. They firmly established John Head's position in Philadelphia's cabinetmaking community. A close relationship between Head and prominent clockmakers Peter and William Stretch is also explored.

The chapter ends with a look at external design features that distinguish Head's work from other contemporaries in Philadelphia. What is particularly refreshing here is the acknowledgment that despite the comprehensive information provided by the ledgers, we still don't have all the answers. Stiefel discusses differences of opinion among his specialist advisors and presents pros and cons to open questions.

Serious students of early American furniture will find chapters 16 and 17 ("To a Chest of Drawers" and "To a Chamber Table") must reading. The object that accounts for more entries than any other furniture form is a chest of drawers, some two hundred examples if my count is correct. This term would apply to those objects that are today called chests, chest-on-chests, and high chests. The author covers every aspect of these entries and classifies them according to today's nomenclature. Since most of the entries are the generic "chest of drawers," and the type of wood is seldom listed, the price debited becomes the all-important factor in attempting to segregate form, wood, and embellishment. This is a difficult task, but Stiefel's conclusions are thoroughly reasoned. Specific forms are discussed as to quantity produced, surviving examples, the indicated wood used in construction, noted sales to Philadelphia citizens, hardware, chalk inscriptions, and—when possible—the transition dates of one form superseded by another. Internal construction characteristics of the shop are described. Of necessity, the text consists of numerous prices and examples that are the basis for the type of chest produced, but the discussion is often confusing to the reader. A summary chart of assumed form, with a breakdown of wood and embellishment, would have helped in understanding different categories. Many people reading this book also may not be fully conversant in woodworking terms: dado, pins and tails of dovetails, and so forth. Small sketches of examples of specialized furniture terms would have been a nice addition.

Most objects illustrated in this chapter incorporate ball feet. At least three and possibly more foot profiles are shown, but it is not stated in each case as to whether the feet are original or restored replacements. For example, chests in figures 17.1 and 17.3 are described as having original feet, but they are of substantially different profile. Did Head refine his turning of feet over time, or did he distinguish between inexpensive and higher-priced pieces in the use of different foot profiles?

Stiefel's analysis of Head's furniture raises several other intriguing questions. For example, why were so few of his case pieces veneered during the second quarter of the eighteenth century (compared, for example, to New England objects of the same period)? It is also noteworthy that furniture made of cherry and cedar was priced at a premium above that of walnut and was comparable in price to mahogany. (Although it commanded a premium price, there is evidence that cedar did not deserve its reputation for repelling insects.)

Chapters are devoted in whole or in part to tables; beds; desks and secretaries; corner cupboards, presses, cradles, and close stools; small chests; miscellaneous articles; and coffins. Unfortunately, no example of any of these forms could firmly be attributed to the Head shop. The author gleans as much information as the account book allows, and the chapters follow the outline in the balance of the book: quantities sold at specific prices (with speculation as to wood used and complexity of form), and the customers (and as much miscellaneous information concerning them as could be determined).

The most comprehensive discussion of a furniture form is covered in chapter 20, "To a Clock Case." It is the best example of the author's diligence in documenting every lead offered by the account book. Characteristics of clock case construction are explained, as are the different levels of design categorized by price charged. Stiefel breaks down when specific forms were introduced; for example, the arched-dial clock was first sold in 1721, much earlier than has been generally recognized. Other features of the clock case that help in dating are analyzed. Five Philadelphia clockmakers are listed by Head in addition to the city's most important clockmakers, the Stretch family. An interesting aspect of these discussions reveals that several surviving clocks have Head cases, but the works are by English artisans not listed in his ledgers.

After twenty years of documenting his cabinet work for Philadelphia's citizens, John Head made his last entry on December 27, 1744. Stiefel notes that Head's writing had become infirm and speculates on his general health and the decline in his business in the final chapter.

In summary, this book represents a decade of dedicated effort by Jay Robert Stiefel and the unwavering support of the American Philosophical Society in documenting every thread of knowledge that could be teased from the discovery and analysis of the account books of Philadelphian John Head. Not only are his cabinetmaking and mercantile interests continuously recorded between 1718 and 1753, but his place in cabinetmaking history has ascended from that of a virtually unknown maker to that of a superior craftsman. As a consequence, many surviving examples of furniture have been attributed to his shop, and it is a virtual certainty that more will be identified in the future.

However, one topic deserves further study and should yield rewarding results: the exploration of connections between a marriage and the purchase of case pieces, particularly tables, chests of drawers, chairs, and beds. This is particularly important because research on New England colonial buying habits has indicated a high percentage of these items were tied either directly to the married couple or close relatives. These acquisitions generally occurred six months prior to a marriage date but up to a year afterwards if a house was being built for the new couple. It is very difficult to tie tables and the few surviving beds to a specific shop due to the lack of shared construction characteristics for objects containing drawers or a chest frame, but knowledge of the buying habits surrounding a marriage may lead to attributions of these elusive forms.[1]

Students of colonial decorative arts will find this book rich in detail and brimming with hitherto unknown facts; it also provides a clear path to further discoveries as a result of its extensive footnote references. One reading of the book is insufficient to absorb its voluminous content, and it is sure to be a key reference in any library.

Kemble Widmer
Newburyport, Massachusetts

1. See, for example, Elisabeth Garrett Widmer, "Brides, Housewives, and Hostesses: Acquiring, Using, Caring for, and Enjoying Mr. Gould's Furniture," in Kemble Widmer and Joyce King, et al., *In Plain Sight: Discovering the Furniture of Nathaniel Gould* (Salem, Mass.: Peabody Essex Museum in association with D Giles Ltd., London, 2014), pp. 47–65.

Recent Writing on American Furniture: A Bibliography

Compiled by
Gerald W. R. Ward

▼ THIS YEAR'S LIST primarily includes works published in 2018 and roughly through early September 2019. As always, a few earlier publications that had escaped notice are also listed. The short title *American Furniture 2018* is used in citations for articles and reviews published in last year's edition of this journal, which is also cited in full under editor Luke Beckerdite's name.

Once again, many people have assisted in compiling this list. I am particularly grateful to Luke Beckerdite, Jonathan Fairbanks, Vonda K. Givens, Joshua Klein, and Barbara McLean Ward, as well as to the scholars who have prepared reviews for this issue. I am also indebted to the librarians of the Museum of Fine Arts, Boston, the Portsmouth Athenaeum, the Massachusetts College of Art and Design, and the Portsmouth Public Library for their ongoing assistance.

I would be glad to receive citations for titles that inadvertently have been omitted from this or previous lists. Information about new publications and review copies of significant works would also be much appreciated.

Albert, Amber C. Review of *Crafting Excellence: The Furniture of Nathan Lumbard and His Circle*, by Christine Jackson, Brock Jobe, and Clark Pearce. In *American Furniture 2018*, 215–17.

Albertson, Karla Klein. "Deco: Luxury to Mass Market." *Antiques and the Arts Weekly* (January 25, 2019): 1C, 10C–11C. Color illus. (Re exhibition at the Wolfsonian, Miami Beach, Florida.)

Ambler, Frances. *Mid-Century Modern: Icons of Design*. New York: Thames and Hudson, 2016. 206 pp.; 96 color and bw illus., index.

Atkins, Robert. "Craftsman Home." *Antiques* 186, no. 4 (July/August 2019): 86–93. Color and bw illus. (Re home of Sam Maloof.)

Auscherman, Amy, Sam Grawe, and Leon Ransmeier, eds. *Herman Miller: A Way of Living*. London: Phaidon Press, 2019. 614 pp.; numerous color and bw illus., index.

Baker, Emerson W., and Nina Maurer. *Forgotten Frontier: Untold Stories of the Piscataqua*. South Berwick, Me.: Old Berwick Historical Society, 2018. 87 pp.; color illus.

Barisione, Silvia. "Around the World with Art Deco." *Antiques* 185, no. 6 (November/December 2018): 90–95. 11 color illus.

Bateman, Vanessa. "Ursus horribilis: Seth Kinsman's Grizzly Chair." *RACAR: revue d'art canadienne/Canadian Art Review* 43, no. 1 (2018): 99–108. 6 illus.

"Bayou Bend's Acquisitions Since 2015." *Antiques and the Arts Weekly* (July 12, 2019): 40. 6 bw illus. (Includes Boston rococo side chair owned by Moses Gill, worktable by Duncan Phyfe, and sewing table of 1877 by William Glosnop of Texas.)

Beach, Laura. "Art of Illinois." *Antiques and the Arts Weekly* (November 23, 2018): 1C, 30–31. Color and bw illus.

———. "A Passion for American Art: Selections from the Carolyn and Peter Lynch Collection." *Antiques and the Arts Weekly* (June 7, 2019): 1C, 12C–13C. Color illus.

Beckerdite, Luke, ed. *American Furniture 2018*. Milwaukee, Wis.: Chipstone Foundation, 2018. vii + 248 pp.; numerous color and bw illus.,

bibliography, index. Distributed by Oxbow Books.

Becksvoort, Christian. *Shaker Inspirations: Five Decades of Fine Craftsmanship*. Fort Mitchell, Ky.: Lost Art Press, 2018. 157 pp.; color and bw illus.

Bennett, Shelley M. *The Art of Wealth: The Huntingtons in the Gilded Age*. San Marino, Calif.: Huntington Library, Art Collections, and Botanical Gardens, 2013. xvi + 363 pp.; numerous color and bw illus., index. (Includes Herter Brothers furniture and many period interiors.)

Birks, Kimberlie. *Design for Children: Play, Ride, Learn, Eat, Create, Sit, Sleep*. London: Phaidon, 2018. Unpaged; numerous color illus., 3 indexes. (Includes some furniture.)

Bittner, Regina, et al. *Desk in Exile: A Bauhaus Object Traversing Different Modernities*. Bauhaus Taschenbuch 20. Leipzig: Spector Books, 2017. 51 pp.; color and bw illus.

Bray, Derin. "Transaction Analysis: Account Books Show Early Cabinetmakers' Business Dealings." *Historic New England* 19, no. 3 (winter 2019): 29–31. 4 color illus.

Brieful, Aviva. "'Freaks of Furniture': The Useless Energy of Haunted Things." *Victorian Studies* 59, no. 2 (winter 2017): 209–34. 3 bw illus.

Burt, Owen H., and Jo Burt. *Walter H. Durfee and His Clocks*. Columbia, Pa.: National Association of Watch and Clock Collectors, 2017. 110 pp.; color illus.

Carlisle, Nancy. "Preserved Seating: How to Restore a Couch." *Historic New England* 19, no. 3 (winter 2019): 23–26. 5 color and 1 bw illus.

Cathcart, Shelley, and Amy Griffin. "On the Trail of Two Cabinetmakers: Reconstructing the Careers of Samuel Wing and Tilly Mead." *Mortise & Tenon Magazine* 3 (2017): 109–15. Color and bw illus.

Cathers, David, et al. *The American Arts and Crafts Chair: "A Message of Honesty and Joy."* Morris Plains, N.J.: Stickley Museum at Craftsman Farms, 2019. 12 pp.; color illus. (Visitors guide to eponymous exhibition; contains entries by Adrienne Spinoza, Kevin W.

Tucker, Jonathan Clancy, Donald A. Davidoff, Ryan Berley, Jill Thomas-Clark, Michael McCracken, Isak Lidenauer, and Tim L. Hansen.)

Chair: 500 Designs that Matter. London: Phaidon, 2018. 655 pp.; numerous color illus., timeline, index.

Chicirda, Tara Gleason. Review of *Opening the Door: Safes of the Shenandoah Valley*, by Kurt C. Ross and Jeffrey S. Evans. In *American Furniture 2018*, 217–20.

Chicirda, Tara Gleason, and Mack Cox. "A Rhode Island Cabinetmaker in Kentucky: Revelations of a Clock Reexamined." In *American Furniture 2018*, 170–92. 31 color and bw illus.

Connors, Michael. "Living with Antiques: Antilles Grace." *Antiques* 186, no. 3 (May/June 2019): 62–69. 12 color illus.

Conversations in Craft: Furniture from The Trustees Collection and North Bennet Street School Artisans. Harvard, Mass.: Fruitlands Museum and North Bennet Street School, 2018. 47 pp.; illus. (Essay by Christine Jackson.)

Cooke, Edward S., Jr. *Inventing Boston: Design, Production, and Consumption, 1680–1720*. New Haven, Conn., and London: Paul Mellon Centre for Studies in British Art, 2019. vix + 222 pp.; numerous color and bw illus., index.

Correia, Ana Paula Rebelo, et al. *Beyond the Mirror*. Lisbon: Calouste Gulbenkian Museum, 2017. 147 pp.; index.

Couch, Dale L., ed. *Folk and Folks: Variations in the Vernacular*. Athens, Ga.: Georgia Museum of Art, 2018. 215 pp.; color and bw illus. (Conference report; see especially "Religion, Land, and Cultural Tradition: Johannes Spitler of the Shenandoah Valley, 1790–1809," by Elizabeth A. Davison; "'The Tree of Life, my soul hath seen': Painted Dower Chests in Walton County, Georgia," by Sumpter Priddy III; and "Under Continental Influences: Current Research into the Long-Block Group of Georgia Furniture," by Dale L. Couch and Joseph D. Litts.)

"Craft and Comfort: Furniture for the

Saco Home." *Antiques and the Arts Weekly* (May 24, 2019): 10. 7 bw illus.

CraftNOW Philadelphia, et al. *Craft Capital: Philadelphia's Culture of Making*. Ed. Glenn Adamson. Atglen, Pa.: Schiffer Books, 2019. 208 pp.; 114 color illus.

"Crocker Museum Acquires Pottier & Stymus Masterpieces Commissioned for Silver Mining Magnate James Flood." *Antiques and the Arts Weekly* (January 25, 2019): 32. 5 bw illus.

Dalati, Sammy. Review of *Art Deco Chicago: Designing Modern America*, edited by Robert Bruegmann. In *Antiques* 186, no. 1 (January/February 2019): 90. 2 color illus.

Dapkus, Mary Jane. "Early 19th-Century Connecticut Clock Making and Freemasonry: A Preliminary Report." *Watch and Clock Bulletin* 60, no. 6 (November/December 2018): 527–35. Color illus., table.

Digital Antiques Journal. https:/ antiquesjournal.com. (On-line successor, issued twice monthly, to *New England Antiques Journal*, which ceased its printed version with vol. 38, no. 4 [November 2018].)

Duffy, Rebecca. "Hamilton & Burr: Who Wrote Their Stories?" *Antiques and Fine Art* 18, no. 3 (autumn 2019): 110–11. 3 color illus. (Includes New York card table, 1800, at Winterthur, with panel inscribed "Jefferson/Burr.")

Encyclopedia of Greater Philadelphia. https://philadelphiaencyclopedia.org/. (The *Encyclopedia* is produced by the Mid-Atlantic Regional Center for the Humanities [MARCH] at Rutgers University-Camden and is an evolving on-line reference [and eventually also a print volume] sponsored by Rutgers University; see in particular individual articles by Colin Fanning and Lisa Minardi cited elsewhere in this list.)

Erby, Adam T. "Reinterpreting Mount Vernon's Front Parlor." *Decorative Arts Trust Magazine* 6, no. 1 (summer 2019): 22–25. 10 color illus.

"Examination of an 18th-Century Mahogany Tea Table." *Mortise & Tenon Magazine* 5 (2018): 90–99. Color illus.

"Examination of Two Period High Chairs." *Mortise & Tenon Magazine* 3 (2017): 70–81. Color illus. (See also https://www.mortiseandtenonmag.com/collections/books/ for more illustrations.)

Fanning, Colin. "Arts of Wharton Esherick." *Encyclopedia of Greater Philadelphia*. ©2016. https://philadelphiaencyclopedia.org/archive/arts-of-wharton-esherick/ (accessed July 23, 2019). Color illus., bibliography, other references.

Feld, Elizabeth, and Stuart P. Feld. *Augmenting the Canon: Recent Acquisitions of American Neo-Classical Decorative Arts at Hirschl & Adler Galleries*. New York: Hirschl and Adler Galleries, 2019. 104 pp.; color illus., bibliography.

———. "Augmenting the Canon: Recent Acquisitions of American Neoclassical Decorative Arts at Hirschl & Adler Galleries." *Antiques and Fine Art* 18, no. 1 (spring 2019): 130–37. Color illus.

Fennimore, Donald F. "Pewter and Clocks: A Miscellany." *Bulletin* (Pewter Collectors' Club of America) 15, no. 9 (summer 2018): 34–38. 6 bw illus.

Fiell, Charlotte, and Peter Fiell. *1000 Chairs*. 1997. Rev. ed. Koln: Taschen, 2017. 664 pp.; numerous color illus.

Fitzgerald, Oscar P. *Little Book of Wooden Boxes: Wooden Boxes Created by the Masters*. East Petersburg, Pa.: Fox Chapel, 2019. 192 pp.; color illus.

Fitzpatrick, Megan. "Woodworking in Classic Literature." *Mortise & Tenon Magazine* 5 (2018): 80–89. Color and bw illus.

Follansbee, Peter. *Joiner's Work*. Covington, Ky.: Lost Art Press, 2019. xiv + 247 pp.; numerous color illus., line drawings, bibliography.

Frank, Caroline. "New England and the World." *Historic Deerfield* 17 (autumn 2018): 2–8. Color illus.

Frishman, Bob. "The Asa Munger Clock Case Mystery." *Maine Antique Digest* 47, no. 6 (June 2019): 152. 1 color illus.

———. "Claggett Clock Reunion." *Watch & Clock Bulletin* 61, no. 2 (March/April 2019): 153–54. 4 color illus.

———. "A Comprehensive Look at the Bond Family of Clockmakers." *Maine Antique Digest* 47, no. 10 (October 2019): 152. 1 color illus.

(Review of *From Celestial to Terrestrial Timekeeping: Clockmaking in the Bond Family*, by Donald Saff.)

———. "Rufus Porter and His Clock." *Watch and Clock Bulletin* 61, no. 1 (January/February 2019): 30–31. 3 color illus.

———. Review of *Claggett: Newport's Illustrious Clockmakers*, by Donald L. Fennimore and Frank L. Hohmann III. In *American Furniture 2018*, 221–25.

———. Review of *The Music of Early American Clocks, 1730–1830*, by Kate Van Winkle Keller and Gary R. Sullivan. In *Watch and Clock Bulletin* 60, no. 6 (November/December 2018): 541–42.

Gaffney, Brendan Bernhardt. "An Unlikely Masterpiece: Examining Chester Cornett's Bookcase Rocking 'Chire.'" *Mortise & Tenon Magazine* 5 (2018): 36–49. Color and bw illlus.

Garvin, James L., and Donna-Belle Garvin. "The Granite State House." *Historical New Hampshire* 71, no. 2 (fall/winter 2018): 66–141. Color and bw illus. (Special issue devoted to bicentennial of the New Hampshire state house, built in 1819; includes some references to federal-period furniture.)

Gevalt, Emelie. "Revisiting Taunton: Robert Crosman, Esther Stevens Brazer, and the Changing Interpretations of Taunton Chests." In *American Furniture 2018*, 106–69. 70 color and bw illus., appendix.

Gronning, Erik K. "Luxury of Choice: Boston's Early Baroque Seating Furniture." In *American Furniture 2018*, 2–105. 181 color and bw illus., appendix.

Guiler, Thomas A. "The Byrdcliffe Library." *Antiques and Fine Art* 18, no. 1 (spring 2019): 146–47. 3 color illus.

Hanson, Margaret. "A Looking Glass for William Claggett: Theology, Self-Representation, and Early Eighteenth-Century Print Culture." *Newport History: Journal of the Newport Historical Society* 90, no. 179 (winter/spring 2019): 31–57. 13 bw illus.

Hardiman, Thomas M., Jr. *Money, Revolution, and Books: A Multi-Generational Perspective on the Portsmouth Athenaeum's Library of John Fisher of London*. Portsmouth, N.H.: Peter E. Randall, 2019.

xiii + 144 pp.; bw illus., appendix, index. (Includes references to rococo furniture in Portsmouth.)

Harp, Clint. *Handcrafted: A Woodworker's Story*. New York: Touchstone, 2018. x + 239 pp.; illus.

Harrison, Michael B. *Collecting Nantucket: Artifacts from an Island Community*. Nantucket, Mass.: Nantucket Historical Society, 2019. xi + 214 pp.; numerous color and bw illus., bibliography, index.

———. "Museum Visit: Treasure Island." *Antiques* 186, no. 1 (January/February 2019): 82–86. Color illus. (Re Nantucket Historical Association.)

Henny, Sundar. "Archiving the Archive: Scribal and Material Culture in 17th-Century Zurich." In Liesbeth Corens, Kate Peters, and Alexandra Walsham, eds., *Archives and Information in the Early Modern World*, 209–35. Proceedings of the British Academy 212 (Oxford: Oxford University Press, 2018). 3 bw illus.

[High Museum]. "Hand to Hand: Southern Craft of the Nineteenth Century." *Antiques and Fine Art* 18, no. 2 (summer 2019): 106–12. Color illus.

[Hirschl and Adler Galleries]. "Current and Coming: Canon Fodder at Hirschl & Adler." *Antiques* 186, no. 1 (January/February 2019): 34. 3 color illus.

"Hirschl & Adler Augments the Canon: Exhibition Examines New Scholarship." *Antiques and the Arts Weekly* (January 4, 2019): 18. 7 bw illus.

"Historic Huguenot Street Presents Online Kasten Exhibit." *Antiques and the Arts Weekly* (December 28, 2018): 9.

Hoffman, Rob. "Shop Talk: Observations on Two Seventeenth Century Eastern Massachusetts Armchairs." *Antiques and the Arts Weekly* (June 7, 2019): 32–33. 6 bw illus.

"The Honesty and Joy of an Arts and Crafts Chair." *Antiques and the Arts Weekly* (June 14, 2019): 9. 1 bw illus. (Re exhibition at the Stickley Museum at Craftsman Farms.)

[Hucker, Thomas]. "Thomas Hucker, Fellow." In "Pinnacle: 2018 American Craft Council Awards." *American Craft* 78, no. 5 (October/November 2018): 52–53. 4 color illus.

Hummel, Charles F. "The Business of Woodworking, 1700 to 1840." *Mortise & Tenon Magazine* 4 (2018): 58–69. Color and bw illus.

[Huntington Library, Art Collection, and Botanical Gardens]. "Huntington Acquires Tiffany Chair, Several Fine Art Works." *Antiques and the Arts Weekly* (July 5, 2019): 38. 1 bw illus. (Re side chair of ca. 1891–93.)

Janowitz, Neil. "Who Owns an Idea?" *American Craft* 79, no. 1 (February/March 2019): 50–55. Color illus. (Re furniture of Greg Klassen.)

Johnson, John P., and Kate McBrien. *Creative Maine: Trade Banners and the Crafts that Built Maine*. Portland, Me.: Maine Historical Society, 2017. 59 pp.; color and bw illus.

"Kasten from Mid-Hudson Valley Collections: An Online Exhibition." https://hudsonvalleykasten.org/ (accessed December 30, 2018). Color illus.

Kirtley, Alexandra. "Taking Inventory: Philadelphia Stories." *Antiques* 186, no. 1 (January/February 2019): 72–79. Color illus.

Klein, Joshua A. "Hand in Hand with Jonathan Fisher." *Mortise & Tenon Magazine* 5 (2018): 122–37. Color illus.

———. "The Spring-Pole Lathe: Design, Construction, and Use." *Mortise & Tenon Magazine* 3 (2017): 18–33. Color and bw illus.

Klein, Joshua A., ed. *Mortise & Tenon Magazine* 3 (2017): 1–144. Numerous color and bw illus. (See also individual articles cited elsewhere in this list.)

———. *Mortise & Tenon Magazine* 4 (2018): 1–144. Numerous color and bw illus. (See also individual articles cited elsewhere in this list.)

———. *Mortise & Tenon Magazine* 5 (2018): 1-144. Numerous color and bw illus. (See also individual articles cited elsewhere in this list.)

Kosinski, Jessica. "Furniture from the [Hudson] Valley." *Journal of Antiques and Collectibles* 20, no. 6 (September 2019): 31. 6 color illus.

Lahikainen, Dean T. "American Art." *Antiques and Fine Art* 18, no. 3 (autumn 2019): 70–79. Color illus. (Re Lynch collection.)

Lahikainen, Dean T., ed. *A Passion for American Art: Selections from the Carolyn and Peter Lynch Collection*. Salem, Mass.: Peabody Essex Museum, 2019. 213 pp.; color illus.

"Landmark Classical Richmond Furniture Exhibition Closes June 30." *Antiques and the Arts Weekly* (June 7, 2019): 39. 1 bw illus.

Lazaro, David E. "Inspired Design: Asian Decorative Arts and Their Adaptations." *Antiques and Fine Art* 18, no. 3 (autumn 2019): 104–9. 7 color illus.

Levy, Bernard, and S. Dean Levy, Inc. *Gallery Catalog XVI, 2019*. New York: Bernard & S. Dean Levy, Inc., [2019]. 33 pp.; color illus.

Lindfield, Peter N. *Georgian Gothic: Medievalist Architecture, Furniture, and Interiors, 1730–1840*. Woodbridge, England: Boydell Press, 2016. xvi + 265 pp.; bw illus., index.

[Liverant, Nathan, and Son]. *Recent Acquisitions 2019*. Colchester, Conn.: Nathan Liverant and Son, LLC, 2019. Unpaged; color illus.

Lovelace, Joyce. "On Her Own Terms." *American Craft* 78, no. 6 (December/January 2019): 66–73. Color illus. (Re Alison Croney Moses.)

———. "Seriously: What Does 'Craft' Mean?" *American Craft* 78, no. 5 (October/November 2018): 62–71. Color and bw illus.

Lupkin, Paula, and Penny Sparke, eds. *Shaping the American Interior: Structures, Contexts, and Practices*. New York: Routledge, 2018. vi + 211 pp.; bw illus., bibliography, index.

[Lynch collection.] "Boston Strong." *Antiques* 186, no. 3 (May/June 2019): 94–101. Color illus. 3C. 3 bw illus.

Martin, Brigitte. "Crafted Lives: Relationship Goals." *American Craft* 78, no. 5 (October/November 2018): 72–79. Color illus. (Interview with Sylvia and Garry Knox Bennett.)

Mayer, Roberta A. "An Exotic Side Chair Attributed to R. W. Bates & Co. of Chicago." *Maine Antique Digest* 46, no. 11 (November 2018): 32C–3

McConnell, Jim. "An Open Question: Designing the Steam-bent Drawer Backs of the Swisegood School of Cabinetmaking." *Mortise & Tenon*

Magazine 4 (2018): 86–95. Color and bw illus.

Merrill, Todd, ed. *Modern Americana: Studio Furniture from High Craft to High Glam.* 2009. Rev. ed. New York: Rizzoli, 2019. 327 pp.; color and bw illus.

Metropolitan Museum of Art. *The Metropolitan Museum of Art Guide.* 2012. Rev. ed. New York: Metropolitan Museum of Art, 2019. 456 pp.; numerous color and bw illus., index. Distributed by Yale University Press, New Haven and London.

[Michener Art Museum]. "Michener Art Museum Pays Tribute to Nakashima and Its Arts and Crafts Roots." *Antiques and the Arts Weekly* (April 19, 2019): 14. 7 bw illus.

———. "200 Years of American Design: 'The Art of Seating' and 'Nakashima Looks' at the Michener." *Antiques and the Arts Weekly* (February 8, 2019): 24. 8 bw illus.

Minardi, Lisa. "Furnituremaking." *Encyclopedia of Greater Philadelphia.* ©2017. https://philadelphiaencyclopedia.org/archive/furnituremaking/ (accessed July 23, 2019). Color illus., bibliography, other references.

Mueller-Merki, Fortunat F. "The Peak of Rhode Island Clock-making." *Watch & Clock Bulletin* 61, no. 2 (March/April 2019): 152–53. 1 color illus. (Re the recent publication on the Claggett family.)

———. Review of *Musical Clocks of Early America, 1730–1830: A Catalogue Raisonné,* by Gary R. Sullivan and Kate Van Winkle Keller. In *Watch and Clock Bulletin* 60, no. 6 (November/December 2018): 540–41. 1 color illus.

Naeem, Asma, et al. *Black Out: Silhouettes Then and Now.* Washington, D.C.: National Portrait Gallery, Smithsonian Institution, in association with Princeton University Press, 2018. xii + 182 pp.; 98 color illus., bibliography, index. (See pp. 9–11 for a comparison [*sic*] of silhouettes and early American furniture.)

Nantucket Historical Association, 125th Anniversary Year: The Winter Show 2019: Collecting Nantucket, Connecting the World. Nantucket, Mass.: Nantucket Historical Association, 2019. 60 pp.; numerous color and bw illus.

"New Hampshire Furniture Maker Wins National Competition." *Antiques and the Arts Weekly* (December 14, 2018): 4. 1 bw illus. (Re Owain Harris, recipient of the Pinnacle Award from the International Society of Furniture Designers, for his *Escape Velocity* cabinet.)

"New Haven Museum Online Collection Catalog Now Available." *Antiques and the Arts Weekly* (August 9, 2019): 29. 1 bw illus. (See https://newhavenmuseum.org/museum-collections/collections-database/.)

Newman, Walter C. "Two Gems Surface at Evans Sale." *Maine Antique Digest* 47, no. 6 (August 2019): 146. 2 color illus. (Includes federal-period cellaret attributed to Micajah Wilkes of eastern North Carolina.)

Orrom, James. *Chair Anatomy: Design and Construction.* London: Thames and Hudson, 2018. 240 pp.; 700+ color illus., designer biographies, glossary, bibliography.

Parks, Sarah, and Catharine Anne Roeber. "Digital Decorative Arts: Celebrating a New Consortium." *Decorative Arts Trust Magazine* 6, no. 1 (summer 2019): 18–19. 4 color illus.

Penick, Monica, and Christopher Long, eds. *The Rise of Everyday Design: The Arts and Crafts Movement in Britain and America.* Austin: Harry Ransom Center at the University of Texas, in association with Yale University Press, 2019. xi + 242 pp.; color and bw illus.

Percier, Charles, with an introduction by Barry Bergdoll. *The Complete Works of Percier and Fontaine.* New York: Princeton University Press in association with the Institute of Classical Architecture and Art, 2018. 441 pp.; color and bw illus., bibliography.

Perlman, Baron. *Come Collect with Me: Musings on Collecting and American Antiques.* New Glarus, Wis.: CK Books, 2019. 336 pp., illus.

"A Personal View." *Olde Hope Collection* 8 (summer 2018): 1–72. Numerous color illus. (See also https://oldehope.com.)

Peteran: Furniture. Guelph, Ontario: Art Gallery of Guelph, 2018. 113 pp.; illus.

Phillips, Bruce. "Vintage Electronics: How We Listened, 1946–1976." *New England Antiques Journal* 38, no. 4 (November 2018): 20–23. Color illus.

Polster, Bernd. *Walter Knoll: The Furniture Brand of Modernity.* Kempen, Germany: TeNeus, 2019. 352 pp.; numerous color and bw illus., index, bibliography.

"Rare Furniture Finds a New Home." *Notes from the Farms: The Journal of the Stickley Museum at Craftsman Farms* 28, no. 2 (spring 2019): 3. 4 color illus.

Resnikoff, Shoshana. "How Modern Architecture Came to Miami Beach." *Antiques* 185, no. 6 (November/December 2018): 96–97. 3 color illus.

"Richmond Furniture." *Maine Antique Digest* 47, no. 5 (May 2019): 182. 1 color illus.

Ritok, Christine. "Exotic Woods in Connecticut River Valley Furniture." *Historic Deerfield* 17 (autumn 2018): 32–35. Color illus.

Ross, Amy Theobald, ed. *Art of Illinois: An Exhibition of Fine and Decorative Arts Presented in the People's House.* Springfield, Ill.: Illinois Executive Mansion Association, 2018. 180 pp.; color and bw illus.

Saff, Donald. *From Celestial to Terrestrial Timekeeping: Clockmaking in the Bond Family.* London: Antiquarian Horological Society, 2019. 424 pp.; numerous color and bw illus., appendices, bibliography, index.

Saunt, Jenny. Review of *The Cabinetmaker's Account: John Head's Record of Craft and Commerce in Philadelphia, 1718–1753,* by Jay Robert Stiefel. *Furniture History Society Newsletter,* no. 214 (May 2019): 20–21. 1 color illus.

Scherer, Barrymore Laurence. "Crazy Eight." *Antiques* 186, no. 5 (September/October 2019): 72–81. 15 color illus. (Re Armour-Stiner house, Irvington, N.Y., 1860s–70s.)

Schinto, Jeanne. Review of *Musical Clocks of Early America, 1730–1830: A Catalogue Raisonné,* by Gary R. Sullivan and Kate Van Winkle Keller. In *American Furniture 2018,* 225–28.

Scott, Amy, ed. *Art of the West: Selected Works from the Autry*

Museum. Norman: University of Oklahoma Press in association with the Autry Museum of the American West, Los Angeles, 2018. xiv + 151 pp.; numerous color and bw illus., bibliography, index.

Simons, D. Brenton. "From Our Collections." *American Ancestors* 19, no. 4 (winter 2019): 60–63. 4 color illus. (Re library table owned by the Rev. John Pierpoint.)

Slough, William. "2018 Crafts Competition." *Watch and Clock Bulletin* 60, no. 6 (November/December 2018): 551–57. Color illus.

Solis-Cohen, Lita. "Augmenting the Canon." *Maine Antique Digest* 47, no. 7 (July 2019): 123. 1 color illus. (Review of Hirschl and Adler catalogue of the same name.)

———. "Chippendale's Drawings for the *Director*." *Maine Antique Digest* 47, no. 7 (July 2019): 148. 2 color illus.

———. "Signed Newport Fly Table Shown in Reopened Museum." *Maine Antique Digest* 47, no. 7 (July 2019): 126. 2 color illus. (Re table by Joseph Sanford.)

———. Review of *Folk and Folks: Variations in the Vernacular*, edited by Dale L. Couch. In *Maine Antique Digest* 46, no. 12 (December 2018): 23D. 1 bw illus.

———. Review of *The Hidden World of Objects: Fewer, Better Things*, by Glenn Adamson. In *Maine Antique Digest* 46, no. 12 (December 2018): 22CS–23CS. 1 color illus.

"Speed Museum Takes Time for Kentucky Tall Case Clocks." *Antiques and the Arts Weekly* (February 15, 2019): 7. 1 bw illus.

Speelberg, Femke. "Dissecting the *Director*: New Insights about Its Production, and Chippendale as Draughtsman." *Furniture History* 54 (2018): 27–42. 13 color illus.

Stiefel, Jay Robert. *The Cabinetmaker's Account: John Head's Record of Craft and Commerce in Colonial Philadelphia, 1718–1753*. Philadelphia: American Philosophical Society Press, 2019. xxi + 298 pp.; numerous color and bw illus., appendix, bibliography, index.

———. "The John Head Project:

Documenting His Clock Cases." *Antiques and Fine Art* 18, no. 2 (summer 2019): 82–87. 8 color illus.

"Studio Craft Takes Wing in San Francisco." *Antiques* 186, no. 5 (September/October 2019): 30. 4 color illus. (Re SFO Museum.)

Sullivan, Gary R., and Benedict Leca, with a prologue by Donald L. Fennimore. *The Claggetts of Newport: Master Clockmakers in Colonial America*. Newport, R.I.: Redwood Library and Athenaeum, 2018. 48 pp.; color illus.

Talley, Anna. "Current and Coming: Artful Craft at the High Museum." *Antiques* 186, no. 1 (January/February 2019): 28–29. 6 color illus.

Taylor, Snowden, and Mary Jane Dapkus. *Antebellum Shelf Clock Making in Farmington and Unionville Villages, Connecticut*. Columbia, Pa.: National Association of Watch and Clock Collectors, 2019. vi + 189 pp.; illus.

Thurlow, Matthew A. Review of *Rather Elegant Than Showy: The Classical Furniture of Robert Vose*, by Robert D. Mussey Jr. and Clark Pearce. In *American Furniture 2018*, 228–32.

Updegraff, Michael. "An Overwhelming Call: The Life & Work of Eric Sloane." *Mortise & Tenon Magazine* 5 (2018): 100–111. Color and bw illus.

[Vogel collection]. *The Collection of Anne H. and Frederick Vogel III*. Sale N10003. New York: Sotheby's, January 19, 2019. Vol. 1, *Important English Pottery*. 151 pp.; numerous color illus. Vol. 2, *Important Early American Furniture, English Silver, Needlework, and Decorative Arts*. 284 pp.; numerous color illus.

[Wadsworth Atheneum Museum of Art]. "New Acquisitions Join Collections of Wadsworth Atheneum." *Antiques and the Arts Weekly* (July 26, 2019): 39. 3 bw illus. (Includes Pembroke table, ca. 1770–95, by Peleg Weeden of Rhode Island.)

Ward, Gerald W. R. "John Head's Account Book." *Maine Antique Digest* 47, no. 6 (June 2019): 130. 1 color illus. (Review of *The Cabinetmaker's Account: John Head's Record of Craft and Commerce in Philadelphia, 1718–1753*, by Jay Robert Stiefel.)

———. *New Hampshire Folk Art: By the People, For the People, and Contemporary NH Folk Art with the League of NH Craftsmen*. Portsmouth Marine Society Press Publication 40. Portsmouth, N.H.: Portsmouth Marine Society Press, 2019. 40 pp.; color illus.

Ward, Gerald W. R., comp. "Recent Writing on American Furniture: A Bibliography." In *American Furniture 2018*, 233–40.

Warren, Elizabeth V., and Stacy Hollander. *Made in New York: The Business of Folk Art*. New York: American Folk Art Museum, 2019. 135 pp.; illus., bibliography.

Wells, K. L. H. "Serpentine Sideboards, Hogarth's *Analysis*, and the Beautiful Self." *Eighteenth-Century Studies* 46, no. 3 (spring 2013): 399–413. 8 illus.

Wentworth-Gardner Tobias Lear Houses Association. "Recent Gift of 18th Century Connecticut Chest-on-Chest." *Wentworth Lear News* (fall 2018): 3. 2 color illus. (Re piece, ca. 1770–80, of the type associated with Samuel Loomis of Colchester.)

"Whitehorse House Museum Reopens with Debut of Recently Acquired Tea Table." *Antiques and the Arts Weekly* (May 31, 2019): 4. 1 bw illus. (Re table signed by Joseph Sanford [1740–1794].)

Wolfe, Heather, and Peter Stallybrass. "The Material Culture of Record-Keeping in Early Modern England." In Liesbeth Corens, Kate Peters, and Akexandra Walsham, eds., *Archives and Information in the Early Modern World*, 179–208. Proceedings of the British Academy 212 (Oxford: Oxford University Press for the British Academy, 2018). 8 bw illus.

Zimmerman, Philip D. "Breaking the Rules: Philadelphia Blockfront and Bombé Furniture." *Antiques and Fine Art* 18, no. 2 (summer 2019): 96–103. 9 color and bw illus.

———. "Dating William Savery's Furniture Labels and Implications for Furniture History." In *American Furniture 2018*, 193–214. 26 color and bw illus., 1 table.

Index

furniture and upholstered goods, 2(fig. 2), 3(&fig.); shaving desk, 32(figs.); summary of goods bought from, 62–68; as suppliers for Belvoir furniture, 13–19

Williams Inn (Centerbrook, Connecticut), 175(&fig.)

Willis, Francis, 40, 41, 76

Wilmington, Delaware. *See* Swedish-American furniture

Wilton Persian carpet, 27(fig.), 28, 34, 37, 61n59

Winchester (Virginia), 10–11, 22

Wine coaster, silver-plated, 85(fig. 6)

Winterthur, 222

Wistar, Caspar, 243

Work table, mahogany, 166, 167(fig. 11)

Worldly sociability, salons and, 84, 85–86

Writing flap, hinged, 219, 220–21(&fig. 7)

Writing table, 125

Yale University Art Gallery, 234

Yellow Chamber, at Belvoir, 24, 34, 70

Yellow drawing room, President's House, 149n43

"Yellow morine," 34

Yellow poplar, looking glass, 114(fig. 38)

Zoffany, Johan, 27(fig.), 37